Decisions
of the
United States
Supreme Court

1970-71 TERM

by
The Editorial Staff
United States Supreme Court Reports,
Lawyers' Edition

THE LAWYERS CO-OPERATIVE PUBLISHING CO.
Rochester, New York 14603

LCP

Library of Congress Catalog Card Number 64–17924

PREFACE

This volume is designed to serve as a quick-reference guide to the work of the United States Supreme Court during its 1970–1971 Term. Its important features are described below.

The Court's Personnel. A list of the operating personnel of the Court is accompanied by photographs and biographical sketches of each Justice serving during the Term.

Survey of the Term. A succinct narrative statement outlines the high spots of the Term.

Summaries of Decisions. Every important decision of the Supreme Court is individually summarized. These summaries (reprinted from Vols. 27–29 L Ed 2d) describe the manner in which the case came before the Court, the facts involved and issues presented, the holding of the Court and the reasons supporting that holding, the name of the Justice who wrote the opinion of the majority, and the names and views of those of the Justices who concurred or dissented.

The Summaries are printed in the order in which the cases were decided by the Court. Notations to each Summary indicate the volume and page at which the full opinion of the Court may be found in the official reports (US) published by the Federal Government, and the privately published United States Supreme Court Reports, Lawyers' Edition (L Ed 2d), and Supreme Court Reporter (S Ct).

Following each Summary is a listing of the attorneys who acted in behalf of the litigants.

Glossary. A glossary of common legal terms defines, in laymen's language, various legal words and phrases used in the Supreme Court's decisions and in the Summaries of those decisions that appear in this volume.

Table of Cases. A complete Table of Cases makes possible the location of the Summary of any case through the name of a party litigant.

Index. A detailed, alphabetical word index makes possible the location of the Summary of any case by consulting the index entries for appropriate factual and conceptual terms.

THE COURT'S PERSONNEL

JUSTICES

OF THE

SUPREME COURT OF THE UNITED STATES

1970–71 Term

Chief Justice
HON. WARREN E. BURGER

Associate Justices
HON. HUGO L. BLACK

HON. WILLIAM O. DOUGLAS

HON. JOHN M. HARLAN

HON. WILLIAM J. BRENNAN, Jr.

HON. POTTER STEWART

HON. BYRON R. WHITE

HON. THURGOOD MARSHALL

HON. HARRY A. BLACKMUN

BIOGRAPHIES OF THE
JUSTICES

Mr. Chief Justice Burger was born in St. Paul, Minnesota, on September 17, 1907, the son of Charles Joseph and Katharine B. (Schnittger) Burger. He married  Elivera Stromberg on November 8, 1933. They have two children, Wade Allan and Margaret Elizabeth.

After attending the public schools of St. Paul, Mr. Chief Justice Burger was a student at the University of Minnesota from 1925 to 1927. He later attended the St. Paul College of Law, receiving an LL.B. degree, magna cum laude, in 1931. After becoming admitted to the Minnesota Bar, he joined the St. Paul law firm of Boyesen, Otis and Faricy (subsequently Faricy, Burger, Moore and Costello) as an associate in 1931, and he became a partner in the firm in 1935. While practicing law in St. Paul, he also was a member of the faculty of the Mitchell College of Law, and he was, at various times, president of the Junior Chamber of Commerce, president of the Council on Human Relations, a member of the Emergency War Labor Board, and a member of the Governor's Interracial Commission.

In 1953, Mr Chief Justice Burger was appointed Assistant Attorney General in charge of the Civil Division of the Department of Justice, and in 1956, he was appointed to a judgeship on the United States Court of Appeals for the District of Columbia Circuit. He has been not only a member but also a committee chairman of the American Bar Association.

Mr. Chief Justice Burger was nominated by President Nixon to be Chief Justice of the United States, and took office on June 24, 1969.

Mr. Justice Black was born in Harlan, Alabama, on February 27, 1886, the son of William LaFayette and Martha Ardellah (Toland)  Black. In 1921 he married Josephine Patterson Foster, who died December 7, 1952. They had three children, Hugo, Jr., Sterling Foster, and Martha Josephine (Mrs. Mario Pesaresi). On September 11, 1957, he married Mrs. Elizabeth Seay DeMeritte.

Mr. Justice Black was educated in the public schools of Ashland, Alabama. After completing a two-year medical course at the University of Alabama in Birmingham, he entered the study of law and received his LL.B. from the University of Alabama Law School in 1906.

Mr. Justice Black entered private practice in Ashland in 1907, and later moved his practice to Birmingham. In 1910 and 1911 he served as a police judge, and from 1915 to 1917 he served as prosecuting attorney for Jefferson County, Alabama. In 1917 he entered Officers' Training School at Fort Oglethorpe, Georgia. During World War I he served as Captain in the 81st Field Artillery and as Adjutant in the 19th Artillery Brigade. After the war he entered the general practice of law in Birmingham. He was elected to the United States Senate in 1926, where he served two terms.

Mr. Justice Black was appointed to the position of Associate Justice of the United States Supreme Court by President Franklin D. Roosevelt on August 12, 1937

Mr. Justice Douglas was born in Maine, Minnesota, on October 16, 1898. His father was William Douglas, and his mother was Julia Bickford Fisk. Mr. Justice Douglas has a daughter, Mrs. Frank Wells, Jr., and a son, William O. Douglas, Jr.

He attended grade and high schools in Yakima, Washington, and received his A.B. from Whitman College, Walla Walla, in 1920, and his LL.B. from Columbia Law School in New York in 1925.

In 1918, Mr. Justice Douglas served as a private in the United States Army (SATC).

Mr. Justice Douglas was a member of the faculty of the Columbia Law School from 1924 to 1928, and the Yale Law School from 1928 to 1936. He served as Commissioner of the Securities and Exchange Commission from 1936 to 1939, and as Chairman of the Securities and Exchange Commission from 1937 to 1939.

Mr. Justice Douglas was nominated by President Roosevelt to be an Associate Justice of the Supreme Court of the United States, and took his seat on April 17, 1939.

Mr. Justice Harlan was born in Chicago, Illinois, on May 20, 1899, the son of John Maynard and Elizabeth Palmer (Flagg) Harlan. He married Ethel Andrews on November 10, 1928. They have one daughter, Eve Harlan Newcomb (Mrs. W. A. Newcomb).

After attending Chicago Latin School, Appleby School, and Lake Placid School, Mr. Justice Harlan graduated from Princeton University in 1920 with an A.B. degree. He attended Balliol College from 1921 to 1923 as a Rhodes Scholar, receiving a B.A. degree in Jurisprudence and an M.A. degree. Upon returning from Oxford, Mr. Justice Harlan attended New York Law School and received an LL.B. degree in 1924.

Mr. Justice Harlan was admitted to the New York Bar in 1925. He joined the firm of Root, Clark, Buckner & Howland (subsequently Root, Ballantine, Harlan, Bushby & Palmer) as an associate in 1923, and was a member of the firm from 1931 to 1954. He served as Assistant U. S. Attorney for the Southern District of New York from 1925 to 1927, and was appointed to the United States Court of Appeals for the Second Circuit in 1954.

He was a Colonel in the United States Army Air Force from 1943 to 1945, serving as Chief of Operations Analysis Section Eighth Air Force, and as a member of Planning Section for the Occupation of Germany, U. S. Strategic Air Forces in Europe.

Mr. Justice Harlan was appointed to the Supreme Court of the United States by President Eisenhower on March 17, 1955, and took office on March 28, 1955.

Mr. Justice Harlan is a member of the American Bar Association, the New York State Bar Association, the Association of the Bar of the City of New York, the New York County Lawyers Association (Director, 1938 to 1942), the American Law Institute, and the National Legal Aid Association (Director).

Mr. Justice Brennan was born in Newark, New Jersey, on April 25, 1906, the son of William Joseph Brennan, Sr. and Agnes (McDermott) Brennan. He married Marjorie Leonard on May 5, 1928.

They have three children, William Joseph Brennan III, Hugh Leonard Brennan, and Nancy Brennan.

Mr. Justice Brennan attended public schools in Newark, and graduated from the University of Pennsylvania in 1928 with a B.S. degree. He earned his LL.B. degree from Harvard University in 1931.

Mr. Justice Brennan was admitted to the New Jersey Bar in 1932, after joining the Newark law firm of Pitney, Hardin & Skinner. Following that, for 10 years, he practiced law in Newark.

In March, 1942, he entered the Army as a Major in the legal division of the Ordnance Department, leaving with the rank of Colonel in September, 1945.

Returning to Newark, he rejoined his law firm and became a name partner in Pitney, Hardin, Ward & Brennan. In 1949 he became a trial judge in the New Jersey Superior Court. After two years he was elevated to a judgeship in the Appellate Division of the same court, and in March, 1952, he was appointed as an Associate Justice of the New Jersey Supreme Court.

President Eisenhower appointed him an Associate Justice of the United States Supreme Court on October 15, 1956, and he took his seat on the Court on October 16, 1956.

Mr. Justice Brennan is a member of the American, New Jersey, Essex County, Hudson County and Monmouth County (N.J.) Bar Associations.

Mr. Justice Stewart was born in Jackson, Michigan, on January 23, 1915, the son of James Garfield Stewart and Harriet Loomis Potter Stewart. He married Mary

Ann Bertles on April 24, 1943. They have a daughter, Harriet Potter Stewart, and two sons, Potter Stewart, Jr., and David Bertles Stewart.

After attending the public schools of Cincinnati, Mr. Justice Stewart attended Hotchkiss School and Yale College, receiving in 1937 a B.A. degree, cum laude. He also attended Cambridge University, England, on a Henry Fellowship, and Yale Law School, receiving an LL.B. degree, cum laude, in 1941.

Mr. Justice Stewart was admitted to the Ohio Bar in 1941, and to the New York Bar in 1942. He was an associate in the firm of Debevoise, Stevenson, Plimpton & Page in New York City from 1941 to 1942, and from 1945 to 1947. Mr. Justice Stewart was an associate in the firm of Dinsmore, Shohl, Sawyer & Dinsmore in Cincinnati, Ohio, in 1947, and was a partner of that firm from 1951 to 1954. He was a member of the Cincinnati City Council from 1950 to 1953, and was Vice Mayor of Cincinnati from 1952 to 1953. Mr. Justice Stewart was appointed to the United States Court of Appeals for the Sixth Circuit in 1954.

He volunteered in the United States Naval Reserve in 1941, and was called into active service in 1942. After serving three years active sea duty, he was honorably discharged as a Lieutenant in 1945.

Mr. Justice Stewart was appointed by President Eisenhower as an Associate Justice of the Supreme Court of the United States on October 14, 1958, during a recess of the Senate, and took his oath of office and his seat on that day. He was nominated as an Associate Justice of the Supreme Court by President Eisenhower on January 17, 1959, was confirmed by the Senate on May 5, 1959, and took the oath of office on May 15, 1959.

Mr. Justice Stewart is a member of the American, Ohio, Cincinnati, and City of New York Bar Associations, the American Law Institute, and the American Judicature Society.

Mr. Justice White was born in Ft. Collins, Colorado, on June 8, 1917, the son of Alpha Albert White and Maud Burger White.   He married Marion Lloyd Stearns on June 15, 1946.   They have two children, Charles Byron and Nancy Pitkin.

Mr. Justice White attended elementary and high schools at Wellington, Colorado. He graduated from the University of Colorado in 1938 with a B.A. degree, and attended Oxford University, Oxford, England, as a Rhodes Scholar, from January, 1939 until October, 1939.   From October, 1939 to October, 1941, and from February, 1946 to November, 1946, he attended Yale University Law School, receiving an LL.B. degree, magna cum laude.

Mr. Justice White volunteered for service in the United States Navy in July 1941 and received a commission as an ensign.   During World War II, he served in the Pacific as an intelligence officer, and was honorably discharged as a Lieutenant Commander in 1946.

Upon graduation from Yale, Mr. Justice White served from 1946 to 1947 as law clerk to Chief Justice Vinson, Supreme Court of the United States.

In 1947, he joined the law firm of Lewis, Grant, Newton, Davis and Henry (now Lewis, Grant and Davis), in Denver, Colorado.   He became a partner and remained with that firm until January 1961, when he was appointed Deputy Attorney General of the United States by President Kennedy.

Mr. Justice White was nominated by President Kennedy as Associate Justice of the Supreme Court of the United States on April 3, 1962, and took his seat on April 16, 1962.

Mr. Justice Marshall was born in Baltimore, Maryland on July 2, 1908, the son of William Marshall and Norma Williams Marshall.

His first wife, the former Vivian Burey, whom he married on September 4, 1929, passed away in February, 1955. On December 17, 1955, the Justice married Cecelia S. Suyat. Mr. Justice Marshall has two sons, Thurgood Marshall, Jr., and John Marshall.

After attending public schools in Baltimore, Mr. Justice Marshall attended Lincoln University, where, in 1930, he received his A.B. degree. He earned his LL.B. in 1933 from Howard University.

The Justice was admitted to the Maryland Bar in 1933 and was engaged in private practice until 1937. He served as Assistant Special Counsel to the National Association for the Advancement of Colored People between 1936–1938 and as Special Counsel until 1950. He directed the N.A.A.C.P.'s Legal Defense and Education Fund between 1940–1961.

In 1961, Mr. Justice Marshall was appointed United States Circuit Judge for the Second Judicial Circuit, a position he left in 1965 to become Solicitor General of the United States.

President Johnson appointed him Associate Justice of the United States Supreme Court in 1967.

He is a member of the American Bar Association, the National Bar Association, the New York City County Lawyers Association, and the Bar Association of the District of Columbia.

Mr. Justice Blackmun was born in Nashville, Illinois, on November 12, 1908, the son of Corwin M. and Theo H. Blackmun. He married Dorothy E. Clark on June 21,

1941. They have three daughters: Nancy, Sally Ann (Mrs. D. Richard Funk), and Susan (Mrs. Roger M. Karl).

After attending Van Buren Grade School and Mechanical Arts High School in St. Paul, Minnesota, Mr. Justice Blackmun attended Harvard College, where, in 1929, he received his A.B. degree, summa cum laude. He earned his LL.B. degree from Harvard Law School in 1932.

He then served for two years as law clerk for Judge John B. Sanborn of the United States Court of Appeals for the Eighth Circuit.

In 1934, he joined the law firm then known as Dorsey, Colman, Barker, Scott & Barber, in Minneapolis, Minnesota. He became a general partner of that firm in 1943 and remained with it until 1950. During this same period he was also an instructor at St. Paul College of Law (now William Mitchell College of Law) (1935–1941), and taught at the University of Minnesota Law School (1945–1947).

In 1950 he became resident counsel of the Mayo Clinic in Rochester, Minnesota, and held that position until 1959, when he was appointed a judge of the United States Court of Appeals for the Eighth Circuit by President Eisenhower.

Mr. Justice Blackmun was nominated by President Nixon as Associate Justice of the United States Supreme Court on April 14, 1970, and took his seat on June 9, 1970.

SURVEY OF THE 1970–1971 TERM

The Supreme Court of the United States heard argument in 151 cases during its October Term, 1970, which lasted until June 30, 1971. Of these cases, 126 were decided by signed opinions, 22 were decided by per curiam opinions, and 3 were set for reargument in the October Term, 1971.

Administrative law questions were presented in several cases, involving the jurisdiction, proceedings, and orders of various agencies, including the Federal Maritime Commission, the Department of Transportation, the Interstate Commerce Commission, and the Federal Power Commission. A decision of the Federal Maritime Commission pertaining to wharf demurrage charges was held to be final, binding, and not subject to judicial review, where the time for direct review of the decision by the Court of Appeals had expired [see p. 20]. A decision of the Secretary of Transportation approving the routing of a proposed interstate highway through a public park was held, in view of federal statutes restricting the use of park lands for such purposes, subject to broad and substantial judicial review [see p. 141]. It was also held that a carrier seeking approval by the Interstate Commerce Commission of a proposed termination of certain interstate train service was required to give statutory notice only to those states where the carrier operated the trains [see p. 3]. And an order of the Federal Power Commission requiring interconnection of two electric utility companies operating within a state, without imposing any annual standby fee against the smaller utility, was held to be supported by the record [see p. 264].

In the field of **admiralty and maritime law,** it was held that a longshoreman injured while loading a ship, through the isolated negligent act of a fellow longshoreman in operating the ship's boom, was not entitled to recover from the shipowner under the doctrine of unseaworthiness [see p. 62], and a seaman's statutory suit for wages was held not to be precluded by his failure to take advantage of the provisions of the Labor-Management Relations Act for the enforcement of grievance and arbitration provisions of collective bargaining agreements [see p. 39].

With regard to **aliens and citizenship,** it was held that an alien who once claimed a draft exemption on the ground of alienage was not thereby debarred from citizenship when he was later drafted but found to be physically unfit [see p. 262]. In another decision, the court held that the provision of the Immigration and Nationality Act of 1952 imposing loss of citizenship on a foreign-born child of an American parent unless the child was present in the United States continuously for 5 years between the ages of 14 and 28 was constitutional [see p. 201]. It was also held that an alien's firm resettlement in a foreign country, following his flight from another foreign country, barred his claim to refugee status under the Immigration and Nationality Act of 1952 [see p. 220].

Several **antitrust** decisions were handed down, the most important of which held that the Clayton Act provisions suspending the statute of limitations on a private antitrust claim during a government antitrust proceeding were applicable to a nonparty in such government proceeding, and that a release of a coconspirator was effective only as to parties intended to be released [see p. 130]. In other decisions, it was held that in a private antitrust action against a union, the "clear proof" requirement of the Norris-LaGuardia Act was applicable only to the union's authorization of, participation in, or ratification of, acts allegedly performed on its behalf, the usual preponderance of evidence rule otherwise applying [see p. 128]; a 1920 consent decree in an antitrust action forbidding meat packers from engaging in the retail food business was held not to preclude a company engaged in such business from acquiring a controlling interest in a meat-packing company [see p. 291]; and § 7 of the Clayton Act was held to be violated by the acquisition by one company engaged in the printing and sale of color comic supplements for newspapers, of another company engaged only in printing such supplements for comic-feature syndicate use [see p. 274].

On the subject of **bankruptcy,** bankrupt wage earners' accrued but unpaid vacation pay was held not to constitute "property" passing to the trustee in bankruptcy under the Bankruptcy Act [see p. 8]; and despite the failure of a debtor in arrangement proceedings under the Act to comply with a court order requiring the deposit of withheld taxes into a special account for the government, it was held that the government's claim for such taxes was not entitled to priority over the administrative expenses of bankruptcy proceedings [see p. 161].

In a **banking** case, it was held that the Glass-Steagall Act was violated by a national bank's operation, pursuant to a regulation of the Comptroller of the Currency, of a collective investment fund in competition with the mutual fund industry [see p. 179].

The court decided a number of **civil rights** cases. In two decisions relating to employment practices, it was held that the Civil Rights Act of 1964 prohibited an employer from imposing as job requirements the possession of a high school diploma and the attaining of a satisfactory intelligence test score, which requirements tended to exclude Negroes and were unrelated to successful job performance [see p. 146], and it was also held that the Act did not permit different hiring policies for male and female parents of pre-school-age children, at least in the absence of a proper showing of relevance to job perform-ance [see p. 73]. The federal civil rights statute au-thorizing recovery of damages for conspiracy was held to be constitutional as applied to an assault on Negroes by private white persons [see p. 305]. And in another case, it was held that a city's closing of public swimming pools rather than desegregating them was not violative of the Thirteenth Amendment or of the equal protection clause of the Fourteenth Amendment [see p. 321]. In a series of school desegregation decisions, a federal court order requiring an Alabama county school board to de-segregate its faculty and staff was affirmed, but the case was remanded for further consideration as to changes in student attendance zones [see p. 211]; a Georgia county school board, in desegregating a dual school system, was held not to be precluded by the equal protection clause or by federal civil rights legislation from considering the students' race in assigning them to new attendance zones [see p. 214]; a North Carolina statute prohibiting the as-signment or busing of students on the basis of race or for the purpose of creating a racial balance or ratio was held unconstitutional [see p. 216]; and federal court orders requiring a North Carolina county school board to adopt plans for desegregating its dual school system were af-firmed where the plans included provisions for the de-segregation of faculty, new attendance zones, and the busing of students [see p. 206].

The court also decided four cases involving the admis-sibility of **confessions and incriminating statements** in criminal prosecutions. In an important decision it was held that an accused's prior statements to the police, which were inconsistent with his trial testimony, were admissible to impeach his credibility notwithstanding that the prior statements had been made to the police under circumstances rendering them inadmissible to establish the prosecution's case in chief under the Miranda rules [see p. 112]. The admission in a state prosecution of a codefendant's alleged out-of-court statement implicating the other defendant at their joint trial was held not to violate such other defendant's Sixth and Fourteenth Amendment rights, where the codefendant took the stand, denied making the statement, was available for cross-examination, and testified favorably as to the other defendant [see p. 285]. It was also held that a state prisoner seeking federal habeas corpus relief was not entitled to a new hearing on the voluntariness of his statements, tape-recorded during a jail conversation with an insurance agent, and admitted at his murder trial [see p. 52]. In another decision it was held that a defendant's constitutional rights were not violated by the admission in evidence at a state murder prosecution of a witness' testimony as to a statement implicating the defendant that had been made by an alleged accomplice while in custody after the murder [see p. 23].

In two **contempt** cases, it was held in the first case that a defendant who disrupted his state criminal trial and repeatedly insulted the judge was entitled under due process to a trial before another judge on contempt charges asserted after the criminal trial [see p. 55], and in the second case, a state court contempt conviction of a civil rights worker, under similar circumstances, was reversed and the case was remanded for a hearing before an unbiased judge [see p. 319].

In a **court-martial** case it was held that crimes of a variety normally tried in civilian courts, which crimes were committed by a serviceman on a military post and violated the security of persons or property on the post, were properly triable by court-martial [see p. 134].

The element of **criminal knowledge** was involved in two decisions. One case held that proof of the defendant's knowledge of a Department of Transportation regulation was not required under a federal statute imposing criminal sanctions for whoever "knowingly" violated administrative regulations pertaining to the transportation of dangerous articles [see p. 277]. In the other case, a prosecution for the possession of unregistered hand grenades in violation of the National Firearms Act, it was held that an allegation of specific intent or knowledge that the hand grenades were unregistered was not necessary [see p. 177].

The absence of state standards to guide a jury's determination in capital cases as to whether the **death penalty** should be imposed, and a single-verdict procedure for determining guilt and penalty, were held to be constitutional [see p. 240].

On the subject of **double jeopardy,** a Federal District Court's dismissal of a criminal information on the ground of double jeopardy, based on the District Court's earlier discharge of the jury and its declaration of a mistrial, was affirmed [see p. 58], and a state appellate court was held to have erred in rejecting the accused's claim of collateral estoppel and double jeopardy without examining the record of a prior trial at which the accused had been acquitted [see p. 336].

Questions relating to **elections and voting rights** were presented in several cases. In a landmark decision, a federal voting-rights statute was upheld insofar as it lowered the minimum voting age to 18 for federal elections, changed residency requirements and absentee voting procedures for presidential elections, and suspended literacy tests throughout the nation, but the statute, insofar as it lowered the minimum voting age for state and local elections, was held to be invalid as not authorized by the Fourteenth Amendment's equal protection clause and enforcement clause [see p. 27]. In other cases, it was held that changes pertaining to the location of polling places, municipal boundaries, and at-large election of aldermen of a city, which city was covered by the Voting Rights Act of 1965, were subject to the federal approval requirement of the Act [see p. 42]; a state election law which required that candidates who did not enter and win a political party's primary, but who wished to have their names printed on the ballots, must obtain the signatures of at least 5 percent of the registered voters on nominating petitions was held to be constitutional [see p. 338]; and a state's constitutional and statutory provisions requiring a 60-percent vote before political subdivisions could issue bonds or raise tax rates was upheld [see p. 295]. In decisions pertaining to apportionment or districting, the Arizona legislature was allowed until November 1, 1971, to enact valid apportionment plans [see p. 307]; a three-judge District Court decree which created a large multi-member Mississippi legislative district was stayed, with instructions to devise a single-district apportionment plan [see p. 294]; legislative districting for a New York county which followed town lines was held to be constitutional in view of longstanding town-county co-operation, notwithstanding an 11.9 percent deviation from voting equality [see p. 312]; and a countywide legislative district for the at-large election of several Indiana legislators was held to be constitutional although a disproportionately small number of legislators resided in a ghetto located in the district [see p. 309].

In a series of important decisions, the court limited **federal jurisdiction** with regard to intervening in state criminal matters. Thus, it was held that a Federal District Court was not authorized, absent a showing of extraordinary circumstances where the danger of irreparable injury was great and immediate, to enjoin a pending, good-faith state prosecution under a state statute which was attacked as being unconstitutional on its face, the accused having an adequate opportunity to assert his constitutional claims in the state prosecution [see p. 84.] Similarly, federal declaratory relief against enforcement of an allegedly unconstitutional state statute in a pending state prosecution was also held to be unauthorized where there was no showing that the plaintiffs would suffer irreparable damages [see p. 87]. Additionally, a Federal District Court was held not to be authorized to grant either declaratory or injunctive relief against an allegedly unconstitutional state statute, in the absence of a showing of any actual or threatened prosecutions under the statute [see p. 90]; and a District Court order suppressing allegedly obscene materials that had been seized in connection with pending criminal prosecutions was held to be improper where there was no showing of irreparable injury justifying federal injunctive interference with state criminal processes [see p. 92]. Other Federal District Court decisions which had granted declaratory or injunctive relief against enforcement of state statutes in pending prosecutions were remanded by the Supreme Court for reconsideration in light of the foregoing decisions [see pp. 106, 109].

The First Amendment rights of **freedom of assembly, association, and belief** were involved in several cases. In three cases dealing with state requirements for admission to the Bar, denial of admission to the Arizona State Bar because of failure to answer a question as to membership in organizations advocating forceful overthrow of the government was held to be violative of the First and Fourteenth Amendments [see p. 76]; and questions on the application for admission to the Ohio State Bar requiring listings of organizations of which the applicant was or had been a member, and a question as to the applicant's membership in organizations advocating forceful overthrow of the government, were also held to be violative of the First Amendment [see p. 80]; whereas New York statutes, rules, and procedures for screening bar applicants, including questions as to the applicants' "knowing" membership in organizations advocating forceful overthrow of the government, were held to be constitutional [see p. 101]. In another decision, a city ordinance punishing sidewalk assemblies "annoying" to passersby was held to be unconstitutional as violating the right of free assembly and association [see p. 283].

Freedom of religion was involved in two important decisions relating to the propriety of government aid to parochial schools. In one case, the statutes of two states under which aid as to secular instruction was furnished to church-related elementary and secondary schools, and to teachers therein, were held to be unconstitutional under the religion clauses of the First Amendment, as fostering excessive entanglement between government and religion [see p. 355]. In the second case, however, it was held that the religion clauses of the First Amendment were not violated by the Federal Higher Education Facilities Act of 1963 insofar as it authorized federal construction grants for secular facilities of church-related colleges and universities, but the Act's limitation of federal interest in the facilities covered to a 20-year period was held to be violative of the First Amendment [see p. 363].

During the term, the court decided a large number of cases involving the First Amendment rights of **freedom of speech and press.** In the highly publicized "Pentagon Papers" case, it was held that the Federal Government was not entitled to an injunction against the publication by newspapers of a classified study relating to the government's Viet Nam policy, where the government had not met its burden of showing justification for the imposition of a prior restraint of expression [see p. 373]. In decisions concerning the constitutional rule requiring proof of "actual malice" in order for a "public official" or a "public figure" to recover in a libel action, it was held that the rule was applicable which regard to candidates for public office and their fitness for office, a newspaper's reference to a public office candidate as a "former small-time bootlegger" being relevant to the candidate's fitness for office [see p. 120]; that a false newspaper story that a mayor who was also a candidate for the office of county tax assessor had been charged with perjury was also relevant to his fitness for office and subject to the rule [see p. 126]; that a magazine's failure to indicate that brutality charges against a policeman were merely allegations in a private civil rights action against him, rather than charges of the United States Civil Rights Commission, did not constitute "falsification" sufficient to sustain a finding of "actual malice" under the rule [see p. 123]; and that the rule was applicable in a libel action based on radio news reports relating to the arrest of a "private" person for possession of obscene materials, precluding recovery in the absence of a showing of knowing or reckless falsity [see p. 301]. In decisions pertaining to federal regulation of obscene matters, 39 USC §§ 4006, 4007, authorizing the Postmaster General to prevent the use of the mails or postal money orders in connection with allegedly obscene materials, were held to be in violation of the First Amendment because of the lack of adequate procedural safeguards [see p. 45]; 18 USC § 1461, prohibiting the use of the mails for the delivery of obscene matter, was held to be constitutional as applied to distribution of such matter to willing, adult recipients [see p. 246]; and after specific time limits were read into 19 USC § 1305(a) as to the institution and completion of judicial proceedings for the forfeiture of obscene materials seized by customs officials, the application of the statute to an importer of pictures for commercial use was upheld [see p. 248]. And in other First Amendment decisions, a state court injunction against the distribution of leaflets which accused a real-estate broker of "panic peddling" activities was held to be unconstitutional as a prior restraint on First Amendment rights [see p. 254]; a state court injunction against a union's furnishing legal advice to members and controlling legal fees by agreement with lawyers was held to be unconstitutional under the First Amendment [see p. 174]; and a state court conviction for disturbing the peace by the defendant's wearing a jacket bearing the words "Fuck the Draft" was held to be violative of the First and Fourteenth Amendments, the words not constituting an obscene expression or "fighting words" [see p. 299].

A guilty plea to second degree murder in a state prosecution was held to be constitutionally valid even though the defendant was motivated by fear of the death penalty upon a jury conviction of first degree murder, and had entered his plea with a protestation of innocence [see p. 10].

In one case, it was held that the Federal Constitution was not violated by a state constitutional provision requiring that each low-income **housing** project be approved by majority vote in a local referendum [see p. 233].

State statutes which barred an acknowledged **illegitimate** child from sharing in the intestate father's estate with legitmate heirs were held not to be violative of due process or equal protection [see p. 168].

In decisions pertaining to the rights of **indigents,** it was held that the equal protection clause of the Fourteenth Amendment was violated by imprisonment of an indigent for nonpayment of fines for traffic offenses [see p. 139]; that the application of state statutes requiring payment of court fees and costs, so as to prevent indigents from suing for divorce, was unconstitutional [see p. 137]; and that the rule of Gideon v Wainwright, requiring appointment of counsel for indigent criminal defendants, was fully retroactive and not dependent upon a request for counsel [see p. 204].

A state statute which authorized the posting of a notice naming a person to whom the sale of **intoxicating liquors** was forbidden was held to be violative of due process because of the failure to provide notice and an opportunity to be heard [see p. 50].

In an important decision, it was held that a jury trial in state **juvenile delinquency proceedings** was not required under the due process clause of the Fourteenth Amendment [see p. 346].

As in past terms, several **labor law** cases were decided. A suspended union member's breach of contract claim against the union for procuring his discharge under the union security clause was held to be within the exclusive jurisdiction of the National Labor Relations Board, even though the claim was predicated on the union's violation of its own constitution [see p. 324]; the secondary boycott provisions of the National Labor Relations Act were held to have been violated where a union which had a work assignment dispute with one subcontractor used coercion and strikes against the neutral general contractor and other subcontractors [see p. 33]; a union member's failure to protest an election rule to the union before filing a complaint with the Secretary of Labor was held to preclude the Secretary's challenge to the rule in a suit under the Labor-Management Reporting and Disclosure Act [see p. 327]; a Tennessee gas utility district was held to be a "political subdivion" exempt from the Labor-Management Relations Act [see p. 281]; review by the National Labor Relations Board of a regional director's determination of an appropriate bargaining unit, prior to the Board's issuance of an unfair labor practice order based on such determination, was held to be discretionary rather than mandatory [see p. 95]; a suit for violation of the Landrum-Griffin bill of rights provisions was held to be within the jurisdiction of a federal court rather than the National Labor Relations Board, but the federal court was held to be without authority to determine whether the union constitution and bylaws had been violated [see p. 114]; and a railway strike, after exhaustion of the Railway Labor Act procedures, was held to be enjoinable for the union's failure to make a reasonable effort to reach agreement [see p. 279].

The constitutionality of the **loan shark** provisions of the Federal Consumer Credit Protection Act, prohibiting extortionate intrastate credit transactions, was upheld under the commerce clause [see p. 236].

It was held that a **loyalty oath** for state employees was constitutional insofar as it required a pledge to support the federal and state constitutions, but was unconstitutional in requiring a disavowal of belief in forceful overthrow of the government, noncompliance resulting in summary dismissal from public employment without a hearing or inquiry required by due process [see p. 317].

In the sole **mining-rights** case, oil shale mining claims under the General Mining Act of 1872 were held to be subject to cancellation by the government for the claimants' failure to substantially satisfy the Act's assessment work requirements [see p. 17].

In three decisions involving the regulation of **motorists,** it was held that a state's suspension of a bankrupt motorist's license because of his failure to satisfy an automobile accident judgment was unconstitutional as conflicting with the Bankruptcy Act [see p. 288]; that the due process clause was violated by a state's procedure for the suspension of the license and registration of an uninsured motorist who was involved in an accident and who did not post the required security [see p. 269]; and that a state statute requiring a motorist to stop and identify himself after being involved in a property damage accident did not violate the privilege against self-incrimination [see p. 256].

In the field of **patent law,** it was held that a determination of the invalidity of a patent in the patentee's suit against an alleged infringer afforded a basis for pleading the defense of collateral estoppel in a subsequent suit by the patentee against a different alleged infringer [see p. 243].

The court, in the exercise of its discretion, refused to exercise its orginal jurisdiction in a **pollution** case, denying Ohio's motion for leave to file a complaint charging contamination of Lake Erie by out-of-state corporations [see p. 158].

In decisions dealing with **poverty and welfare laws,** the refusal by a recipient of Aid to Families with Dependent Children to permit a caseworker's visit to the recipient's home was held sufficient to warrant termination of welfare benefits pursuant to state procedure [see p. 37]; the statutes of two states, denying welfare benefits to resident aliens who had not resided in the United States for a specified number of years, were held to be unconstitutional [see p. 332]; a state's denial of unemployment benefits pending the employer's appeal from the award was held to be violative of the Social Security Act [see p. 230]; and written reports adverse to a social security disability claimant, which reports were prepared by licensed physicians who did not appear at the administrative hearing, were held to be admissible and sufficient to sustain a finding of nondisability [see p. 251].

The court decided several cases involving **searches and seizures and arrests.** A federal tax investigator's affidavit based partially on the accused's reputation and on information received from an informer was held sufficient to establish probable cause for the issuance of a search warrant for nontaxpaid liquor [see p. 351]. Probable cause for an arrest was held to be lacking where information in a police radio bulletin, on which the arresting officer acted, was based on an uncorroborated informer's tip [see p. 171]. Electronic monitoring by the police of a conversation between the accused and an informant, by means of a radio transmitter concealed on the informant's person, was held not to be violative of the Fourth Amendment [see p. 193]. A warrant authorizing the search of an automobile, issued by the state attorney general acting as a justice of the peace, was held to be invalid as not having been issued by a neutral magistrate, and the search and seizure of the automobile were held unconstitutional, there being no valid warrant or exigent circumstances [see p. 340]. A federal cause of action for damages was held to be stated by a complaint alleging injuries resulting from federal narcotics agents' violations of the plaintiff's Fourth Amendment rights [see p. 343]. A caseworker's visit to the home of a welfare recipient was held not to constitute a "search" within the meaning of the Fourth Amendment [see p. 37]. And in two cases, it was held that the constitutional principles announced in Chimel v California, narrowing the permissible scope of search incident to an arrest, were not retroactively applicable [see pp. 183, 196], the latter case also upholding a search, despite the mistaken identity of the person arrested.

As to **selective service** issues, it was held that the statutory conscientious objector exemption was applicable only to persons opposed to participation in all wars rather than a particular war, and that such statutory exemption did not violate the religion clauses of the First Amendment [see p. 148]. In other decisions, it was held that a registrant who asserted a conscientious objector claim after receipt of his induction notice, but before induction, was not entitled to a preinduction determination of his claim by the draft board, but it was required to submit the claim to postinduction determination by a military review board [see p. 227], that a registrant's failure to take an administrative appeal from a denial of his conscientious objector claim precluded his raising the claim in a prosecution for refusing induction [see p. 260]; and that a conviction for refusing induction must be reversed where the administrative denial of the registrant's conscientious objector claim might have been based on the Justice Department's erroneous advice to the state appeal board [see p. 368].

It was held that the registration provisions of the amended National Firearms Act did not violate the privilege against **self-incrimination** [see p. 177]. It was also held that although Supreme Court decisions which had invalidated a federal wagering tax statute as violative of the privilege against self-incrimination were retroactively applicable on direct review of forfeiture proceedings [see p. 190], nevertheless such decisions were not retroactively applicable on collateral review of a conviction for income tax evasion [see p. 187].

In two **standing to sue** cases, a group of travel agents was held to have standing to challenge a ruling of the Comptroller of the Currency which allowed national banks to provide travel services for bank customers [see p. 15], and investment companies and an association thereof were held to have standing to challenge a regulation of the Comptroller which authorized banks to operate collective investment funds [see p. 179].

In decisions dealing with **tax** matters, it was held that a "grandfather clause" of the Internal Revenue Code, limiting the income tax exemption of certain nonprofit, mutual insurers to those organized before a specified date, was constitutional [see p. 1]; that a wife was liable for federal income taxes on half of the community income, despite her subsequent exercise of a state statutory right to renounce the community [see p. 314]; that a payment by a state-chartered savings and loan association to the Federal Savings and Loan Insurance Corporation of an "additional premium" under the National Housing Act was not deductible for income tax purposes as an ordinary and necessary business expense [see p. 329]; and that a taxpayer was not entitled to intervene in a Federal District Court proceeding involving the enforcement of summonses that had been issued by a special agent of the Internal Revenue Service requesting records from the taxpayer's former employer [see p. 67].

It was held that the prohibition of the **Travel Act** against interstate travel in furtherance of certain criminal activity was not violated by the interstate travel of persons to place bets, or by persons conducting a gambling operation, even though such operation was frequented by out-of-state bettors [see p. 199].

In three decisions the court was faced with determining the constitutionality of criminal statutes or ordinances challenged on the ground of **vagueness.** In one case, a District of Columbia abortion statute, after being construed as permitting abortions for both physicial and mental health reasons, was upheld as not being unconstitutionally vague [see p. 223]. In the other cases, it was held was that a city's "suspicious person ordinance" was unconstitutionally vague as applied to a parked motorist who was talking on a two-way radio late at night [see p. 271], and that another city's ordinance punishing sidewalk assemblies that were "annoying" to passersby was unconstitutional on its face as violating the due process standard of vagueness [see p. 283].

A state's criminal law which, because a misdemeanor rather than a felony was charged, denied the defendant an opportunity of showing that in view of community prejudice, a change of **venue** should be granted for a jury trial, was held to be unconstitutional [see p. 65].

†

SUMMARIES OF DECISIONS

UNITED STATES, Appellant,

v

MARYLAND SAVINGS-SHARE INSURANCE
CORPORATION

400 US 4, 27 L Ed 2d 4, 91 S Ct 16

October 19, 1970

Decision: "Grandfather clause" of 26 USC § 501(c) (14)(B), limiting income tax exemption of certain nonprofit, mutual insurers to those organized before September 1, 1957, held constitutional.

SUMMARY

A nonprofit, mutual insurance corporation, chartered in 1962 by the Maryland Legislature for the purpose of insuring the accounts of shareholders of member savings and loan associations, instituted an action to recover federal income taxes in the United States District Court for the District of Maryland, attacking the constitutionality of the cutoff date of September 1, 1957, found in § 501 (c)(14)(B) of the Internal Revenue Code of 1954, which grants an exemption from the payment of income taxes to organizations similar to the plaintiff corporation, but only if they were organized before the cutoff date provided in the statute. The District Court allowed recovery, holding that the statutory cutoff date was arbitrary and violative of the plaintiff's right to due process under the Fifth Amendment (308 F Supp 761).

On direct appeal, the United States Supreme Court reversed. In a per curiam opinion expressing the view of eight members of the court, it was held that the cutoff date provided in § 501(c)(14)(B) was not arbitrary or unconstitutional, since Congress had a rational basis relating to the protection of federal programs for its refusal to broaden the exemption by extending the cutoff date.

Harlan, J., would have set the case for argument on the ground that the issues deserved plenary consideration.

———————

UNITED STATES et al., Appellants,

v

CITY OF CHICAGO et al. (No. 386)

UNITED STATES et al., Appellants,

v

TENNESSEE PUBLIC SERVICE COMMISSION
et al. (No. 387)

LOUISVILLE & NASHVILLE RAILROAD
COMPANY, Appellant,

v

TENNESSEE PUBLIC SERVICE COMMISSION
et al. (No. 396)

CHICAGO & EASTERN ILLINOIS RAILROAD
et al., Appellant,

v

CITY OF CHICAGO et al. (No. 410)

400 US 8, 27 L Ed 2d 9, 91 S Ct 18
October 19, 1970

Decision: Carrier seeking ICC approval of proposed termination of interstate train service, held required to give notice under 49 USC § 13a(1) only to states where carrier operated trains.

SUMMARY

The Interstate Commerce Commission, by terminating its investigation proceedings, approved the proposed discontinuance of a railroad's portion of the operation of certain interstate train runs, such railroad's portion of the operation having been confined to two states, while a second railroad continued the runs by operation in three other states (331 ICC 447). Thereafter, the Commission, in separate proceedings, similarly approved the second railroad's proposed termination of other interstate train runs which connected with the runs involved in the first proceeding (333 ICC 720). Suits to review the Commission's actions were instituted in the United States District Court for the Northern District of Illinois by various cities, state agencies, and other interested parties. The District Court dismissed such suits on the ground that the Commission's decisions were not subject to judicial review (294 F Supp 1103, 1106), but the United States Supreme Court reversed (24 L Ed 2d 340). Thereafter, the District Court remanded the proceedings involving the first railroad back to the Interstate Commerce Commission, holding that under the provisions of § 13a(1) of the Interstate Commerce Act—requiring that a carrier proposing discontinuance or change of train operation or service must give notice of the proposed discontinuance or change to the governor of each state in which the train operated, and must post such notice in every station, depot, or other facility served by the train—the railroad's compliance with the statutory requirements as to only the states in which it operated the train runs was inadequate, since the notice requirements should also have been met as to the other states involved in the continued operation of the runs by the second railroad. The District Court also remanded the proceedings involving the second railroad to the Commission, because of the close relationship with the first proceedings.

On appeals by the government, the Interstate Commerce Commission, and the railroads, the United States Supreme Court reversed and remanded. In a per curiam opinion expressing the view of seven members of the court, it was held that under § 13a(1) of the Interstate Commerce Act, the first railroad was required to give notice in only the states in which the railroad operated the train runs, and was not required to give notice to the states served by the second railroad's continuation of the runs.

Harlan, J., joined by **Black, J.**, dissented on the ground that the cases should not be summarily disposed of without benefit of briefs and oral argument by the parties.

EDDIE ODOM, Petitioner,

v

UNITED STATES

400 US 23, 27 L Ed 2d 122, 91 S Ct 112

November 9, 1970

Decision: Certiorari to consider retroactivity of earlier Supreme Court decision dismissed as improvidently granted.

SUMMARY

After reversal of a conviction of a federal offense upon trial in the United States District Court for the Middle District of Florida, the defendant's second conviction upon retrial in the same District Court, resulting in the imposition of a more severe sentence than had been originally imposed, was affirmed by the Court of Appeals for the Fifth Circuit (403 F2d 45). The United States Supreme Court granted a writ of certiorari limited to the question of the retroactivity of the decision in North Carolina v Pearce, 395 US 711, 23 L Ed 2d 656, 89 S Ct 2072, relative to the propriety of the imposition of a more severe sentence upon a defendant after reconviction on a new trial (399 US 904, 26 L Ed 2d 559, 90 S Ct —).

The writ of certiorari was dismissed as improvidently granted, in a per curiam opinion, expressing the view of eight members of the court, on the ground that an order of the District Court judge, which was dated after the grant of certiorari and which denied the petitioner's motion to set aside his second sentence as illegally imposed under North Carolina v Pearce, made it clear that the greater severity of the second sentence was based on the petitioner's conduct occurring after the time of the original sentencing proceeding, and that the new information was specifically referred to at resentencing.

Douglas, J., expressed the view that the case should be decided on the merits, since North Carolina v Pearce required that the factual data upon which the increased sentence was based must be made part of the record, which had not been done in the case at bar.

———————

KAL W. LINES, Trustee, etc., Petitioner,

v

KENNETH ROBERT FREDERICK and
Clarence Harris

400 US 18, 27 L Ed 2d 124, 91 S Ct 113

November 9, 1970

Decision: Bankrupt's accrued but unpaid vacation pay held not to constitute "property" passing to trustee under § 70a(5) of Bankruptcy Act.

SUMMARY

Referees in bankruptcy, in two separate proceedings, entered turnover orders requiring bankrupt wage earners to pay to the trustees in bankruptcy on receipt, the bankrupts' vacation pay accrued but unpaid at the time of the filing of the bankruptcy petitions, except for amounts thereof exempt under state law.   The United States District Court for the Northern District of California affirmed the referee in each case, but the Court of Appeals for the Ninth Circuit reversed, holding that the accrued vacation pay was not "property" under § 70a(5) of the Bankruptcy Act (425 F2d 215).

Granting certiorari, the Supreme Court of the United States affirmed.   In a per curiam opinion, expressing the view of seven members of the court, it was held that accrued but unpaid vacation pay of a bankrupt wage earner did not pass to the trustee in bankruptcy as "property" under § 70a(5) of the Bankruptcy Act, since the function of accrued vacation pay was to support the basic requirements of life for the bankrupt and his family during vacation periods or in the event of layoff, and since a wage-earning bankrupt required to take vacation without pay or to forgo vacation would not achieve the new opportunity in life, unhampered by the pressure and discouragement of pre-existing debt, which it was the purpose of the Bankruptcy Act to provide.

Burger, Ch. J., was of the opinion that the petition for writ of certiorari should have been denied.

Harlan, J., dissented, stating that the case should have been set for argument, rather than decided summarily.

———————

NORTH CAROLINA, Appellant,

v

HARRY C. ALFORD

400 US 25, 27 L Ed 2d 162, 91 S Ct 160

Reargued October 14, 1970. Decided
November 23, 1970.

Decision: Guilty plea to second degree murder in North
Carolina prosecution held constitutionally valid notwithstanding defendant was motivated by fear of
death penalty upon jury conviction of first degree
murder, and entered plea with protestation of innocence.

SUMMARY

The defendant was indicted for first degree murder
under North Carolina statutes which, at the time, provided that the penalty upon conviction was death unless
the jury recommended life imprisonment, and that upon
acceptance of a guilty plea to first degree murder, the
penalty would be life imprisonment. Upon the defendant's plea of guilty to the reduced charge of second degree
murder, the trial court heard the defendant's testimony
that although he had not committed the murder, he was
pleading guilty, as recommended by court-appointed
counsel who had explained the consequences of the plea
and the rights waived thereby, in order to avoid a possible
death penalty upon a jury conviction of first degree murder, and to limit the penalty to the 30-year maximum
sentence provided by statute for second degree murder.
Before accepting the guilty plea, the trial court heard further testimony which strongly indicated the defendant's
guilt. After being sentenced to 30 years' imprisonment,

and after earlier unsuccessful attempts to obtain post-conviction relief in both state and federal courts, the defendant petitioned for a writ of habeas corpus in the United States District Court for the Middle District of North Carolina, which denied relief on the ground that the defendant's guilty plea was voluntary. On appeal the Court of Appeals for the Fourth Circuit reversed, holding that the guilty plea was involuntary because its principal motivation was fear of the death penalty under the unconstitutional statutory framework (405 F2d 340).

On appeal, the United States Supreme Court vacated the judgment of the Court of Appeals, and remanded the case. In an opinion by **White, J.**, expressing the view of six members of the court, it was held that (1) the fact that a defendant would not have pleaded guilty except for the opportunity to limit the possible penalty did not necessarily demonstrate that the plea was not the product of a free and rational choice, especially where the defendant was represented by a competent counsel whose advice was that the plea would be to the defendant's advantage, and (2) there was no constitutional error in accepting a guilty plea which contained a protestation of innocence when, as in the case at bar, the defendant intelligently concluded that his interests required entry of a guilty plea and the record before the judge contained strong evidence of actual guilt.

Black, J., concurred in the judgment and in substantially all of the opinion.

Brennan, J., joined by **Douglas** and **Marshall, JJ.**, dissented on the ground that the defendant's guilty plea was not voluntary, since the record showed that the plea was induced by the influence of the unconstitutional threat of the death penalty, the defendant's denial of guilt also being a relevant factor in determining whether the plea was voluntarily and intelligently made.

COUNSEL

Jacob L. Safron reargued the cause for appellant. With him on the briefs were Robert Morgan, Attorney General of North Carolina, and Andrew A. Vanore, Jr., joined in and adopted by the Attorneys General for their respective States as follows: Joe Purcell of Arkansas, David P. Buckson of Delaware, William J. Scott of Illinois, John B. Breckinridge of Kentucky, Joe T. Patterson of Mississippi, and Robert L. Woodahl of Montana; by the Government of the Virgin Islands; and by the National District Attorneys Association.

Doris R. Bray, by appointment of the Court, 394 US 1010, 23 L Ed 2d 37, 89 S Ct 1628, reargued the cause and filed briefs for appellee.

Jack Greenberg, James M. Nabrit III, Michael Meltsner, Norman C. Amaker, Charles Stephen Ralston, Anthony G. Amsterdam, J. LeVonne Chambers, and James E. Ferguson II filed a brief for Albert Bobby Childs et al. as amici curiae.

ARTURO FORNARIS, Jr., Appellant,

v

RIDGE TOOL CO. et al.

400 US 41, 27 L Ed 2d 174, 91 S Ct 156

November 23, 1970*

Decision: Federal District Court held required to refrain from deciding constitutionality of Puerto Rican statute until Puerto Rican Supreme Court ruled on local law question.

SUMMARY

A dealer brought suit in a Puerto Rican court for damages for breach of his distributorship contract with a manufacturer, relying on the Dealer's Contract Law enacted by the Legislature of Puerto Rico, which statute imposes liability on a manufacturer for unilaterally terminating a contract with a local dealer, regardless of the terms of the contract itself, for other than "just cause" as defined by the statute. The suit was removed on the basis of diversity of citizenship to the United States District Court for the District of Puerto Rico, which denied a motion to dismiss based on a claim that the statute was unconstitutional. Allowing an interlocutory appeal, the Court of Appeals for the First Circuit held that the statute placed substantial liability on a manufacturer as to contracts which could have been terminated without liability prior to enactment of the statute, and that such retrospective impact of the statute violated the due process clause of the Federal Constitution (423 F2d 563).

The United States Supreme Court reversed, directing the Court of Appeals to remand the case to the District

---

* Together with No. 543, Puerto Rico v The Ridge Tool Co. et al.

Court with instructions. In a per curiam opinion, expressing the unanimous view of the court, it was held that (1) the appeal from the judgment of the Court of Appeals was improper under 28 USC § 1254(2), which provides for appeals to the Supreme Court by a party relying on a "State statute" held to be unconstitutional by a Court of Appeals, since the Puerto Rican statute was not a "State statute"; (2) although the appeal was improper, the jurisdictional statements therein would be treated as petitions for writs of certiorari and granted on that basis; and (3) the District Court should be instructed to hold its hand until the Puerto Rican Supreme Court, which had not yet construed the statute, authoritatively ruled on the local law question in light of the federal claims.

ARNOLD TOURS, Inc., et al., Petitioners,

v

WILLIAM B. CAMP et al.

400 US 45, 27 L Ed 2d 179, 91 S Ct 158

November 23, 1970

Decision: Travel agents held to have standing to challenge Comptroller's ruling allowing national banks to provide travel services for bank customers.

SUMMARY

A group of independent travel agents, asking for declaratory and injunctive relief against the Comptroller of the Currency and a national bank, sought to invalidate a ruling by the Comptroller allowing national banks to provide travel services for their customers, which ruling, the travel agents contended, had caused them to lose substantial business and profits and was in excess of the Comptroller's authority. The United States District Court for the District of Massachusetts dismissed the complaint for lack of standing to sue (286 F Supp 770) and the Court of Appeals for the First Circuit affirmed (408 F2d 1147). In earlier proceedings, the United States Supreme Court vacated and remanded the case for reconsideration (397 US 315, 25 L Ed 2d 333, 90 S Ct 1109) and the Court of Appeals reaffirmed its previous decision.

Granting certiorari, the United States Supreme Court reversed and remanded. In a per curiam opinion, expressing the view of seven members of the court, it was held that the travel agents had standing to maintain the action, since § 4 of the Bank Service Corporation Act of 1962, providing that no bank service corporation may engage in any activity other than the performance of bank services for banks, arguably brings a competitor within the zone of interests protected by it, and since national banks are competitors of travel agents when they begin to provide travel services for bank customers.

Burger, Ch. J., and **Harlan, J.,** would have set the case for argument.

WALTER J. HICKEL, Secretary of the
Interior, Petitioner,

v

OIL SHALE CORPORATION et al.

400 US 48, 27 L Ed 2d 193, 91 S Ct 196

Argued October 22, 1970. Decided December 8, 1970.

Decision: Oil shale mining claims under General Mining
Act of 1872 held subject to cancellation by government for failure to substantially satisfy Act's assessment work requirements.

SUMMARY

Separate actions, instituted by claimants of certain oil
shale mining claims and consolidated for trial in the
United States District Court for the District of Colorado,
presented the issue whether the claims, asserted under the
General Mining Act of 1872, had been validly canceled
by the Department of the Interior in 1930 for failure
to comply with the statutory requirement that at least
$100 worth of labor or improvements be expended annu-
ally on each claim, notwithstanding the further provision
of the Act that failure to comply with the assessment
work requirements results in the claim's being subject to
relocation by others. The Mineral Lands Leasing Act
of 1920 restricts disposition of oil shale lands to leasing,
rather than to location and acquisition of title, but the
savings clause of § 37 of the 1920 Act, which the claimants
contended was applicable, makes available for patent,
valid pre-existing claims that are maintained in compliance with the laws under which they were initiated.
The District Court granted the relief sought, which included the issuance of patents that had previously been

administratively denied to some of the claimants and the expunging of the administrative rulings canceling the claims (261 F Supp 954), and the Court of Appeals for the Tenth Circuit affirmed (406 F2d 759), both courts holding that the administrative cancellations of the claims were void under earlier Supreme Court decisions to the effect that failure to do assessment work under the 1872 Act inured only to the benefit of relocators, and gave the government no grounds to cancel the claims.

On certiorari, the United States Supreme Court reversed and remanded. In an opinion by **Douglas, J.**, expressing the views of four members of the court, it was held that (1) relocation of oil shale claims under the 1872 Act upon default in assessment work was impossible after the 1920 Act, which made the United States the beneficiary of all invalid claims, (2) the earlier Supreme Court decisions should be construed to preclude the government's cancellation of claims only where there was substantial compliance with the assessment work requirements of the 1872 Act, and (3) cancellation of claims was proper where the assessment work did not substantially satisfy the statutory requirements, as was indicated by the record in the case at bar.

Burger, Ch. J., and **Stewart, J.**, dissented on the ground that the Court of Appeals had correctly construed and applied the earlier Supreme Court decision.

Harlan, White, and **Marshall, JJ.**, did not participate.

COUNSEL

Peter L. Strauss argued the cause for petitioner. With him on the briefs were Solicitor General Erwin N. Griswold, Assistant Attorney General Kashiwa, S. Billingsley Hill, Thos. L. McKevitt, and Edmund B. Clark.

[Supreme Ct Sum]

Fowler Hamilton argued the cause for respondents. With him on the briefs for respondents Oil Shale Corp. et al. were Richard W. Hulbert and Donald L. Morgan. John D. Knodell, Jr., Fred M. Winner, and Warren O. Martin filed a brief for respondents Umpleby et al.

PORT OF BOSTON MARINE TERMINAL
ASSOCIATION et al., Petitioners,

v

REDERIAKTIEBOLAGET TRANSATLANTIC

400 US 62, 27 L Ed 2d 203, 91 S Ct 203

Argued October 22, 1970.   Decided December 8, 1970.

Decision: Federal Maritime Commission decision pertaining to wharf demurrage charges held final, binding, and not subject to judicial review, where time
for Court of Appeals' direct review of decision had
expired.

SUMMARY

Without obtaining prior approval from the Federal
Maritime Commission, a marine terminal association
changed its allocation of wharf demurrage charges so as
to impose certain charges upon shipowners when the
failure to remove cargo resulted from a longshoremen's
strike.   After several shipowners had refused to pay these
charges, the terminal association brought suit in a state
court, and the action was removed to the United States
District Court for the District of Massachusetts.   The
defendants consisted of a shipping association and its
members, including the agent of the respondent shipowner.   The shipping association contended that the
change in the charges was invalid in the absence of the
Commission's prior approval, and the District Court
stayed the proceedings to allow the shipping association
to obtain a ruling by the Commission on the validity of
the change.   After a full evidentiary hearing, the Commission issued a report and order to the effect that the

change was valid despite the failure to obtain the Commission's prior approval (10 FMS 409). The shipping association petitioned the Court of Appeals for the District of Columbia Circuit for review, but the petition was dismissed as untimely because it was filed after the expiration of the 60-day period specified in the Administrative Orders Review Act. The respondent applied to the Commission for reconsideration, but the application was denied as untimely because it was filed after the expiratio: of the 30-day period specified in a Commission rule. Tl respondent did not seek direct judicial review of the Commission's denial of the application for reconsideration, but intervened in the action still pending in the District Court. The District Court, holding that it lacked authority to review the merits of the Commission's decision, rendered judgment against the defendants, including the respondent's agent. The respondent appealed to the Court of Appeals for the First Circuit, which, reversing the District Court's judgment, held that (1) since the respondent was not a party to the Commission proceedings, the Commission's decision was not entitled to binding effect as against the respondent, and (2) the Commission's position on the merits was erroneous (420 F2d 419).

On certiorari, the United States Supreme Court reversed. In an opinion by **Marshall, J.**, expressing the unanimous views of the court, it was held that since the time for the Court of Appeals' direct review of the Commission's order had expired, and the respondent had had every opportunity to participate in the Commission proceedings and to seek timely review, the Commission's decision was final and was binding upon the respondent, and the merits of the decision were not subject to review by the District Court, the Court of Appeals, or the Supreme Court.

COUNSEL

John M. Reed argued the cause and filed briefs for petitioners.

George F. Galland argued the cause and filed a brief for respondent.

Daniel M. Friedman argued the cause for the United States et al. as amici curiae. On the brief were Solicitor General Erwin N. Griswold, Assistant Attorney General McLaren, Deputy Solictor General Springer, Irwin A. Seibel, and Gordon M. Shaw.

A. L. DUTTON, Warden, Appellant,

v

ALEX S. EVANS

400 US 74, 27 L Ed 2d 213, 91 S Ct 210

Reargued October 15, 1970. Decided
December 15, 1970.

Decision: Admission in Georgia murder prosecution of witness' testimony as to statement made by defendant's alleged accomplice while in custody after murder, held not violative of defendant's constitutional rights.

SUMMARY

Upon jury trial in a Georgia court, the defendant was convicted of murder, the state having presented 20 witnesses, including an eyewitness, who described in detail the defendant's participation with others in the murder. The trial court, overruling the defendant's objection on the ground that the testimony was hearsay and thus violated the defendant's right of confrontation, admitted testimony of a prosecution witness that an alleged accomplice of the defendant, after the accomplice's arraignment on the murder charge, had told the witness, who was a fellow prisoner in a federal penitentiary, that if it had not been for the defendant, "we wouldn't be in this now," the alleged accomplice not having appeared as a witness at the defendant's trial. Such testimony was admitted on the basis of a Georgia statute allowing admission of a conspirator's statements against other conspirators, which statute was construed to allow evidence of a coconspirator's out-of-court statement made during the concealment phase of the conspiracy. After the judgment of conviction was affirmed by the Supreme Court of Georgia (222 Ga 392, 150 SE2d 240), the defendant instituted habeas corpus proceedings in the United States District Court for the Northern District of Georgia, again asserting that the admission of the evidence of the accomplice's statement violated the defendant's constitutional right of confrontation. The District Court denied the writ, but the Court of Appeals for the Fifth Circuit reversed, upholding the defendant's claim because it found no cogent reasons for the hearsay exception applied by the Georgia courts, and noting that such exception was broader than that applicable in federal conspiracy trials, under which a conspirator's out-of-court statements, made during the concealment phase of the conspiracy, were not admissible against a coconspirator (400 F2d 826).

On appeal, the United States Supreme Court reversed and remanded. Five members of the court, although not agreeing on an opinion, agreed that the defendant's constitutional rights had not been violated by the admission of the evidence under the Georgia statute.

Stewart, J., announced the judgment of the court, and in an opinion joined by Burger, Ch. J., White, J., and Blackmun, J., expressed the views that (1) the evidentiary rule applied by the state did not violate the confrontation clause of the Sixth Amendment as applicable under the Fourteenth Amendment merely because it did not exactly coincide with the hearsay exception applicable in the decidedly different context of a federal prosecution for the substantive offense of conspiracy, and (2) the defendant's right of confrontation was not otherwise violated under the circumstances of the case at bar, particularly since the accomplice's statement was not "crucial" or "devastating" in view of the other evidence, the defendant had been given full opportunity for cross-examination of all the prosecution witnesses, and there were "indicia of reliability" warranting admission of the statement even though there was no confrontation of the declarant.

Blackmun, J., joined by **Burger, Ch. J.**, concurred in the opinion of **Stewart, J.**, stating as an additional reason for the result reached that under the record, the admission of the evidence as to the accomplice's statement constituted harmless error, if it was error at all.

Harlan, J., concurring in the result, expressed the view that the due process requirement of the Fourteenth Amendment, rather than the confrontation clause, was the proper constitutional standard for testing rules of evidence, and that the application of the Georgia statute in the case at bar satisfied the due process requirement of a fair trial.

Marshall, J., joined by **Black, Douglas**, and **Brennan, JJ.**, dissented on the ground that the defendant had been denied his constitutional guaranty of the right to confront and cross-examine all the witnesses against him, since the incriminatory extrajudicial statement of the alleged accomplice was so inherently prejudicial that it should not be introduced unless there was an opportunity to cross-examine the declarant, whether or not the statement fell within a genuine exception to the hearsay rule.

COUNSEL

Alfred L. Evans, Jr., Assistant Attorney General of Georgia, reargued the cause for appellant. With him on the brief were Arthur K. Bolton, Attorney General, and Marion O. Gordon and Mathew Robins, Assistant Attorneys General.

Robert B. Thompson reargued the cause and filed a brief for appellee.

Solicitor General Erwin N. Griswold, by invitation of

the Court, argued the cause for the United States as amicus curiae on the reargument. With him on the brief were Assistant Attorney General Wilson, Jerome M. Feit, Beatrice Rosenberg, and Roger A. Pauley.

STATE OF OREGON, Plaintiff,

v

JOHN N. MITCHELL, Attorney General of
the United States (No. 43, Orig.)

STATE OF TEXAS, Plaintiff,

v

JOHN N. MITCHELL, Attorney General of
the United States (No. 44, Orig.)

UNITED STATES, Plaintiff,

v

STATE OF ARIZONA (No. 46, Orig.)

UNITED STATES, Plaintiff,

v

STATE OF IDAHO (No 47, Orig.)

400 US 112, 27 L Ed 2d 272, 91 S Ct 260

Argued October 19, 1970. Decided December 21, 1970.

Decision: Federal voting rights statute held valid insofar
as it lowers minimum voting age to 18 for federal
elections, changes residency requirements and absentee voting procedures for presidential elections, and
suspends literacy tests throughout nation, but statute
held invalid insofar as it lowers minimum voting age
for state and local elections.

SUMMARY

A 1970 federal voting rights statute provided that the minimum voting age would be lowered from 21 to 18 for both federal elections and state and local elections, that the use of literacy tests would be suspended throughout the United States for both federal elections and state and local elections, that the states would be prohibited from disqualifying voters from presidential and vice presidential elections because of failure to meet state residency requirements, and that there would be uniform national rules for absentee registration and voting in presidential and vice presidential elections.

Invoking the original jurisdiction of the United States Supreme Court, the United States sought to enjoin certain states from noncompliance with the statute, and certain states sought to enjoin the United States Attorney General from enforcing the statute. In an opinion by **Black, J.**, announcing the judgments of the court, it was held (1) expressing the view of five members of the court, that the provision lowering the minimum voting age from 21 to 18 was valid as applied to federal elections, (2) expressing the view of five members of the court, that as applied to state and local elections, the provision lowering the voting age from 21 to 18 was not authorized by the Fourteenth Amendment's equal protection clause and enforcement clause and was invalid, (3) expressing the unanimous view of the court, that the provision suspending the use of literacy tests for both federal elections and state and local elections was valid, and (4) expressing the view of eight members of the court, that the provisions pertaining to residency requirements and absentee registration and voting in presidential and vice presidential elections were valid.

Black, J., expressing his own views, would base holding (1) above on Art 1 § 4 of the Constitution and on Art 2

§ 1 and the necessary and proper clause of Art 1 § 8 cl 18, would base holding (3) on the equal protection clause of the Fourteenth Amendment, § 1 of the Fifteenth Amendment, and the enforcement clauses of the Fourteenth and Fifteenth Amendments, and would base holding (4) on Art 2 § 1 of the Constitution and the necessary and proper clause of Art 1 § 8 cl 18.

Douglas, J., concurring in holdings (1), (3), and (4) above, but dissenting from holding (2), would hold that on the basis of the Fourteenth Amendment's equal protection clause and enforcement clause, the provisions lowering the voting age and suspending the use of literacy tests were valid in both federal elections and state and local elections, and that on the basis of the Fourteenth Amendment's privileges and immunities clause and enforcement clause, the provision pertaining to residency requirements in presidential elections was valid.

Harlan, J., concurring in holdings (2) and (3) above, but dissenting from holdings (1) and (4), would hold that the suspension of the use of literacy tests was an appropriate means of enforcing the Fifteenth Amendment, but that neither the Fourteenth Amendment nor any other source of congressional power authorized Congress to lower the voting age as fixed by state laws, or to alter state laws on residency, registration, and absentee voting, with respect to either federal elections or state and local elections.

Brennan, J., joined by **White** and **Marshall, JJ.**, concurring in holdings (1), (3), and (4) above, but dissenting from holding (2), would hold that on the basis of the Fourteenth Amendment's equal protection clause and enforcement clause, the provision lowering the voting age was valid with respect to both federal elections and state and local elections, that on the basis of the Fifteenth Amendment and its enforcement clause, the provision suspending the use of literacy tests was valid, and that on the basis of the constitutional right of interstate travel and the enforcement clause of the Fourteenth Amendment, the provision pertaining to residency requirements was valid.

Stewart, J., joined by Burger, Ch. J., and Blackmun, J., concurring in holdings (2), (3), and (4) above, but dissenting from holding (1), would hold that on the basis of the Fifteenth Amendment and its enforcement clause, the provision suspending the use of literacy tests was valid, and that on the basis of the power of Congress to protect the constitutional right of interstate travel, the provision pertaining to residency requirements was valid, but that the provision lowering the voting age for federal elections and for state and local elections exceeded Congress' constitutional power.

COUNSEL

Lee Johnson, Attorney General of Oregon, argued the cause for plaintiff in No. 43, Orig. With him on the briefs were Diarmuid F. O'Scannlain, Deputy Attorney General, Jacob B. Tanzer, Solicitor General, and Al J. Laue and Thomas H. Denney, Assistant Attorneys General. Charles Alan Wright argued the cause for plaintiff in No. 44, Orig. With him on the brief were Crawford C. Martin, Attorney General of Texas, Nola White, First Assistant Attorney General, Alfred Walker, Executive Assistant Attorney General, and J. C. Davis, W. O. Shultz II, and John Reeves, Assistant Attorneys General. Solicitor General Griswold argued the cause for defendant in Nos. 43, Orig., and 44, Orig., and for the United States in Nos. 46, Orig., and 47, Orig. With him on the briefs were Attorney General Mitchell, pro se, Assistant Attorney General Leonard, and Peter L. Strauss.

Gary K. Nelson, Attorney General of Arizona, and John M. McGowan II, Special Assistant Attorney General, argued the cause and filed a brief for defendant in No. 46, Orig. Robert M. Robson, Attorney General of Idaho, argued the cause for defendant in No. 47, Orig. With him on the brief was Richard H. Greener, Assistant Attorney General. Brief of amicus curiae in all cases was filed by A. F. Summer, Attorney General, Delos Burks, First Assistant Attorney General, William A. Allain, Assistant Attorney General, and Charles B. Henley for the State of Mississippi. Briefs of amici curiae in Nos. 43, Orig., 46, Orig., and 47, Orig., were filed by Melvin L. Wulf for the American Civil Liberties Union, and by John R. Cosgrove for Citizens for Lowering the Voting Age et al. Brief of amicus curiae in Nos. 43, Orig., and 46, Orig., was filed by William A. Dobrovir, Joseph L. Rauh, Jr., David Rubin, Stephen I. Schlossberg, John A. Fillion, Nathaniel R. Jones, Clarence Mitchell, and J. Francis Pohlhaus for the Youth Franchise Coalition et al. Briefs of amici curiae in No. 43, Orig., were filed by Joseph A. Califano, Jr., and Clifford L. Alexander for the Democratic National Committee, and by Messrs. Jones, Mitchell, and Pohlhaus for the Department of Armed Services and Veterans Affairs of the National Association for the Advancement of Colored People. Brief of amicus curiae for the State of Indiana in support of plaintiff in No. 44, Orig., was filed by Theodore L. Sendak, Attorney General, Richard C. Johnson, Chief Deputy Attorney General, and William F. Thompson, Assistant Attorney General, joined by the Attorneys General for their respective States, as follows: Joe Purcell of Arkansas, Robert M. Robson of Idaho, Jack P. F. Gremillion of Louisiana, Clarence A. H. Meyer of Nebraska, Warren B. Rudman of New Hampshire, Robert Morgan of North Carolina, Helgi Johanneson of North Dakota, Paul W. Brown of Ohio, Gordon Mydland of South Dakota, Vernon B.

Romney of Utah, Slade Gorton of Washington, Chauncey H. Browning, Jr., of West Virginia, and James E. Barrett of Wyoming. Brief of amicus curiae in No. 47, Orig., was filed by Andrew P. Miller, Attorney General, and Anthony F. Troy and Walter A. McFarlane, Assistant Attorneys General, for the Commonwealth of Virginia.

NATIONAL LABOR RELATIONS BOARD,
Petitioner,

v

LOCAL 825, INTERNATIONAL UNION OF
OPERATING ENGINEERS, AFL-CIO
(No. 40)

BURNS AND ROE, Inc., et al., Petitioners,

v

LOCAL 825, INTERNATIONAL UNION OF
OPERATING ENGINEERS, AFL-CIO
(No. 42)

400 US 297, 27 L Ed 2d 398, 91 S Ct 402

Argued November 18, 1970. Decided January 12, 1971.

Decision: Secondary boycott provision of § 8(b)(4)(B) of National Labor Relations Act held violated where union, which had work assignment dispute with one subcontractor, used coercion and strikes against neutral general contractor and other subcontractors.

SUMMARY

A union, members of which were employed by subcontractors on a construction project, became involved in a dispute with one of the subcontractors, who refused to assign certain jobs to the union's members rather than to the members of another union. After the general contractor on the project refused to execute a contract which would bind both the general contractor and all the subcontractors and which would give the union jurisdiction over the disputed work assignments, the union threatened the general contractor and all of the subcontractors with work stoppages unless the union's demands were met. Upon the employers' refusal, the union induced and conducted strikes by its members employed by both the neutral subcontractors and the subcontractor involved in the primary dispute, thus shutting down the whole construction project. In unfair labor practice proceedings against the union (162 NLRB 1617), the National Labor Relations Board found that § 8(b)(4)(B) of the National Labor Relations Act as amended, which makes it an unfair labor practice for a union to engage in certain secondary activity, including strikes or coercive conduct, where an object of such activity is to force any person to cease doing business with another person, had been violated by the union's coercion of the general contractor and by its encouragement of strikes by its members employed by the neutral subcontractors, for the purpose of forcing the subcontractor involved in the primary dispute to assign the disputed work to union members. The Board also found that the union, by inducing the strikes by its members employed by all the subcontractors, had violated § 8(b)(4)(D) of the Act, which makes it an unfair labor practice for a union to induce or engage in a strike to force an employer to assign particular work to the union's members rather than to members of another union. The United States Court of Appeals for the Third Circuit, in proceedings to enforce the Board's order, approved the latter finding, but set aside the finding as to § 8(b)(4)(B), on the ground that the union's objective was only to force the subcontractor involved in the primary dispute to change its work assignment policy, rather than to force the general contractor to terminate its relationship with the subcontractor, as required by the "cease doing business" provision of the statute (410 F2d 5).

On certiorari, the United States Supreme Court reversed and remanded. In an opinion by **Marshall, J.**, it was held (1) expressing the view of seven members of the court, that the union's activities with regard to the general contractor and the neutral subcontractors constituted secondary conduct proscribed by § 8(b)(4)(B), since even though the union did not expressly demand termination of the relationship between the general contractor and the subcontractor involved in the primary dispute, nevertheless the clear implication of the union's demands was that the general contractor should either force a change in the subcontractor's policy or terminate its contract, and (2) expressing the unanimous view of the court, that although § 8(b)(4)(D) was also applicable to the union's conduct, nevertheless such section did not provide the exclusive remedy, neither of the sections involved having exclusive application.

Douglas, J., joined by **Stewart, J.**, dissented as to holding (1) above, while agreeing with holding (2).

COUNSEL

Arnold Ordman argued the cause for the National Labor Relations Board, petitioner in No. 40 and respondent in No. 42. With him on the brief were Solicitor General Erwin N. Griswold, Peter L. Strauss, Dominick L. Manoli, and Norton J. Come. Vincent J. Apruzzese argued the cause for petitioners in No. 42. With him on the brief were Francis A. Mastro and Merritt T. Viscardi.

Earl S. Aronson argued the cause for respondent Local 825, International Union of Operating Engineers, in both cases. With him on the brief was Thomas E. Durkin, Jr.

Laurence Gold argued the cause for the American Federation of Labor and Congress of Industrial Organizations as amicus curiae urging affirmance in both cases. With him on the brief were J. Albert Woll and Thomas E. Harris.

Briefs of amici curiae urging reversal in both cases were filed by William B. Barton and Harry J. Lambeth for Associated Builders & Contractors, Inc., and by Winthrop A. Johns and Lawrence T. Zimmerman for the Associated General Contractors of America et al.

GEORGE K. WYMAN, Individually and as Commissioner of the State of New York, Department of Social Services, Appellant,

v

BARBARA JAMES, etc.

400 US 309, 27 L Ed 2d 408, 91 S Ct 381

Argued October 20, 1970. Decided January 12, 1971.

Decision: Caseworker's visit to welfare recipient's home held not unreasonable search, and recipient's refusal to permit visit held to warrant termination of welfare benefits.

SUMMARY

The plaintiff, a recipient of Aid to Families with Dependent Children, was notified that her home would be visited by a caseworker. The plaintiff offered to supply information relevant to her need for public assistance, but she refused to permit the caseworker to visit her home, and pursuant to New York statutory and administrative provisions, her AFDC benefits were terminated because of such refusal. Granting the plaintiff's request for injunctive relief, a three-judge United States District Court for the Southern District of New York held that since the visit to the plaintiff's home would, in the absence of a warrant, have been an unconstitutional search, the plaintiff's refusal to permit the visit did not justify terminating her AFDC benefits (303 F Supp 935).

On appeal, the United States Supreme Court reversed and directed that a judgment of dismisal be entered. In an opinion by **Blackmun, J.**, it was held (1) expressing the view of five members of the court, that the caseworker's home visit was not a "search" within the meaning of the Fourth Amendment, and (2) expressing the view of six members of the court, that even if the visit was a search, it was not unreasonable, it served a valid and proper administrative purpose for the dispensation of the AFDC program, it was not an unwarranted invasion of personal privacy, and it violated no right guaranteed by the Fourth Amendment.

White, J., concurring in the judgment, joined in the court's opinion except as to holding (1) above.

Douglas, J., dissenting, would affirm the judgment below.

Marshall, J., joined by **Brennan, J.**, dissenting, would hold a nonconsensual home visit by a caseworker violative of regulations of the Department of Health, Education, and Welfare, and would hold, if it was necessary to reach the constitutional question, that the home visit was a search, and that, absent a warrant, the search was unreasonable.

COUNSEL

Brenda Soloff, Assistant Attorney General of New York, argued the cause for appellant Wyman. With her on the brief were Louis J. Lefkowitz, Attorney General, and Samuel A. Hirshowitz, First Assistant Attorney General, for appellant Wyman, and J. Lee Rankin for appellant Goldberg, Commissioner of Social Services of the City of New York.

Jonathan Weiss argued the cause for appellee. With him on the brief was David Gilman.

Briefs of amici curiae urging affirmance were filed by Stephen F. Gordon and Ernest Fleischman for the Social Service Employees Union Local 371, AFSCME, AFL-CIO, and by the Legal Aid Society of San Mateo County.

U. S. BULK CARRIERS, Inc., Petitioner,

v

DOMINIC B. ARGUELLES

400 US 351, 27 L Ed 2d 456, 91 S Ct 409

Argued November 12, 1970.   Decided January 13, 1971.

Decision: Seaman's suit for wages under 46 USC § 596 held not precluded by his failure to take advantage of § 301 of Labor Management Relations Act providing for enforcement of grievance and arbitration provisions of collective bargaining agreements.

SUMMARY

Instead of pursuing his claim for wages accruing from services rendered in foreign commerce through the grievance and arbitration procedures for disputed claims contained in the collective bargaining agreement which governed the conditions of his employment, a seaman brought suit in admiralty for the wages alleged to be due him, in the United States District Court for the District of Maryland, under 46 USC §§ 596–597, which provides, in essence, that every master or owner of a vessel who fails without sufficient cause to make payment, in the manner and amount provided by the statute, of wages due a seaman, shall pay to such seaman a sum equal to 2 days' pay for each day during which payment, is delayed beyond the prescribed period, and which further states that such sum is recoverable as wages "in any claim made before the court."   The District Court granted the employer's motion for summary judgment, on the ground that the seaman's claim had to be processed in accordance with the procedures established in the collective bargaining agreement, and while it could enforce the grievance procedure or any award which might be given, it had no jurisdiction to adjudicate the maritime claim. The Court of Appeals for the Fourth Circuit reversed (408 F2d 1065), holding that, in spite of § 301 of the Labor Management Relations Act of 1947, which provides for the enforcement of grievance and arbitration procedures contained in collective bargaining agreements in industries affecting commerce, the seaman was entitled to have his claim for wages brought under 46 USC §§ 596–59 adjudicated by the court.

On certiorari, the United States Supreme Court affirmed. In an opinion by **Douglas, J.**, expressing the views of five members of the court, it was held that while § 301 of the Labor Management Relations Act of 1947 provided an optional method of resolving the controversy, it did not displace the earlier and distinctly different alternative method for collecting seamen's wages contained in 46 USC §§ 596–597.

Black, J., while concurring in the judgment and opinion of the court, adhered to his dissent in Republic Steel Corp. v Maddox (1965) 379 US 650, 13 L Ed 2d 580, 85 S Ct 614, in which he expressed the view that the Labor Management Relations Act should never be construed so as to require an individual employee, after he is out of a job, to submit a claim involving wages to grievance and arbitration proceedings, or to surrender his right to sue his employer in court for the enforcement of his claim.

Harlan, J., concurring in the judgment and opinion of the court, expressed the further view that an individual employee whose substantive rights derive solely from a labor agreement cannot bypass the grievance procedures and arbitral forum in a suit brought "simply on the contract"; but that where, as in the case of the seaman, an employee's substantive rights derive from a federal statute as well as a labor agreement, then he has an option to choose between the arbitral and judicial forums where he states a claim under both the labor agreement and the statute.

White, J., joined by **Brennan, Stewart,** and **Marshall, JJ.**, dissented, expressing the view that nothing in 46 USC §§ 596–597 warranted dispensing with the grievance procedure and arbitration provided for in the labor agreement under which the seaman was employed; that it would not be in derogation of such statutes to require that the penalties provided therein as wage claims be presented like any other wage claims after exhausting internal remedies; and that the seaman should have been required to process his claim through arbitration, since there was no indication that Congress, in passing the Labor Management Relations Act of 1947, intended that seamen should be treated any differently from their nonmaritime counterparts.

COUNSEL

George W. Sullivan argued the cause and filed a brief for petitioner.

I. Duke Avnet argued the cause and filed a brief for respondent.

ERNEST PERKINS et al., Appellants,

v

L. S. MATTHEWS, Mayor of the City of Canton, et al.

400 US 379, 27 L Ed 2d 476, 91 S Ct 431

Argued October 20, 1970.   Decided January 14, 1971.

Decision: City's changes as to location of polling places, municipal boundaries, and at-large election of aldermen held subject to federal approval requirement of § 5 of Voting Rights Act of 1965.

SUMMARY

Voters and candidates for election to offices in the city of Canton, Mississippi, instituted an action in the United States District Court for the Southern District of Mississippi to enjoin 1969 city elections, on the ground that the city, which was covered by the Voting Rights Act of 1965, sought to enforce certain changes with respect to voting procedures, which changes had not been first submitted for federal approval under the requirement of § 5 of the Act that states or political subdivisions covered by the Act must obtain approval of voting procedures different from those in effect on November 1, 1964, by obtaining a declaratory judgment as to the nondiscriminatory purpose and effect of the changes from the District Court for the District of Columbia, or by submitting the proposed changes to the United States Attorney General. The plaintiffs alleged that voting requirements for the 1969 elections differed from those in effect at the last city elections in 1965 because of (1) changes in locations of polling places, (2) changes in the municipal boundaries through annexations of adjacent areas which enlarged the number of eligible voters, and (3) a change from ward to at-large election of aldermen, even though a 1962 state statute, which had been ignored by the city in the 1965 elections, required at-large elections. A three-judge District Court, was convened, which dismissed the complaint on the ground that the challenged changes did not have a discriminatory purpose or effect (301 F Supp 565). The elections were thereafter held with the challenged changes in effect.

On direct appeal, the United States Supreme Court reversed and remanded. In an opinion by **Brennan, J.**, it was held (1) expressing the view of six members of the court, that the District Court should have limited its inquiry in the instant proceedings merely to the determination whether the voting changes, without regard to discriminatory purpose or effect, were covered by § 5 of the Act and must be submitted for federal approval, which determination, in view of the adequacy of the record, would be made by the Supreme Court, (2) expressing the view of five members of the court, that any change in election procedure, no matter how small, was subject to § 5 scrutiny, (3) expressing the view of six members of the court, that the city's change in the locations of polling places was subject to the federal approval requirements of § 5, (4) expressing the view of five members of the court, that § 5 also applied to the change in the city's boundary lines by annexations and to the change from ward to at-large elections of aldermen, and (5) expressing the view of seven members of the court, that the Supreme Court would not order new elections, but would remand to the District Court for the initial determination of the appropriate remedy.

Blackmun, J., joined by **Burger**, Ch. J., concurred in the judgment of reversal and in the order of remand, in view of the decision in Allen v State Board of Elections, 393 US 544, 22 L Ed 2d 1, 89 S Ct 817, which held that the election laws there involved were subject to the approval requirements of § 5.

Harlan, J., concurring in part and dissenting in part, agreed with holdings (1) and (3) above, but disagreed with holdings (2) and (4) on the grounds that § 5 should not be construed to apply to matters such as annexations, which affect voting only incidentally or peripherally, and that the change to at-large elections of the city's aldermen should be considered as having occurred on the effective date of the 1962 state statute, thus not requiring § 5 approval.

Black, J., dissented, expressing the view that (1) § 5 of the Act violated the Federal Constitution insofar as it deprived a few states and their political subdivisions of the power to make their own laws and govern themselves without advance federal approval, and (2) in any event, the remand of the case for determining whether a new election should be held was inappropriate, since the Supreme Court should decide the question by upholding the 1969 elections, the alleged violations of the Act being technical and there being no proof of actual discrimination.

COUNSEL

Armand Derfner argued the cause and filed a brief for appellants.

Robert L. Goza argued the cause for appellees. With him on the brief were A. F. Summer, Attorney General of Mississippi, and William A. Allain, Assistant Attorney General.

WINTON M. BLOUNT, Postmaster General of the
United States, et al., Appellants,

v

TONY RIZZI, dba The Mail Box (No. 55)

UNITED STATES et al., Appellants,

v

THE BOOK BIN (No. 58)

400 US 410, 27 L Ed 2d 498, 91 S Ct 423

Argued November 10, 1970. Decided January 14, 1971.

Decision: First Amendment held violated because of lack
of adequate procedural safeguards under federal
statutes (39 USC §§ 4006, 4007) authorizing Postmaster General to prevent use of mails or postal
money orders in connection with allegedly obscene
materials.

SUMMARY

A federal statute (39 USC § 4006) authorized the
Postmaster General, after the completion of administrative proceedings, to return mail to the sender or to forbid
the payment of postal money orders in connection with
the sale of allegedly obscene materials. Another federal
statute (39 USC § 4007) authorized the Postmaster General, upon a showing of probable cause to believe the
§ 4006 was being violated, to obtain from a United States
District Court a temporary restraining order and preliminary injunction directing the detention of the seller's
incoming mail pending the administrative proceedings
under § 4006. After a § 4006 administrative order was

entered against a seller of allegedly obscene magazines the seller, suing in the United States District Court for the Central District of California, obtained from a three judge District Court (1) a declaratory judgment that § 4006 was unconstitutional because of a lack of adequate procedural safeguards, and (2) an injunction against enforcement of the administrative order (305 F Supp 634). With respect to another seller of allegedly obscene magazines, the Postmaster General applied to the United States District Court for the Northern District of Georgia for a § 4007 order, pending the completion of § 4006 administrative proceedings against the seller, but a three-judge District Court held that both § 4006 and § 4007 were unconstitutional because of a lack of adequate procedural safeguards (306 F Supp 1023).

On appeal, the United States Supreme Court affirmed each of the judgments below. In an opinion by **Brennan, J.**, expressing the view of eight members of the court, §§ 4006 and 4007 were held violative of the First Amendment because of a lack of adequate procedural safeguards, since the statutes neither required the Postmaster General to seek a prompt judicial determination of the obscenity of the magazines before barring them from the mail nor provided any assurance of prompt judicial review of administrative proceedings.

Black, J., concurred in the result.

COUNSEL

Peter L. Strauss argued the cause for appellants in both cases. With him on the brief were Solicitor General Erwin N. Griswold, Assistant Attorney General Ruckelshaus, Robert V. Zener, Donald L. Horowitz, David Nelson, and Charles D. Hawley.

Stanley Fleishman argued the cause for appellee in No. 55. With him on the brief was Sam Rosenwein. Robert Eugene Smith argued the cause for appellee in No. 58. With him on the brief was Hugh W. Gilbert.

———————

ROBERT KENNERLY and Helen Kennerly,
Petitioners,

v

DISTRICT COURT OF THE NINTH
JUDICIAL DISTRICT OF
MONTANA et al.

400 US 423, 27 L Ed 507, 91 S Ct 480
January 18, 1971

Decision: Montana court held to lack jurisdiction in civil case involving debt of Blackfeet Indian defendants to grocery store located within Indian reservation.

SUMMARY

A suit was commenced in a Montana state court against members of the Blackfeet Indian Tribe, who resided on an Indian reservation in Montana, to recover on a debt arising from the Indians' purchase of food on credit from a grocery store located on the reservation. In 1967, the Blackfeet Tribal Council enacted a tribal law providing that the Tribal Court and the state should have concurrent jurisdiction over all actions wherein the defendant was a member of the Tribe. However, the state thereafter took no action under a 1953 federal statute (67 Stat 590) which authorized any state, not otherwise jurisdiction in Indian country located therein, to assume such jurisdiction by affirmative legislative action. Furthermore, there had not been any tribal consent given to the state's assumption of jurisdiction, by a majority vote of the affected adult Indians voting at a special election called for such purpose, as was required by Title IV of the Civil Rights Act of 1968, which repealed the 1953 statute except as to jurisdiction previously acquired thereunder. The trial court overruled the defendants' motion to dismiss on the ground that the state courts lacked jurisdiction because the defendants were members of the Blackfeet Tribe and the transaction took place on the reservation, and the Supreme Court of Montana affirmed such ruling.

Granting certiorari, the United States Supreme Court vacated the judgment of the Supreme Court of Montana, and remanded the case. In a per curiam opinion expressing the view of seven members of the court, it was held that the unilateral action of the Tribal Council in enacting the tribal law conferring concurrent jurisdiction on the state was insufficient to vest the state with civil jurisdiction either under the 1953 statute, the state not having taken the required affirmative legislative action, or under Title IV of the Civil Rights Act of 1968, there never having been held any election to obtain tribal consent as required thereby.

STATE OF WISCONSIN, Appellant,

v

NORMA GRACE CONSTANTINEAU

400 US 433, 27 L Ed 2d 515, 91 S Ct 507

Argued December 10, 1970. Decided January 19, 1971.

Decision: Due process held violated by failure to provide
notice and opportunity to be heard before posting
of notice naming person to whom sale of liquor is
forbidden, and Federal District Court held not required to abstain from deciding constitutionality of
state statute.

SUMMARY

A Wisconsin statute provided that various persons
could forbid in writing the sale or gift of intoxicating
liquors to one who, by excessive drinking, produced
described conditions or exhibited specified traits, such
as exposing himself or his family to want or becoming
dangerous to the peace of the community. Pursuant
to this statute, a police chief, without giving the appellee
advance notice or an opportunity to be heard, caused
to be posted in all local retail liquor outlets a notice forbidding sales or gifts of liquor to the appellee. Suing
in the United States District Court for the Eastern District of Wisconsin, the appellee sought injunctive relief
against the enforcement of the statute. A three-judge
District Court granted injunctive relief, holding the
statute violative of procedural due process because of
the failure to provide notice of the intent to post and an
opportunity to be heard (302 F Supp 861).

On appeal, the United States Supreme Court affirmed.
In an opinion by **Douglas, J.**, expressing the views of six

members of the court, it was held (1) that the label or characterization given a person by posting the notice, though a mark of serious illness to some, was to others such a stigma or badge of disgrace that procedural due process required notice and an opportunity to be heard, and (2) that since there was no ambiguity in the state statute, the Federal District Court had acted properly in not abstaining from deciding the appellee's federal constitutional claim.

Burger, Ch. J., joined by **Blackmun, J.**, dissented on the ground that on the basis of the policy of steering around head-on collisions with the states by avoiding unnecessary constitutional decisions, the Federal District Court should have abstained from deciding the appellee's federal constitutional claim until resort to state courts was exhausted.

Black, J., joined by **Blackmun, J.**, dissented, expressing substantial agreement with **Burger, Ch. J.**, and adding that the state courts might, without reaching constitutional questions, confine the state statute to its proper limits on the basis of state law provisions, and that it was unfair to deny the state courts such an opportunity.

COUNSEL

Benjamin Southwick, Assistant Attorney General of Wisconsin, argued the cause for appellant. With him on the brief were Robert W. Warren, Attorney General, and Robert D. Martinson, Assistant Attorney General.

S. A. Schapiro argued the cause and filed a brief for appellee.

R. K. PROCUNIER, Director, California
Department of Corrections, Petitioner,

v

VERON ATCHLEY

400 US 446, 27 L Ed 2d 524, 91 S Ct 485

Argued November 18, 1970. Decided
January 19, 1971.

Decision: State prisoner seeking federal habeas corpus
relief held not entitled to new hearing on voluntariness of statements tape-recorded during jail conversation with insurance agent and admitted at
murder trial.

SUMMARY

Upon trial in a California state court in 1959, the defendant was convicted of murdering his wife. The trial
court, over the defendant's objection based on involun-
tariness, admitted in evidence a police tape recording
of incriminating statements made by the defendant during a conversation with an insurance agent, which conversation occurred while the defendant was in jail and
related to an insurance policy on the defendant's wife.
The Supreme Court of California, affirming the conviction, rejected the defendant's contention that the statement was inadmissible as an involuntary confession (53
Cal 2d 160, 346 P2d 764). In 1967, the defendant
initiated habeas corpus proceedings in the United States
District Court for the Northern District of California,
renewing his assertion that the recorded statement, as
an involuntary confession, had been unconstitutionally
admitted into evidence. Ruling that the defendant was
entitled to a new hearing in the state courts on the issue

of voluntariness, the District Court concluded that although it was not able to say that the confession was involuntary, nevertheless the trial court had not reliably determined the voluntariness of the confession, since it had excluded certain pertinent evidence, including evidence as to whether the defendant had been denied counsel, had been advised of his right to remain silent, and had known that the conversation was being recorded (300 F Supp 68). The Court of Appeals for the Ninth Circuit affirmed on the District Court's opinion (412 F2d 230).

On certiorari, the United States Supreme Court reversed. In an opinion by **Stewart, J.**, expressing the view of eight members of the court, it was held that (1) an applicant for federal habeas corpus was not entitled to a new hearing on the voluntariness issue, in either the federal or state courts, merely because he pointed to shortcomings in procedures used to decide the issue in the state courts, but he must also show that his version of events, if true, would require the conclusion that his confession was involuntary; and (2) the applicant in the case at bar was not entitled to a new hearing, since he had not made such showing, and since the state courts had given full consideration to the issue of the voluntariness of his statement and had applied correct constitutional standards in upholding its admission in evidence.

Black, J., concurred in the judgment and substantially all of the opinion.

COUNSEL

Robert R. Granucci, Deputy Attorney General of California, argued the cause for petitioner. With him on the briefs were Thomas C. Lynch, Attorney General, Albert W. Harris, Jr., Assistant Attorney General, and William D. Stein, Deputy Attorney General.

Charles A. Legge argued the cause and filed a brief for respondent.

———————

RICHARD MAYBERRY, Petitioner,

v

STATE OF PENNSYLVANIA

400 US 455, 27 L Ed 2d 532, 91 S Ct 499

Argued December 17, 1970. Decided
January 20, 1971

Decision: Defendant who disrupted state criminal trial
and repeatedly insulted judge, held entitled under
due process to trial before another judge on criminal
contempt charges asserted after criminal trial.

SUMMARY

During the defendant's criminal trial in a Pennsylvania
state court, the defendant, who had an appointed counsel
as an adviser but who represented himself, repeatedly
engaged in disruptive conduct and made insulting and
slanderous remarks to the judge—including calling him
"dirty sonofabitch," "dirty tyrannical old dog," "stum-
bling dog," and "fool," charging him with running a
"Spanish Inquisition," and telling him to "Go to hell"
and "Keep your mouth shut." When the defendant was
brought in for sentencing after a jury verdict of guilty
on the criminal charges, the trial judge pronounced him
guilty of 11 criminal contempts arising from his conduct
during the trial, and sentenced him to a total of 11 to
22 years thereon. The Supreme Court of Pennsylvania
affirmed (434 Pa 478, 255 A2d 131).

On certiorari, the United States Supreme Court vacated and remanded. In an opinion by **Douglas, J.**, it
was held (1) expressing the view of seven members of the
court, that the trial judge could have acted instantly as
the defendant's acts and outbursts occurred to hold him

in contempt, but (2) expressing the view of eight members of the court, that under the due process clause of the Fourteenth Amendment, the defendant in the case at bar was entitled to a public trial before another judge on the contempt charges entered at the conclusion of the criminal trial, since the insults involved were such as to strike at the most vulnerable and human qualities of the trial judge's temperament.

Black, J., concurred in the judgment and with all of the opinion except as to holding (1) above.

Burger, Ch. J., concurring, joined the court's opinion, noting additionally that summary removal of the defendant from the courtroom would have been the most salutary remedy; that in view of the public interest in protecting the integrity of the trial process, a trial judge, upon the defendant's refusal of counsel, was well advised to appoint "standby counsel," as in the case at bar; and that where available, statutes punishing obstruction of justice might also be used to cope with grave misconduct of persons in the courtroom.

Harlan, J., concurred in the judgment of the reversal solely on the ground that the contempt convictions must be regarded as infected by the fact that the unprecedented long sentence of 22 years was imposed by the judge who was the victim of the defendant's shockingly abusive conduct, such circumstance depriving the contempt proceeding of the appearance of even-handed justice which was at the core of due process.

COUNSEL

Curtis R. Reitz, by appointment of the Court, 398 US 902, 26 L Ed 2d 60, 90 S Ct 1696, argued the cause and filed a brief for petitioner.

Carol Mary Los argued the cause for respondent, pro hac vice. With her on the brief was Robert W. Duggan.

UNITED STATES, Appellant,

v

MILTON C. JORN

400 US 470, 27 L Ed 2d 543, 91 S Ct 547

Argued January 12, 1970. Reargued October
22, 1970. Decided January 25, 1971

Decision: Federal District Court's dismissal of criminal
information on ground of former jeopardy, based
on court's earlier discharge of jury and declaration of mistrial, held appealable by government to
Supreme Court; and dismissal of information affirmed.

SUMMARY

The defendant was brought to trial in the United
States District Court for the District of Utah on an information charging him with willfully assisting in the
preparation of fraudulent income tax returns. The
trial judge, acting on his own motion without the defendant's consent, discharged the jury and declared a
mistrial when he concluded that taxpayers who were
to be called as witnesses by the government, and who
allegedly had been aided by the defendant in preparing
their returns, had not been properly advised on initial
contact by the Internal Revenue Service of their constitutional rights against self-incrimination and thus
should be allowed to consult with attorneys, notwithstanding that the first taxpayer to be called as a government witness and the prosecuting attorney both stated
that the taxpayers had been warned of their constitutional rights when first contacted. The case was set for
retrial, but on motion by the defendant, the trial judge

dismissed the information on the ground of double jeopardy.

On direct appeal by the government, the United States Supreme Court affirmed. Although not agreeing on an opinion, seven members of the court agreed that the District Court's judgment was appealable by the government, and six members agreed that the judgment must be affirmed.

Harlan, J., announced the judgment of the court, and concluded (1) expressing the view of seven members of the court, that the District Court decision was appealable by the government as a decision "sustaining a motion in bar, when the defendant has not been put in jeopardy" within the meaning of the applicable provisions of the Criminal Appeals Act, since the dismissal of the information on the former jeopardy plea occurred prior to the impaneling of a second jury, (2) expressing the view of four members of the court, that absent a motion by the defendant for a mistrial in circumstances such as in the case at bar, the trial judge must not foreclose the defendant's option under the double jeopardy provision of the Fifth Amendment to have his trial completed by a particular tribunal until a scrupulous exercise of judicial discretion resulted in the conclusion that the ends of public justice would not be served by a continuation of the proceedings, and (3) expressing the view of four members of the court, that the district judge, who had given no consideration to the possibility of a trial continuance in the instant case, had abused his discretion in discharging the jury and declaring a mistrial, thus rendering reprosecution of the defendant violative of the double jeopardy provision of the Fifth Amendment.

Black and **Brennan, JJ.**, were of the opinion that the court lacked jurisdiction over the appeal under the

Criminal Appeals Act, because the trial judge's action amounted to an acquittal of the defendant, but joined the judgment of the court in view of the decision by the majority of the court to reach the merits.

Burger, Ch. J., concurring, joined the opinion and judgment of the court, expressing reluctance, however, since the case represented a plain frustration of the right to have the case tried, attributable solely to the trial judge's conduct.

Stewart, J., joined by **White** and **Blackmun, JJ.,** dissented, stating that while the court had jurisdiction of the appeal for the reasons set out in the plurality opinion, nevertheless (1) in determining whether the trial judge had abused his discretion in declaring the mistrial, the real question was whether there had been an abuse of the trial process resulting in prejudice to the accused such as to outweigh society's interest in the punishment of crime, and (2) even assuming that the trial judge's action in the case at bar was improper by standards of good trial practice, the circumstances of the declaration of mistrial, which could not possibly have injured the defendant, did not involve abuse of a kind to invoke the constitutional guaranty against double jeopardy.

COUNSEL

Richard B. Stone reargued the cause for the United States.   Louis F. Claiborne argued the cause for the United States on the original argument.   With Mr. Stone on the brief on the reargument were Solicitor General Erwin N. Griswold and Assistant Attorney General Walters.   On the brief on the original argument were Solicitor General Erwin N. Griswold, Assistant Attorney General Walters, Peter L. Strauss, and Joseph M. Howard.

Denis R. Morrill, by appointment of the Court, 396 US 899, 24 L Ed 2d 176, 90 S Ct 210, argued the cause and filed briefs for appellee on the original argument and on the reargument.

JOSEPH CHARLES USNER, Petitioner,

v

LUCKENBACH OVERSEAS CORPORATION et al.

400 US 494, 27 L Ed 2d 562, 91 S Ct 514

Argued November 18, 1970. Decided
January 25, 1971.

Decision: Longshoreman, injured while loading ship
through isolated negligent act of fellow longshoreman in operating ship's boom, held not entitled to
recover from shipowners under unseaworthiness
doctrine.

SUMMARY

A longshoreman, employed by an independent steve-
doring contractor, was injured while working on a barge
alongside a ship which he and his fellow longshoreman
were loading with cargo. The injury occurred when the
longshoreman was struck by a sling attached to the
ship's boom, which was being operated by a fellow
longshoreman and which was lowered too fast and too
far. The injured longshoreman instituted an action to
recover damages against the shipowner in the United
States District Court for the Eastern District of
Louisiana, alleging that his injuries had been caused by
the ship's unseaworthiness. The District Court denied
the shipowner's motion for summary judgment, which
motion was based on the ground that a single negligent
act by a fellow longshoreman could not render the ship
unseaworthy. On interlocutory appeal, the United
States Court of Appeals for the Fifth Circuit reversed,
directing that the shipowner's motion for summary judgment be granted (413 F2d 984).

On certiorari, the United States Supreme Court affirmed the judgment of the Court of Appeals. In an opinion by **Stewart, J.**, expressing the view of five members of the court, it was held that (1) liability based upon unseaworthiness is wholly distinct from liability based upon negligence, unseaworthiness being a condition and it being irrelevant how the condition causing unseaworthiness came into existence, whether by negligence or otherwise; (2) the condition of unseaworthiness includes, in addition to any defective condition of a ship itself, such circumstances as defective gear or appurtenances, an unfit or insufficient crew, and an improper method of loading or stowing cargo; and (3) the longshoreman could not recover under the doctrine of unseaworthiness in the case at bar, since his injuries were not caused by any such conditions of unseaworthiness, but instead were caused by the single, wholly unforeseeable act of negligence by a fellow longshoreman in operating the ship's boom.

Douglas, J., joined by **Black** and **Brennan, JJ.**, dissented on the ground that the case should be controlled by the established concept of unseaworthiness resulting from operational negligence, under which it is the obligation of a shipowner to furnish seaworthy appliances in addition to a seaworthy ship.

Harlan, J., dissented on the ground that the particular issue in the case had already been decided in Crumady v The J. H. Fisser, 358 US 423, 3 L Ed 2d 413, 79 S Ct 445, where it was held that a stevedore's negligence with a winch, which caused injuries to an employee of the stevedore when a rope sling broke, rendered the vessel pro tanto unseaworthy.

COUNSEL

H. Alva Brumfield argued the cause for petitioner. With him on the brief were Evangeline M. Vavrick and H. Alva Brumfield III.

Charles Kohlmeyer, Jr., argued the cause for respondents. With him on the brief were Thomas W. Thorne, Jr., and Benjamin W. Yancey.

Arthur J. Mandell filed a brief for the American Trial Lawyers Association as amicus curiae urging reversal.

JAMES EDMUND GROPPI, Appellant,

v

STATE OF WISCONSIN

400 US 505, 27 L Ed 2d 571, 91 S Ct 490

Argued December 7, 1970. Decided
January 25, 1971

Decision: Denial of opportunity to show that change
of venue was required because of community prejudice held unconstitutional in misdemeanor case
tried by jury.

SUMMARY

Prior to the defendant's jury trial in a Wisconsin state
court for the misdemeanor of resisting arrest, the defendant filed a motion requesting that venue be changed
to a different county because the local news media's mas-
sive coverage of the defendant's activities had resulted
in community prejudice against the defendant. The
motion was denied by the trial judge on the ground that
a Wisconsin statute, which expressly authorized a change
of venue in a felony case, did not permit a change of
venue in a misdemeanor case. Affirming the defendant's
conviction, the Wisconsin Supreme Court held not only
that the trial judge had correctly construed Wisconsin
law as precluding the possibility of a change of venue
in misdemeanor cases, but also that Wisconsin law, as so
construed, was constitutionally valid (41 Wis 2d 312, 164
NW2d 266, 34 ALR3d 787).

On appeal, the United States Supreme Court vacated
the judgment below and remanded the case for further
proceedings. In an opinion by **Stewart, J.**, expressing the
view of six members of the court, it was held that under

the Fourteenth Amendment, the right to an impartial
jury necessitated that a defendant who was to be tried
by a jury for a misdemeanor be given an opportunity to
show that a change of venue was required because of
community prejudice.

Blackmun, J., joined by **Burger,** Ch. J., concurring,
and joining in the court's judgment, stated that although
the defendant was to have an opportunity to demonstrate
community prejudice and the likelihood of an unfair trial,
the judgment of conviction could be reinstated if the defendant failed, or refused to attempt, to make such a
demonstration.

Black, J., dissenting, stated that since such devices as
continuances and challenges to jurors were available to
protect the constitutional right to an impartial jury, and
since the defendant could obtain a new trial on the grounds
of jury prejudice if such devices were insufficient, the
constitutional right to an impartial jury did not necessarily include the right to a change of venue, but that since
the defendant had a right to bring forth any relevant
evidence to show that the jury which tried him was not
impartial, the case should be remanded for a hearing on
a motion for a new trial.

COUNSEL

Elizabeth B. Dubois argued the cause for appellant.
With her on the briefs were Jack Greenberg, Michael
Meltsner, Anthony G. Amsterdam, Thomas M. Jacobson,
and Robert E. Sutton.

Sverre O. Tinglum, Assistant Attorney General of
Wisconsin, argued the cause for appellee. With him on
the brief were Robert W. Warren, Attorney General, and
Roy G. Mita, Assistant Attorney General.

KEVIN L. DONALDSON, fka Merton H. Sweet,
Petitioner,

v

UNITED STATES et al.

400 US 517, 27 L Ed 2d 580, 91 S Ct 534

Argued November 19, 1970. Decided
January 25, 1971.

Decision: Taxpayer held not entitled to intervene in Federal District Court proceedings involving enforcement of Internal Revenue Service special agent's summonses requesting records from taxpayer's former employer.

SUMMARY

In connection with an investigation of a taxpayer's income tax returns for certain years, an Internal Revenue Service special agent, purportedly acting under the authority of § 7602 of the 1954 Internal Revenue Code —which authorized the examination of books and witnesses and the issuance of summonses for the purpose of determining a person's tax liability—issued summonses to a company which had allegedly employed the taxpayer and to the company's accountant. The summonses requested the company and the accountant to appear before the special agent and to produce records concerning such matters as payments which had been made to the taxpayer. In the United States District Court for the Middle District of Florida, the taxpayer obtained temporary restraining orders enjoining the company and the accountant from complying with the summonses. Subsequently, the United States and the special agent petitioned the District Court for judicial enforcement of the summonses. The taxpayer, relying on Rule 24(a)(2) of the Federal Rules of Civil Procedure, filed motions to intervene in the enforcement proceedings, on the grounds that the sole purpose of the investigation was to obtain evidence of criminal violations and that the summonses were therefore not within the scope of § 7602. The District Court denied the motions to intervene and ordered the company and the accountant to comply with the summonses, and the Court of Appeals for the Fifth Circuit affirmed (418 F2d 1213).

On certiorari, the United States Supreme Court affirmed. In an opinion by **Blackmun, J.**, expressing the views of seven members of the court, it was held that the taxpayer's interest in the records which were requested from the company and the accountant was not of sufficient magnitude to entitle the taxpayer to intervene as of right under Rule 24(a)(2), and that although the special agent's investigation had the potentiality of resulting in a recommendation that a criminal prosecution be instituted against the taxpayer, the summonses, having been issued in good faith and prior to any recommendation for criminal prosecution, were within the scope of § 7602 and could be issued in aid of the investigation.

Brennan, J., concurred in the result, expressing the belief that under the facts of the case, the taxpayer had established no right to intervene.

Douglas, J., concurred in the result, stating that although a hearing before the special agent could proceed on the summonses issued, such a hearing should not be held without affording the taxpayer an opportunity to attend, to cross-examine, and to rebut.

COUNSEL

Robert E. Meldman argued the cause for petitioner. With him on the briefs was Louis L. Meldman.

Lawrence G. Wallace argued the cause for the United States et al. On the brief were Solicitor General Erwin N. Griswold, Assistant Attorney General Walters, Deputy Solicitor General Springer, Samuel Huntington, Joseph M. Howard, and John P. Burke.

RALPH PICCIRILLO, Petitioner,

v

STATE OF NEW YORK

400 US 548, 27 L Ed 2d 596, 91 S Ct 520

Argued November 9, 1970. Decided
January 25, 1971.

Decision: Certiorari to consider whether "transactional,"
as opposed to "use," immunity is required to compel
witness to testify before state grand jury over claim
of self-incrimination privilege, dismissed as improvidently granted.

SUMMARY

The defendant, who had pleaded guilty to assault
by the use of tire irons and was sentenced to imprisonment, upon being later called to testify before a New
York State grand jury investigating the assault and conspiracies arising in connection therewith, was granted immunity and testified as to the assault. A police officer
later testified before the grand jury that he had arrested
the defendant and another and took the tire irons from
them, and that the defendant then had offered him a bribe
to change his testimony and to get rid of the tire irons.
The defendant was subsequently indicted for bribery,
and, after an unsuccessful motion to dismiss based on the
grant of immunity, pleaded guilty to attempted bribery
and was convicted. The New York Court of Appeals
affirmed the conviction (24 NY2d 598, 301 NYS2d 544,
249 NE2d 412). The United States Supreme Court
granted a writ of certiorari to resolve the question whether
it is necessary to accord "transactional" immunity to compel a witness to give testimony before a state grand jury

over his claim of the privilege against self-incrimination, or whether mere "use" immunity suffices to that end (397 US 933, 25 L Ed 2d 114, 90 S Ct 957).

The writ of certiorari was dismissed as improvidently granted, in a per curiam opinion expressing the view of five members of the court, on the ground that an intervening decision of the New York Court of Appeals made clear that transactional immunity is required in New York and also indicated that such court's decision in the instant case may have rested on that premise, so that no controversy any longer existed between the parties as to the question which impelled the granting of the writ, even though technically speaking issues remained in the case concerning the kind of immunity required by federal law and, if "transactional" rather than "use" immunity in such a case as the instant one, the proper scope of such immunity.

Black, J., dissented from the dismissal of the writ as improvidently granted, and would vacate the judgment below and remand the case for reconsideration in light of the New York Court of Appeals' intervening decision.

Douglas, J., with whom **Marshall, J.,** concurred, dissented from dismissing the writ as improvidently granted and would reverse the conviction, expressing the view that the case was a clear one for honoring of the transactional test of immunity.

Brennan, J., joined by **Marshall, J.,** dissented from the dismissal of the writ as improvidently granted and would reverse the conviction on the merits and remand the case with directions to dismiss the indictment, on the grounds that the case presented a record which compelled the court to decide the question of the limitations required by the Fifth Amendment's self-incrimination clause upon subsequent state prosecutions of an individual compelled by the state to answer incriminating questions, and that the specific question before the court was whether the Fifth Amendment, as applied to the states by the Fourteenth Amendment, permitted the present conviction to stand in light of the substance of the compelled testimony and the nature and basis of that conviction, this being a matter of federal constitutional law which did not depend upon the interpretation of the New York immunity statute.

COUNSEL

Malvine Nathanson argued the cause for petitioner. With her on the briefs was William E. Hellerstein.

Stanley M. Meyer argued the cause for respondent. With him on the brief was Eugene Gold.

IDA PHILLIPS, Petitioner,

v

MARTIN MARIETTA CORPORATION

400 US 542, 27 L Ed 2d 613, 91 S Ct 496

Argued December 9, 1970. Decided
January 25, 1971.

Decision: Section 703(a) of the Civil Rights Act of 1964
held not to permit different hiring policies for male
and female parents of pre-school age children, at
least in absence of proper showing of relevance to
job performance under § 703(e).

SUMMARY

Petitioner, a woman with pre-school age children, was
informed by a corporation with which she sought employment that it was not accepting job applications from
women with pre-school age children, although it did employ men with pre-school age children. Petitioner thereafter commenced an action in the United States District
Court for the Middle District of Florida under Title VII
of the Civil Rights Act of 1964, alleging that she had been
denied employment because of her sex. The District
Court granted a summary judgment for the employer,
concluding that, inasmuch as 70–75 percent of the applicants for the position petitioner sought were women
and 75–80 percent of those hired for the position were
women, no question of bias against women as such was
presented. The Court of Appeals for the Fifth Circuit
affirmed (411 F2d 1) and denied a rehearing en banc (416
F2d 1257).

On certiorari, the United States Supreme Court vacated and remanded. In a per curiam opinion expressing

the views of eight members of the court, it was held that (1) § 703(a) of the Civil Rights Act of 1964, which requires that persons of like qualifications be given employment opportunities irrespective of their sex, could not be read as permitting one hiring policy for women and another for men, where each had pre-school age children, (2) although conflicting family obligations, if demonstrably more relevant to job performance for women than for men, could arguably be a basis for distinction under § 703(e) of the Act, nevertheless the record in the case at bar was inadequate for resolution of such issue and the summary judgment was thus improper.

Marshall, J., concurring with the view that the case should be remanded for full development of the facts, expressed disagreement with the court's indication that it was arguably possible to establish a bona fide occupational qualification reasonably necessary to the normal operation of the employer's business by showing that some women with pre-school age children have family responsibilities that interfere with job performance and that men do not usually have such responsibilities.

COUNSEL

William L. Robinson argued the cause for petitioner. With him on the briefs were Jack Greenberg, James M. Nabrit III, Norman C. Amaker, and Earl M. Johnson.

Donald T. Senterfitt argued the cause for respondent. With him on the brief were William Y. Akerman, Paul A. Porter, Victor H. Kramer, Dennis G. Lyons, James A. Dobkin, Clark C. Vogel, James T. Ellison, J. Thomas Cardwell, and George T. Eidson, Jr.

Lawrence G. Wallace argued the cause for the United States as amicus curiae urging reversal. With him on the brief were Solicitor General Erwin N. Griswold, Assistant Attorney General Leonard, Robert T. Moore, and Stanley P. Hebert.

Briefs of amici curiae urging reversal were filed by Dororthy Kenyon, Norman Dorsen, Pauli Murray, and Melvin L. Wulf for the American Civil Liberties Union; by Gilbert Feldman for the Air Line Stewards and Stewardesses Association, Local 550, Transport Workers Union of America, AFL-CIO; by Jacob D. Hyman, Faith A. Seidenberg, Marguerite Rawalt, and Phineas Indritz for the Legal Defense and Education Fund, Inc.; and by Sylvia Ellison for Human Rights for Women, Inc.

SARA BAIRD, Petitioner,

v

STATE BAR OF ARIZONA

401 US 1, 27 L Ed 2d 639, 91 S Ct 702

Reargued October 14, 1970. Decided
February 23, 1971.

Decision: Denial of admission to Arizona State Bar because of failure to answer question as to membership
in organizations advocating forceful overthrow of
Government, held violative of First and Fourteenth
Amendments.

SUMMARY

An applicant for admission to the State Bar of Arizona,
after passing the prescribed examination, and after listing, in response to a question on the Bar Committee's
questionnaire, all organizations to which she had belonged
since the age of 16, refused to answer a question on the
questionnaire as to whether she had ever been a member
of the Communist Party or any organization that advocated overthrow of the United States Government by
force or violence. Because of such refusal, the Bar Committee declined to further process her application or to
recommend her admission, and the Arizona Supreme
Court denied the applicant's petition for an order to the
Committee to show cause why she should not be admitted
to practice law.

On certiorari, the United States Supreme Court reversed and remanded. Five members of the court, although not agreeing on an opinion, agreed that under the
First and Fourteenth Amendments, the applicant could
not be denied admission to the Bar merely because she had

refused to answer the question as to membership in any organization that advocated forceful overthrow of the United States Government.

Black, J., announced the judgment of the court, and in an opinion joined by **Douglas, Brennan,** and **Marshall, JJ.,** expressed the view that under the First Amendment, a state could not inquire about a person's views or associations solely for the purpose of withholding a right or benefit because of what he believed, and thus the State Bar's inquiry as to the applicant's organization membership was unconstitutional, notwithstanding the Bar Committee's assertion that an affirmative answer to the question would not result in automatic rejection of the application, but would instead lead to further inquiry as to the applicant's present view with regard to violent overthrow of the government, and notwithstanding the assertion that the question also served a legitimate function as to identifying the nature of the organizations listed in response to the question as to the applicant's affiliations since the age of 16.

Stewart, J., concurring, stated that although there was authority for the view that under some circumstances simple inquiry into present or past Communist Party membership of a Bar applicant was not, as such, unconstitutional, nevertheless, inquiry as to membership in organizations that advocated forceful overthrow of the United States Government was unconstitutional under the First and Fourteenth Amendments, since (1) such inquiry was required to be confined to knowing membership, mere membership in an organization not constituting, by itself, sufficient ground for a state's imposition of civil disabilities, and (2) the State Bar had stated that it would recommend denial of admissions solely because of an applicant's beliefs which the State Bar found objectionable.

White, J., dissented on the grounds that (1) the Constitution did not require a state to admit to practice an applicant who believed in violence and intended to implement such belief in his practice of law and advice to clients, (2) a state could properly ask preliminary questions permitting further investigation as to whether the applicant would or would not advocate lawless conduct as a practicing lawyer, and (3) the inquiries in the case at bar were designed to ascertain whether the applicant expected actively to support illegal violence, Arizona having no intention of barring applicants on the basis of beliefs alone.

Blackmun, J., joined by **Burger, Ch. J.**, **Harlan, J.**, and **White, J.**, dissenting, expressed the view that on the basis of the record, the judgment of the Supreme Court of Arizona should be affirmed, and emphasized that (1) the question as to the applicant's organization membership, realistically read, disclosed that it was directed not at mere belief, but at advocacy and at the call to violence and force in pursuit of that advocacy, (2) the record clearly showed the State Bar Committee's view to be that if the question had been answered in the affirmative, automatic denial of admission would not have resulted, but instead would have led to further inquiry as to the applicant's expectation to actively support the objective of overthrow, with there being no legal basis for refusing admission if the applicant's membership was of a nominal character and she did not participate in the advocacy views, and (3) the state could legitimately inquire as to whether the applicant at least professed to refrain from forceful and violent overthrow of the government.

Harlan, J., dissented, stating that (1) although states were prevented, under the First and Fourteenth Amendments, from denying admission to Bar candidates merely because of theoretical beliefs in the "right" of revolution, nevertheless there was no constitutional barrier to denying admission to those seeking entry to the profession for the very purpose of doing away with the orderly processes of law, and (2) thus temperate inquiry into the character of an applicant's beliefs in such regard, as in the case at bar, was relevant and permissible.

COUNSEL

Peter D. Baird reargued the cause for petitioner. With him on the brief were John P. Frank and Paul G. Ulrich.

Mark Wilmer reargued the cause and filed a brief for respondent.

IN THE MATTER OF APPLICATION OF MARTIN ROBERT STOLAR

401 US 23, 27 L Ed 2d 657, 91 S Ct 713

Reargued October 14 and 15, 1970. Decided February 23, 1971.

Decision: Questions on application for admission to Ohio State Bar requiring listings of organizations of which applicant was or had been member, and question as to applicant's membership in organizations advocating forceful overthrow of Government, held violative of First Amendment.

SUMMARY

An applicant for admission to the Ohio State Bar furnished the Ohio Bar Committee with all of the information which he had previously given to the New York Bar Committee upon his admission to practice in New York a year earlier, including answers as to the applicant's belief in the principles underlying the form of government of the United States, his loyalty to the government, and his never having been a member of any organization pledged to effect changes in the form of government or engaged in advancing the interest of a foreign country. Although the applicant stated on oral interrogation by the Ohio Committee that he was not and never had been a member of the Communist Party or any socialist party, nevertheless he declined to answer a question on the Ohio application as to whether he was or had been a member of any organization which advocated overthrow of the government of the United States by force, and he refused to respond to questions requiring the listing of all organizations of which he was or had been a member, and of all organizations of which he was or had become a member since registering as a law student. The Ohio Committee recommended that the application to take the Ohio Bar examination be denied, and the Ohio Supreme Court approved such recommendation.

On certiorari, the United States Supreme State reversed and remanded. Five members of the court, although not agreeing on an opinion, agreed that the questions on the Ohio application as to the applicant's organization membership violated the First Amendment.

Black, J., announced the judgment of the court, and in an opinion joined by **Douglas, Brennan,** and **Marshall, JJ.**, expressed the views that (1) the questions requiring the applicant to list organizations of which he was or had been a member were impermissible in light of the First Amendment's protection of freedom of association, the listing of an organization considered by the bar committee to be controversial being likely to cause extensive interrogation or denial of admission, with law students thus being encouraged to protect their future by shunning unpopular or controversial organizations, and (2) under the First Amendment's prohibition against a state's penalizing a man solely because of his membership in a particular organization, the question as to whether the applicant was or had been a member of any organization which advocated the overthrow by force of the United States government was also impermissible.

Stewart, J., concurring, stated that the judgment must be reversed since (1) the questions requiring listing of organizations of which the applicant was or had been a member were unconstitutional under Shelton v Tucker, 364 US 479, 5 L Ed 2d 231, 81 S Ct 247, which held unconstitutional a state statute requiring public school teachers to list all organizations of which they were members, and (2) the question as to membership in any organization advocating forceful overthrow of the government was unconstitutional under Baird v State Bar of Arizona, 401 US 1, 27 L Ed 2d 639, 91 S Ct 702.

White, J., dissented on the grounds that (1) the Constitution did not require a state to admit to practice an applicant who believed in violence and intended to implement such belief in his practice of law and advice to clients, (2) a state could properly ask preliminary questions permitting further investigation as to whether the applicant would or would not advocate lawless conduct as a practicing lawyer, and (3) the inquiries in the case at bar were designed to ascertain whether the applicant expected to actively support illegal violence.

Blackmun, J., joined by **Burger**, Ch. J., **Harlan, J.**, and **White, J.**, dissented, stating that even assuming the impropriety of the questions that required the listing of organizations of which the applicant was or had been a member, nevertheless the judgment should be affirmed on the basis of the applicant's refusal to answer the written question about membership in organizations advocating overthrow of the government by force, particularly in view of (1) the inconsistency of his willingness to state at the Ohio oral interview that he was not and never had been a member of the Communist Party and his unwillingness to respond to the related written question, (2) the fact that the written question, although it could have been better phrased, was not a mere question of membership present or past, which Ohio conceded was not in itself conclusive upon the issue of admission to the bar, but instead was a threshold question relating to knowing membership and willingness to participate in forceful destruction of the government, and (3) the irrelevancy to the application for admission to the Ohio Bar of the applicant's responses to similar inquiries upon his admission to the New York Bar a year earlier.

Harlan, J., dissented, exrpessing the views that (1) although states were prevented, under the First and Fourteenth Amendments, from denying admission to bar candidates merely because of theoretical beliefs in the "right" of revolution, neverthless there was no constitutional barrier to denying admission to those seeking entry to the profession for the very purpose of doing away with the orderly processes of law, and (2) thus temperate inquiry into the character of any applicant's beliefs in such regard, as in the case at bar, was relevant and permissible.

COUNSEL

Leonard B. Boudin reargued the cause for petitioner. With him on the briefs was David Rosenberg.

Robert D. Macklin, Assistant Attorney General, reargued the cause for the State of Ohio and the Columbus Bar Association. With him on the brief were Paul W. Brown, Attorney General, Shelby V. Hutchins, and William H. Schneider.

EVELLE J. YOUNGER, Appellant,

v

JOHN HARRIS, JR., et al.

401 US 37, 27 L Ed 2d 669, 91 S Ct 746

Reargued November 16, 1970. Decided
February 23, 1971.

Decision: Federal District Court held not authorized,
in absence of showing of extraordinary circumstances, to enjoin pending California prosecution
under criminal syndicalism statute allegedly unconstitutional on its face.

SUMMARY

The plaintiff, having been indicted in a California state
court on charges of criminal syndicalism, requested the
United States District Court for the Central District of
California to grant injunctive relief against the state
criminal prosecution, on the grounds that the prosecution
and even the presence of the California criminal syndicalism statute violated the First and Fourteenth Amendments by inhibiting the plaintiff in the exercise of his
rights of free speech and press. A three-judge District
Court held the criminal syndicalism statute void for
vagueness and overbreadth in violation of the First and
Fourteenth Amendments and enjoined the further prosecution against the plaintiff of the pending state proceedings (281 F Supp 507).

On appeal, the United States Supreme Court reversed
and remanded the case. In an opinion by **Black, J.**, expressing the views of five members of the court, it was held
that the possible unconstitutionality of the state statute
on its face did not in itself justify an injunction against

good-faith attempts to enforce it, and that since the threat to the plaintiff's federal constitutional rights could be eliminated by his defense against a single criminal prosecution, and the only injury which he faced in connection with the state prosecution was that incidental to every criminal proceeding brought lawfully and in good faith, the District Court's injunction violated the federal policy forbidding federal courts from enjoining pending state criminal proceedings except under extraordinary circumstances where the danger of irreparable injury is great and immediate.

Stewart, J., joined by **Harlan, J.,** concurring, emphasized that the decision dealt only with the proper policy to be followed by a federal court when asked to enjoin a criminal prosecution which was contemporaneously pending in a state court.

Brennan, J., joined by **White** and **Marshall, JJ.,** concurring in the result, stated that since the plaintiff had not alleged that the state prosecution was brought in bad faith to harass, and since his constitutional contentions could be adequately adjudicated in the state criminal proceeding, federal intervention in the pending criminal prosecution was improper.

Douglas, J., dissented on the ground that special circumstances warranting federal intervention in a state criminal proceeding existed where the state statute being enforced was unconstitutional on its face.

COUNSEL

Clifford K. Thompson, Jr., Deputy Attorney General of California, argued the cause for appellant on the second reargument. Albert W. Harris, Jr., Assistant Attorney General, argued the cause for appellant on the original argument and on the first reargument.   With them on the briefs were Thomas C. Lynch, Attorney General, and Evelle J. Younger, pro se.

A. L. Wirin argued the cause for appellees on the re-arguments.   With him on the briefs were Fred Okrand and Frank S. Pestana.   Sam Rosenwein argued the cause for appellees on the original argument.   With him on the brief was Mr. Pestana.

GEORGE SAMUELS et al., Appellants,

v

THOMAS J. MACKELL, District Attorney, et al (No. 7)

FRED FERNANDEZ, Appellant,

v

THOMAS J. MACKELL, District Attorney, et al. (No. 9)

401 US 66, 27 L Ed 2d 688, 91 S Ct 764

Reargued November 16, 1970. Decided February 23, 1971.

Decision: Federal District Court held required, where state prosecutions were pending, to deny declaratory relief without considering merits of constitutional challenge to New York criminal anarchy statutes.

SUMMARY

The plaintiffs, having been indicted in a New York state court on charges of criminal anarchy, requested the United States District Court for the Southern District of New York to grant injunctive relief and a declaratory judgment to the effect that the New York criminal anarchy statutes were unconstitutional under the First and Fourteenth Amendments. The plaintiffs alleged that the state criminal proceedings would harass them and cause them to suffer irreparable damages. A three-judge District Court, dismissing the plaintiffs' complaint, held that the New York criminal anarchy statutes were constitutional (288 F Supp 348).

On appeal, the United States Supreme Court affirmed. In an opinion by **Black, J.**, expressing the views of six members of the court, it was held that since there was no sufficient showing in the record that the plaintiffs had suffered or would suffer irreparable damages, not only would it have been impermissible for the District Court to issue an injunction against the prosecution of the pending state criminal proceedings, but also the District Court should have denied declaratory relief without considering the merits of the plaintiffs' challenge to the constitutionality of the New York criminal anarchy statutes.

Douglas, J., concurring, stated that since certain of the overt acts with which the plaintiffs had been charged were plainly unprotected by the First Amendment, the criminal cases against them could not be considered palpably unconstitutional, and it was for the state courts to preserve such First Amendment rights as might be involved.

Stewart, J., joined by **Harlan, J.**, concurring, emphasized that the decision dealt only with the proper policy to be followed by a federal court when asked to intervene by injunction or declaratory judgment in a criminal prosecution which was contemporaneously pending in a state court.

Brennan, J., joined by **White** and **Marshall, JJ.**, concurring in the result, stated that since the plaintiffs had not alleged facts amounting to bad-faith harassment, neither a declaratory judgment nor an injunction would be proper.

COUNSEL

Victor Rabinowitz argued the cause for appellants in No. 7 on the original argument and on the rearguments.

With him on the briefs were Leonard B. Boudin, Michael Standard, and Dorian Bowman. Eleanor Jackson Piel argued the cause and filed briefs for appellant in No. 9 on the original argument and on the rearguments.

Frederick J. Ludwig argued the cause for appellee Mackell in both cases on the original argument and on the rearguments. With him on the briefs was Thomas J. Mackell, pro se. Maria L. Marcus, Assistant Attorney General, argued the cause for appellee Attorney General of New York in both cases on the original argument and on the rearguments. With her on the briefs were Louis J. Lefkowitz, Attorney General, pro se, Samuel A. Hirshowitz, First Assistant Attorney General, and Hillel Hoffman, Assistant Attorney General.

JOHN S. BOYLE, Chief Judge of the
Circuit Court of Cook County,
Illinois, et al., Appellants,

v

LAWRENCE LANDRY et al.

401 US 77, 27 L Ed 2d 696, 91 S Ct 758

Reargued November 16, 1970. Decided
February 23, 1971.

Decision: Federal District Court held not authorized
to grant declaratory or injunctive relief against allegedly unconstitutional Illinois intimidation statute
in absence of showing of any actual or threatened
prosecutions under statute.

SUMMARY

In an action in the United States District Court for
the Northern District of Illinois, the plaintiffs sought
declaratory and injunctive relief against the enforcement of an Illinois statute which prohibited the intimidation of a person by threats to commit any criminal
offense. A three-judge District Court declared the
statute invalid as an overly broad restriction on freedom
of speech (280 F Supp 938), and the District Court
granted an injunction against the enforcement of the
statute.

On appeal, the United States Supreme Court reversed
and remanded the case. In an opinion by **Black, J.,**
expressing the views of six members of the court, it was
held that since no plaintiff had even been prosecuted,
charged, or arrested under the intimidation statute, and
the complaint contained no mention of any specific threat
by any officer or official to arrest or prosecute any of the

plaintiffs under the statute, the allegations of the plaintiffs' complaint fell far short of showing any irreparable injury from threats or actual prosecutions under the intimidation statute or from any other conduct by state or city officials, and that it was therefore improper for the District Court to grant declaratory or injunctive relief.

Brennan and **White**, JJ., concurred in the result.

Douglas, J., dissented on the ground that the unconstitutionality of the state statute on its face warranted federal intervention.

COUNSEL

Thomas E. Brannigan argued the cause for appellants on the second reargument. Dean H. Bilton argued the cause for appellants on the first reargument. Ronald Butler argued the cause for appellants on the original argument. With Ronald Butler and Dean H. Bilton on the brief were Daniel P. Coman and Daniel W. Weil.

Ellis E. Reid argued the cause for appellees on the original argument and on the rearguments. With him on the brief were Robert L. Tucker and Stanley A. Bass.

LEANDER H. PEREZ, Jr., et al., Appellants,

v

AUGUST M. LEDESMA, Jr., et al.

401 US 82, 27 L Ed 2d 701, 91 S Ct 674

Argued November 17, 1970. Decided
February 23, 1971.

Decision: Federal District Court held not authorized to
order suppression of allegedly obscene materials
seized in connection with pending Louisiana criminal
prosecutions; Supreme Court held not to have jurisdiction over direct appeal from declaratory judgment invalidating local obscenity ordinance.

SUMMARY

After criminal proceedings had been instituted against
the plaintiffs in a Louisiana state court for displaying
obscene materials for sale, the plaintiffs requested on
federal constitutional grounds that the United States
District Court for the Eastern District of Louisiana grant
declaratory and injunctive relief. Holding a Louisiana obscenity statute constitutional on its face, but ruling that
the arrests of the plaintiffs and the seizure of the allegedly obscene materials were invalid for lack of a
prior adversary hearing on the character of the seized
materials, a three-judge District Court ordered such
materials to be suppressed as evidence and to be returned
to the plaintiffs. Though stating that it was not a
function of a three-judge District Court to determine
the constitutionality of a local ordinance, the three-judge
court expressed the view that a local obscenity ordinance
was unconstitutionally vague, and this view was adopted
by reference in an opinion by a single district judge, who

ordered judgment to be entered decreeing the ordinance unconstitutional. (304 F Supp 662.)

On appeal, the United States Supreme Court reversed in part, vacated in part, and remanded the case. In an opinion by **Black, J.**, it was held (1) expressing the view of eight members of the court, that the orders relating to the suppression of evidence and the return of seized materials constituted improper federal interference with a state prosecution and therefore had to be reversed, and (2) expressing the view of six members of the court, that the court had no jurisdiction to review on direct appeal the validity of a declaratory judgment against a local ordinance, and that insofar as the constitutionality of the local ordinance was concerned, the judgment below had to be vacated and the case remanded to the District Court with instructions to enter a fresh decree from which the parties could appeal to the Court of Appeals if they so desired.

Stewart, J., joined by **Blackmun, J.**, concurred, joining in the court's opinion and stating additional reasons in support of each of the court's holdings.

Douglas, J., dissenting in part, agreed with holding (2) above, but disagreed with holding (1).

Brennan, J., joined by **White** and **Marshall, JJ.**, concurring in part and dissenting in part, agreed with holding (1) above, but disagreed with holding (2) on the ground that the three-judge court had properly exercised its discretion in issuing a declaratory judgment upon the constitutionality of the local ordinance.

COUNSEL

Charles H. Livaudais argued the cause for appellants. With him on the brief was Robert J. Klees.

Jack Peebles argued the cause for appellees. With him on the brief were Stanley Fleishman and Robert Eugene Smith.

———————

MAGNESIUM CASTING COMPANY, Petitioner,

v

NATIONAL LABOR RELATIONS BOARD

401 US 137, 27 L Ed 2d 735, 91 S Ct 599

Argued January 18 and 19, 1971. Decided
February 23, 1971.

Decision: Review by NLRB of regional director's determination of appropriate bargaining unit, prior to NLRB's issuance of unfair labor practice order based on determination, held discretionary rather that mandatory.

SUMMARY

A union filed a petition requesting a representation election among the production and maintenance employees at the petitioner employer's plant. Pursuant to § 9(c)(1) of the National Labor Relations Act, a regional director of the NLRB, under the authority delegated to him by § 3(b), held a hearing at which he determined that three out of four individuals, who were classified as "assistant foremen," were, under § 2(11) of the Act, employees rather than supervisors, and includable within the bargaining unit. The regional director therefore ordered an election in a unit consisting of all the employees, including the three, and the employer, contending that the determination was clearly erroneous, filed a request with the NLRB to review the regional director's decision, which request was denied. An election was held, resulting in the union's certification as the exclusive bargaining representative of the employees; the employer refused to bargain with the union; the union filed an unfair labor practice with the NLRB; the trial examiner found for the union; the NLRB affirmed; the employer moved for reconsideration, claiming that the NLRB had to review the regional director's representation determination before issuing an unfair labor practice based on it; and the motion was denied. The Court of Appeals for the First Circuit enforced the NLRB's order (427 F2d 114).

On certiorari, the United States Supreme Court affirmed. In an opinion by **Douglas, J.**, expressing the unanimous view of the court, it was held that under § 3(b) of the National Labor Relations Act, as amended, Congress allowed the NLRB to delegate its authority over determination of appropriate bargaining units to its regional directors, and that although the NLRB has discretion to review determinations made by the regional directors, such reviews are not mandatory and the NLRB need not review a regional director's representation determination before issuing an unfair labor practice order based on it.

COUNSEL

Louis Chandler argued the cause for petitioner. With him on the brief was Jerome H. Somers.

Norton J. Come argued the cause for respondent. With him on the brief were Solicitor General Erwin N. Griswold, Wm. Terry Bray, Arnold Ordman, and Dominick L. Manoli.

Briefs of amici curiae urging reversal were filed by Jerry Kronenberg and Alan Raywid for the Terminal Freight Cooperative Association, and by William L. Dennis for Olson Bodies, Inc.

Briefs of amici curiae urging affirmance were filed by Bernard Kleiman, Elliot Bredhoff, Michael H. Gottes-

man, and George H. Cohen for the United Steelworkers
of America, AFL-CIO, and by Benjamin Rubenstein for
International Union, U. A. W.

———————

LELIA MAE SANKS et al., Appellants,

v

STATE OF GEORGIA et al.

401 US 144, 27 L Ed 2d 741, 91 S Ct 593

Reargued November 17 and 18, 1970. Decided February 23, 1971.

Decision: Appeal dismissed where, prior to reargument, tenants contesting summary eviction procedure voluntarily vacated premises and statutory scheme had been repealed.

SUMMARY

Under a Georgia statutory scheme, a landlord seeking summary eviction could file an affidavit, alleging that his tenant was unlawfully refusing to vacate the premises, after which the sheriff was required to deliver a warrant to the tenant ordering him, after a 4-day grace period, to deliver the premises to the owner. The tenant could prevent summary eviction only by filing a counter-affidavit, alleging one of several specified defenses, and by filing a surety bond for double the amount due at the end of the trial; and the landlord was entitled to the double rent if the tenant should lose his case. Two tenants, each of whom had been served with dispossessory warrants, obtained a "rule nisi," permitting them to remain in possession of their respective premises pending the outcome of their cases, and the local court declared both the bond posting and double rent provisions of the statute unconstitutional. On interlocutory appeal, the local court's judgment was reversed by the Supreme Court of Georgia (225 Ga 88, 166 SE2d 19). The United States Supreme Court noted probable jurisdiction (395 US 974, 23 L Ed 2d 763, 89 S Ct 2150) because the case appeared to raise substantial questions under the Fourteenth Amendment, and after initial argument, set the case for reargument (399 US 922, 26 L Ed 2d 788, 90 S Ct 2229), at which time it became apaprent that (1) both of the tenants had voluntarily removed themselves from the premises, and (2) the Georgia General Assembly had repealed virtually the entire statutory scheme.

On appeal, the United States Supreme Court dismissed and remanded the case to the Supreme Court of Georgia. In an opinion by **Harlan, J.**, expressing the views of eight members of the court, it was held that (1) the tenants' voluntary removal from the premises rendered moot their insistence that they, rather than their landlords, had the right to lawful possession of the premises pending the outcome of the litigation, and (2) subsequent events having made it impossible for the court to predict to what extent adjudication of the issues originally presented would be material to any further litigation that might ensue on remand, due respect for the proper functioning of the court required dismissal of the appeal and no adjudication of the issues on which the appeal had originally been granted.

Black, J., concurred in the judgment of the court dismissing the appeal, but did so specifically on the ground that it was now moot.

COUNSEL

Michael D. Padnos argued the cause for appellants on the original argument and on the reargument. With him on the brief were Nancy S. Cheves and John William Brent.

Alfred L. Evans, Jr., Assistant Attorney General of Georgia, argued the cause for appellees on the original argument and on the reargument. With him on the brief were Arthur K. Bolton, Attorney General, Harold N. Hill, Jr., Executive Assistant Attorney General, and A. Joseph Nardone, Jr., Assistant Attorney General.

Frank B. Zeigler filed a brief for the Legal Aid Office of Savannah, Inc., as amicus curiae urging reversal.

LAW STUDENTS CIVIL RIGHTS RESEARCH COUNCIL, Inc., et al., Appellants,

v

LOWELL WADMOND et el.

401 US 154, 27 L Ed 2d 749, 91 S Ct 720

Argued October 15, 1970. Decided
February 23, 1971.

Decision: New York statutes, rules, and procedures for
screening bar applicants, including questions as to
applicants' knowing membership in organizations
advocating forceful overthrow of Government, held
constitutional.

SUMMARY

Organizations and individuals purportedly representing a class of law students and law graduates similarly
situated, instituted two actions for declaratory and injunctive relief in the United States District Court for
the Southern District of New York, attacking the constitutionality of New York's statutes, rules, and screening procedures for determining the character and fitness
of applicants for admission to the New York Bar. The
defendants were two state committees on character and
fitness, their individual members, two Appellate Divisions
of the Supreme Court of New York, and their individual
justices. The plaintiffs, although not contending that
any applicant had ever been unjustifiably denied admission to the New York Bar under the screening system,
asserted that the system worked a chilling effect upon
the exercise of constitutional rights such as the right of
free speech and association, particularly with regard to
the state's procedures involving questioning of an ap-

plicant as to his willingness to take an oath to support the federal and state constitutions, his good faith in doing so, his knowing membership in organizations advocating violent overthrow of the government, and his specific intent to further such aims. A three-judge District Court consolidated the suits, found certain items of the state's questionnaires to be of doubtful constitutional validity, granted partial relief on the basis of such findings, approved revised questions submitted by the defendants, and otherwise upheld the statutes and rules as valid on their face (299 F Supp 117).

On direct appeal by the plaintiffs, the United States Supreme Court affirmed. In an opinion by **Stewart, J.**, it was held, expressing the view of seven members of the court, that (1) there was no constitutional infirmity in the statutory requirement that bar applicants must possess the character and general fitness requisite for an attorney, and (2) an oath requiring the applicant to swear or affirm his support of the federal and state constitutions before admission to the bar was valid; and it was held, expressing the view of five members of the court, that (3) an applicant's right to privacy was not violated by an inquiry on a form for third-party affidavits attesting to the applicant's good moral character, which inquiry asked the affiant to state whether and how often he had visited the applicant's home, (4) a state rule providing that an applicant could not be admitted to the bar "unless he shall furnish satisfactory proof" that he "believes in the form of the government of the United States and is loyal to such government" was constitutionally valid, since even though the language of the rule itself might raise substantial constitutional questions, nevertheless the defendants had interpreted the rule as placing no burden of proof upon applicants and as referring only to an applicant's willingness and ability, in good faith, to take an oath to support the Constitution,

(5) a two-part question on the state's bar application questionnaire as to whether the applicant had ever organized or been a member of an organization which the applicant, during his membership, knew advocated forceful, violent, or unlawful overthrow of the government, and if so, whether the applicant, during his membership, had the specific intent to further such organization's aims, was constitutionally permissible on its face, (6) a question as to whether the applicant could conscientiously and did affirm that he was, without mental reservation, loyal to and ready to support the Constitution, was valid on its face, since it was merely supportive of the task of ascertaining the good faith with which the applicant could take the constitutional oath, and since there was no indication that an applicant would not be given the opportunity to explain any mental reservation and still gain admission to the bar, and (7) the state's screening system could not be declared invalid as necessarily resulting in chilling effects upon the exercise of constitutional freedoms, it appearing that the state's agents had been scrupulous in the use of their powers and had shown willingness to keep their investigations within constitutionally permissible limits.

Harlan, J., concurring, joined the court's opinion and also expressed the views that although states were prevented, under the First and Fourteenth Amendments, from denying admission to bar candidates merely because of theoretical beliefs in the "right" of revolution, nevertheless there was no constitutional barrier to denying admission to those seeking entry to the profession for the very purpose of doing away with the orderly processes of law; and that temperate inquiry into the character of an applicant's beliefs in such regard, as in the case at bar, was therefore relevant and permissible.

Black, J., joined by **Douglas, J.**, although agreeing with holdings (1) and (2) above, dissented from holdings (4), (5), and (6), expressing the views that the state's rule and questions involved in the latter holdings related to an applicant's political associations and beliefs; that the First Amendment absolutely prohibited a state from inquiring as to such beliefs, and from penalizing a man because of such beliefs; that exclusion of a bar applicant because he had belonged to organizations advocating violent overthrow of the government, even if his membership was "knowing," and he shared the organization's aims, was prohibited by the First Amendment; and that when a state sought to deny an applicant admission to the bar, it was required to proceed according to the most exacting demands of due process of law.

Marshall, J., joined by **Brennan, J.**, dissented from holdings (4), (5), (6), and (7) above, stating that the First Amendment precluded investigation of a bar applicant's beliefs and political affiliations; that such investigation could not be justified as being necessary to protect the integrity of an oath of constitutional support; that the state's rules and questions were overbroad and sanctioned overreaching official inquiry undertaken with a view to predicating the denial of a public benefit on activity protected by the First Amendment; and that the state's screening system thus placed an impermissible burden on the exercise of fundamental rights.

COUNSEL

Norman Dorsen argued the cause for appellants. On the brief for appellants Law Students Civil Rights Research Council, Inc. et al. were Alan H. Levine, Jeremiah S. Gutman, Melvin L. Wulf, and Sanford Jay Rosen. On the brief for appellants Wexler et al. were

Leonard B. Boudin, Victor Rabinowitz, and David Rosenberg.

David W. Peck argued the cause for appellees. With him on the brief were Louis J. Lefkowitz, Attorney General of New York, Daniel M. Cohen, Assistant Attorney General, and Michael M. Maney.

FRANK DYSON, Chief of Police, City of
Dallas, et al., Appellants,

v

BRENT STEIN

401 US 200, 27 L Ed 2d 781, 91 S Ct 769

Reargued November 16, 1970. Decided
February 23, 1971.

Decision: Federal District Court decision granting declaratory and injunctive relief against Texas obscenity statutes, on which pending state criminal proceedings were based, remanded for determination whether irreparable injury was threatened.

SUMMARY

The plaintiff, having been charged in a Texas state court with possession of obscene materials in violation of Texas statutory provisions, requested on federal constitutional grounds that the United States District Court for the Northern District of Texas grant declaratory and injunctive relief against the state obscenity statute. After remanding certain issues to a single District Judge, a three-judge District Court held the state statute unconstitutional and granted declaratory and injunctive relief (300 F Supp 602).

On appeal, the United States Supreme Court vacated the judgment below and remanded the case. In a per curiam opinion expressing the views of five members of the court, it was held that since federal intervention affecting pending state criminal prosecutions, either by injunction or by declaratory judgment, was proper only where irreparable injury was threatened, and since the District Court had made no findings of any irreparable injury, the District Court's judgment had to be vacated and the case remanded in light of Supreme Court decisions defining such irreparable injury.

White, J., concurred in the result.

Stewart, J., joined by **Harlan, J.**, concurring, emphasized that the decision dealt only with the proper policy to be followed by a federal court when asked to intervene by injunction or declaratory judgment in a criminal prosecution which was contemporaneously pending in a state court.

Brennan, J., joined by **Marshall, J.**, concurring in the result, stated that the questions discussed in the dissenting opinion by **Douglas, J.**, were not before the Supreme Court, because the three-judge District Court had remanded to a single judge all questions advanced by the plaintiff except the contention that the obscenity statute was unconstitutional on its face.

Douglas, J., dissented on the grounds that raids conducted in the instant case constituted illegal searches and seizures; that the court was dealing with plain error, as the state statute was unconstitutional on its face; and that the court should put an end to lawless raids under the statute.

COUNSEL

Lonny F. Zwiener, Assistant Attorney General of Texas, argued the cause for appellants on the original argument and on the reargument. With him on the brief were Crawford C. Martin, Attorney General, Nola White, First Assistant Attorney General, Pat Bailey, Executive Assistant Attorney General, Robert C. Flowers, Assistant Attorney General, Henry Wade, pro se, Wilson

Johnston, N. Alex Bickley, Thomas B. Thorpe, and Preston Dial.

David R. Richards argued the cause for appellee on the original argument and on the reargument. With him on the briefs was Melvin L. Wulf.

Stanley Fleishman filed a brief pro se et al. as amicus curiae urging affirmance.

GARRETT H. BYRNE et al., Appellants,

v

SERAFIM KARALEXIS et al.

401 US 216 , 27 L Ed 2d 792, 91 S Ct 777

Reargued November 17, 1970. Decided
February 23, 1971.

Decision: Federal District Court decision granting preliminary injunction against Massachusetts obscenity statute, on which pending state criminal proceeding were based, remanded for reconsideration.

SUMMARY

The owners of a motion-picture theater, having been indicted in a Massachusetts state court for exhibiting an allegedly obscene film, requested on federal constitutional grounds that the United States District Court for the District of Massachusetts grant declaratory and injunctive relief against the Massachusetts obscenity statute on which the indictments were based. Holding that there was a probability that the plaintiffs would ultimately prevail on their contention that the obscenity statute was unconstitutional, a three-judge District Court granted a preliminary injunction (306 F Supp 1363).

On appeal, the United States Supreme Court vacated the District Court's judgment and remanded the case. In a per curiam opinion, expressing the views of five members of the court, it was held that since the District Court had made no finding that the threat to the plaintiffs' federally protected rights was one which could not be eliminated by their defense against a single criminal prosecution, and since the District Court was without the guidance provided by certain Supreme Court decisions, the judgment below had to be vacated and the case remanded for reconsideration in light of such decisions.

Stewart, J., joined by **Harlan, J.**, concurring, emphasized that the decision dealt only with the proper policy to be followed by a federal court when asked to enjoin a criminal prosecution which was contemporaneously pending in a state court.

Brennan, J., joined by **White** and **Marshall, JJ.**, dissenting, would reverse the District Court's judgment rather than merely remand for reconsideration.

Douglas, J., did not participate.

COUNSEL

Robert H. Quinn, Attorney General of Massachusetts, pro se, argued the cause for appellants on the original argument and on the reargument. With him on the brief were Joseph J. Hurley, First Assistant Attorney General, John J. Irwin, Jr., Ruth I. Abrams, and Lawrence P. Cohen, Assistant Attorneys General, Garrett H. Byrne, pro se, and Theodore A. Glynn, Jr.

Nathan Lewin and Alan M. Dershowitz argued the cause for appellees on the reargument. Edward de Grazia and Mr. Lewin argued the cause for appellees on the original argument. With them on the brief was Herbert S. Swartz.

Peter L. Strauss argued the cause for the United States on the reargument as amicus curiae urging reversal. Francis X. Beytagh, Jr., argued the cause for the United States on the original argument. With them on the brief were Solicitor General Erwin N. Griswold, Assistant Attorney General Wilson, Jerome M. Feit, and Roger A. Pauley.

Briefs of amici curiae urging affirmance were filed by Stanley Fleishman and Sam Rosenwein for National General Corp. et al., and by Thomas R. Asher, Michael Schneiderman, and Melvin L. Wulf for the American Civil Liberties Union et al.

———————

VIVEN HARRIS, Petitioner,

v

STATE OF NEW YORK

401 US 222, 28 L Ed 2d 1, 91 S Ct 643

Argued December 17, 1970. Decided
February 24, 1971.

Decision: Accused's prior statements inconsistent with
his trial testimony held admissible to impeach his
credibility, although police had obtained statements
without giving accused warnings required by
Miranda v Arizona.

SUMMARY

The accused, who was indicted for selling heroin and
was tried before a jury in the County Court of Westchest-
er County, New York, had been questioned by the police
when taken into custody, but had not been warned of his
right to appointed counsel. After the accused testified
at the trial, prior inconsistent statements which he had
made to the police were admitted in evidence for the purpose of impeaching his credibility, and the jury was instructed that such statements could be considered only
in passing on the accused's credibility, and not as evidence
of guilt. The jury found the accused guilty, and his conviction was affirmed by the Appellate Division, Second
Department (31 App Div 2d 828, 298 NYS2d 245), and
by the New York Court of Appeals (25 NY2d 175, 303
NYS2d 71, 250 NE2d 349).

On certiorari, the United States Supreme Court affirmed. In an opinion by **Burger,** Ch. J., expressing the
view of five members of the court, it was held that although the accused's prior inconsistent statements, which

he did not claim were coerced or involuntary, had been made to the police under circumstances rendering them inadmissible to establish the prosecution's case in chief under Miranda v Arizona (1966) 384 US 436, 16 L Ed 2d 694, 86 S Ct 1602, 10 ALR3d 974, such statements could properly be used to impeach his credibility, since the shield provided by the Miranda Case could not be perverted into a license to use perjury by way of a defense, free from the risk of confrontation with prior inconsistent utterances.

Black, J., dissented without opinion.

Brennan, J., joined by **Douglas** and **Marshall, JJ.**, dissenting, stated that it was monstrous that courts should aid lawbreaking police officers, and that the court's decision in the instant case went far toward undoing much of the progress made in conforming police methods to the Constitution.

COUNSEL

Joel Martin Aurnou argued the cause and filed a brief for petitioner.

James J. Duggan argued the cause for respondent. With him on the brief was Carl A. Vergari.

Sybil H. Landau argued the cause for the District Attorney of New York County as amicus curiae urging affirmance. With her on the brief was Frank S. Hogan, pro se, and Michael R. Juviler.

INTERNATIONAL BROTHERHOOD OF BOILER-
MAKERS, IRON SHIPBUILDERS, BLACK-
SMITHS, FORGERS AND HELPERS,
AFL-CIO, Petitioner,

v

GEORGE W. HARDEMAN

401 US 233, 28 L Ed 2d 10, 91 S Ct 609

Argued December 16, 1970. Decided
February 24, 1971.

Decision: Suit for violation of Landrum-Griffin bill of
rights provisions held within federal court rather
than NLRB jurisdiction, but federal court held without authority to determine whether union constitution and bylaws had been violated.

SUMMARY

A union member who assaulted the local's business
manager in a job referral dispute was charged with violating the local's constitutional provision against attempting to create dissension or working against the union's
interest and harmony, and the local's bylaw against
threatening or using force against any union officer to
prevent him from properly discharging the duties of his
office. A local committee found him "guilty as charged,"
the local membership approved and voted him suspended
indefinitely, and the international denied his appeal.
Thereafter, he sued the international in the United States
District Court for the Southern District of Alabama for
consequential and punitive damages. The District Court
instructed the jury that there was no evidence that the
member violated the union's constitution, and since the

union tribunals had returned only a general verdict on the two charges, the member had been deprived of the "full and fair hearing" guaranteed by § 101(a)(5)(C) of the Labor-Management Reporting and Disclosure Act (29 USC § 411(a)(5)(C)). The jury awarded damages of $152,150, and the United States Court of Appeals for the Fifth Circuit affirmed (420 F2d 485).

On certiorari, the Supreme Court of the United States reversed. In an opinion by **Brennan, J.**, expressing the views of eight members of the court, it was held that (1) the subject matter of the suit was not within the exclusive competence of the National Labor Relations Board, even though the altercation arose over a job referral dispute normally within the NLRB's exclusive competence, because the critical issue was whether the member had received a "full and fair hearing" under § 101 (a)(5)(C), which is a claim referred to the Federal District Courts by § 102 of the LMRDA (29 USC § 412); (2) under § 101(a)(5) of the LMRDA (29 USC § 411 (a)(5)), which establishes fair notice and hearing requirements for union disciplinary proceedings, a federal court may not determine the scope of offenses for which a union may discipline its members, much less construe a union's constitution and bylaws to determine whether they forbid particular conduct; (3) the union's notice of charges, which not only stated or cited the constitutional and by-law provisions involved, but also contained a detailed statement of the facts relating to the altercation, satisfied the requirements of § 101(a)(5); and (4) the union charges that the member attacked the business manager without warning, and continued to beat him for some time, were supported by some evidence, so as to satisfy the "full and fair hearing" requirement of § 101(a)(5) (C), because the business manager so testified, and was corroborated by a witness, and the accused admitted having struck the first blow.

White, J., while joining the court's opinion, filed a concurring opinion stating that the decision did not reaffirm the doctrine that the NLRB has primary jurisdiction of conduct arguably prohibited by the Labor-Management Relations Act.

Douglas, J., dissented on the ground that there was no evidence that the member's assault on the business manager violated the union's constitution, and since the expulsion could have been predicated on a violation of the union's constitution, it was unlawful.

COUNSEL

Louis Sherman argued the cause for petitioner. With him on the brief were Elihu I. Leifer and Bernard Cushman.

Robert E. McDonald, Jr., argued the cause and filed a brief for respondent.

J. Albert Woll, Laurence Gold, and Thomas E. Harris filed a brief for the American Federation of Labor and Congress of Industrial Organizations, AFL-CIO, as amicus curiae urging reversal.

———

UNITED STATES, Appellant,

v

THOMAS WILLIAM WELLER

401 US 254, 28 L Ed 2d 26, 91 S Ct 602

Argued December 10, 1970.   Decided
February 24, 1971.

Decision: Direct appeal under Criminal Appeals Act held improper where Federal District Court's dismissal of indictment was based upon neither "construction of the statute" nor "motion in bar" provisions of Act.

SUMMARY

In Selective Service proceedings leading up to his induction notice, the defendant, seeking conscientious objector status, specifically requested that his lawyer be allowed to accompany him at the time of his personal appearance before the draft board, but the board, relying on a Selective Service regulation which prohibited a registrant from being represented before a local board by anyone acting as his attorney or legal counsel, denied the request.   Subsequently, the board declined to reopen the defendant's I–A classification; and the defendant, having refused to submit to induction when ordered to do so, was thereafter indicted for violation of § 12(a) of the Military Selective Service Act of 1967.   Before trial, he moved to dismiss the indictment on the ground, inter alia, that the board had deprived him of due process of law under the Fifth Amendment by denying him the right to counsel. The United States District Court for the Northern District of California, without deciding the constitutional claim, granted the motion to dismiss, on the ground that the regulation prohibiting representation by counsel was not authorized by the Military Selective Service Act of 1967 nor by any of the various provisions of the Act conferring rulemaking power on the President (309 F Supp 50). The United States filed a notice of appeal pursuant to the Criminal Appeals Act, which provided, inter alia, that the United States could take an appeal from a Federal District Court direct to the Supreme Court of the United States in all criminal cases involving (1) a decision or judgment dismissing any indictment where the decision or judgment was based upon the construction of the statute upon which the indictment was founded, or (2) a decision or judgment sustaining a motion in bar, when the defendant has not been put in jeopardy. After filing its notice of appeal, the United States reconsidered its position, concluding that the Supreme Court lacked jurisdiction over the appeal, and asked that the case be remanded to the United States Court of Appeals for the Ninth Circuit. The defendant, insisting that the case was properly before the Supreme Court, resisted the motion to remand.

On appeal, the United States Supreme Court remanded the case to the United States Court of Appeals for further proceedings. In an opinion by **Stewart, J.**, expressing the views of eight members of the court, it was held that the court had no jurisdiction to entertain the appeal under either the "construction of the statute" or the "motion in bar" provisions of the Criminal Appeals Act, because (1) the judgment dismissing the indictment was based upon construction of a Selective Service regulation, rather than a statute, and the regulation and statute involved were not so inextricably intertwined that it could be said that construction of the regulation would necessarily involve construction of the statute, and (2) the motion in bar to which the statute referred was some extraneous factor which would prevent the prosecution of a defendant for committing acts which were admittedly a crime, rather than, as was here being urged, some factor (the denial of counsel) which might prevent defendant's act (refusal to be induced) from being a crime.

Douglas, J., dissenting on the ground that the court had jurisdiction to decide the appeal, stated that, in his view, the regulation upon which the dismissal of the indictment was based was so inextricably intertwined with the statute itself that the dismissal of the indictment could be held to involve the construction of the statute.

COUNSEL

James van R. Springer argued the cause for the United States. On the brief were Solicitor General Erwin N. Griswold, Assistant Attorney General Wilson, Beatrice Rosenberg, Philip R. Monahan, and Roger A. Pauley.

Marvin M. Karpatkin argued the cause for appellee. With him on the brief were Michael N. Pollet, Melvin L. Wulf, and Rhoda H. Karpatkin.

MONITOR PATRIOT CO. et al., Petitioners,

v

ROSELLE A. ROY, Etc.

401 US 265, 28 L Ed 2d 35, 91 S Ct 621

Argued December 17, 1970. Decided
February 24, 1971.

Decision: Newspaper's reference to candidate for public
office as "former small-time bootlegger" held relevant
to candidate's fitness for office, and subject to constitutional rule requiring showing of actual malice
in libel action.

SUMMARY

A libel action was instituted in a New Hampshire state
court against a newspaper and the distributor of a syndi-
cated column, based on a column, published in the newspaper, that had referred to the plaintiff, a candidate for
the United States Senate in a primary election, as a "former small-time bootlegger." The trial court instructed
the jury to the effect that the plaintiff was required to
show that the article was false and had been published
with knowledge of its falsity or with a reckless disregard
of whether it was false or true, if the libel was in the
"public sector" and concerned the plaintiff's fitness for
office; but that if the libel did not relate to the plaintiff's
fitness for office, and was instead in the "private sector,"
the plaintiff need only show that the article was false
and had not been made in good faith for a justifiable purpose with a belief founded on reasonable grounds of the
truth of the matter published. The jury was also instructed that if the alleged libel was in the "public sector,"
the distributor could not be found liable, since there was

no showing that it had engaged in knowing or reckless falsehood. Judgment was entered on a verdict against both defendants, and the New Hampshire Supreme Court affirmed, holding that the trial judge had properly submitted to the jury the question whether the alleged libel was relevant to the plaintiff's fitness for office. (109 NH 441, 254 A2d 832).

On certiorari, the United States Supreme Court reversed and remanded. In an opinion by **Stewart, J.**, expressing the view of seven members of the court, it was held that (1) the rule, required by the First and Fourteenth Amendments, prohibiting a "public official" from recovering damages for a defamatory falsehood relating to his official conduct unless he proved that the statement was made with actual malice, that is, with knowledge that it was false or with reckless disregard of whether it was false or not, was applicable with regard to candidates for public office, and included anything which might touch on the candidate's fitness for office; (2) as a matter of constitutional law, a charge of criminal conduct, no matter how remote in time or place, could never be irrelevant to a candidate's fitness for office; and (3) the judgment in the case at bar must be reversed, and the cause remanded, since the jury had been improperly permitted to determine that the charge of prior criminal activity was not relevant to the plaintiff's fitness for office.

White, J., concurring, stated that the constitutional rule, by imposing on libel and slander plaintiffs the burden of showing knowing or reckless falsehood in specified situations, would inevitably result in extending constitutional protection to lies and falsehoods which, though neither knowing nor reckless, did severe damage to personal reputation, and that the sole basis for protecting publishers who spread false information was that otherwise the truth would too often be surpressed.

Black, J., joined by **Douglas, J.**, concurred in the judgment, but dissented from permitting the case to be tried again under different jury instructions, expressing the view that the First Amendment was intended to leave the press free from the harassment of libel judgments.

COUNSEL

Edward Bennett Williams argued the cause for petitioners.   With him on the briefs were Harold Ungar and Joseph A. Millimet.

Stanley M. Brown argued the cause and filed a brief for respondent.

TIME, Incorporated, Petitioner,

v

FRANK PAPE

401 US 279, 28 L Ed 2d 45, 91 S Ct 633

Argued December 16, 1970. Decided
February 24, 1971.

Decision: Magazine's failure to indicate in article on
United States Civil Rights Commission's report that
brutality charges against policeman were merely
allegations in private civil rights action against him,
rather than Commission's charges, held not to constitute "falsification" sufficient to sustain finding of
"actual malice" under constitutional rule in libel
action.

SUMMARY

A libel action was instituted on diversity of citizenship
grounds in the United States District Court for the Northern District of Illinois by a Chicago police officer against a
magazine, based on a magazine article which had discussed a report on police brutality by the United States
Commission on Civil Rights. The magazine article had
reported as a Commission charge or finding of brutality,
material which had in fact appeared in the Commission's
report as a mere description of allegations of brutality in
a private civil rights action against the police officer.
At the trial, both the author and the researcher of the
magazine article testified that although the wording of the
Commission's report had been admittedly altered, nevertheless they had concluded that the Commission took the
charges to be true. The District Court granted the magazine's motion for a directed verdict (294 F Supp 1087),

but the Court of Appeals for the Seventh Circuit reversed, holding that it was for the jury to determine whether the magazine's failure to indicate that the questioned material consisted of allegations in a complaint, rather than charges or findings of the Commission, showed "actual malice" under the constitutional rule prohibiting a public official from recovering damages for a defamatory falsehood relating to his official conduct unless he proved that the statement was made with "actual malice," that is, with knowledge that it was false or with reckless disregard of whether it was false or not (419 F2d 980).

On certiorari, the United States Supreme Court reversed and remanded. In an opinion by **Stewart, J.**, expressing the view of six members of the court, it was held that under the circumstances of the case, the magazine, by failing to state that the Commission report was technically confined to the "allegations" of a complaint, had not engaged in a "falsification" sufficient in itself to create a jury issue, or sustain a jury finding, of "actual malice," particularly since there was a logical implication from the totality of the Commission's report, which was ambiguous, that the Commission must have believed that the incidents described had in truth occurred, the magazine's conduct thus reflecting at most an error of judgment rather than reckless disregard of the truth.

Black, J., joined by **Douglas, J.**, concurred in the judgment, expressing the view that the First Amendment was intended to leave the press free from the harassment of libel judgments.

Harlan, J., dissented, expressing the views that (1) the judgment should be affirmed for the reasons stated in the Court of Appeals' decision (419 F2d 980), and (2) the Supreme Court should not undertake to judge on the specific facts of the case whether a jury could reasonably find that there was sufficient inaccuracy in the magazine's characterization of the Commission's report to permit the concomitant finding that the magazine article had been published with malice, the Court of Appeals having properly defined the requisite quality of proof, and having applied the correct standard of review in passing upon the trial judge's decision to grant a directed verdict.

COUNSEL

Don H. Reuben argued the cause for petitioner. With him on the briefs were Harold R. Medina, Jr., and Lawrence Gunnels.

Patrick W. Dunne argued the cause for respondent. With him on the brief were Robert J. Nolan and Edward J. Hladis.

OCALA STAR-BANNER COMPANY
et al., Petitioners,

v

LEONARD DAMRON

401 US 295, 28 L Ed 2d 57, 91 S Ct 628

Argued December 17, 1970. Decided
February 24, 1971.

Decision: False newspaper story that mayor, who was
also candidate for office of county tax assessor, had
been charged with perjury, held relevant to plaintiff's
fitness for office, and subject to constitutional rule
requiring showing of actual malice in libel suit.

SUMMARY

A libel action was instituted in a Florida state court
against a newspaper, based on a false story that the plaintiff, who at the time of the story was city mayor and a
candidate for the office of county tax assessor, had been
charged in a federal court with perjury in a civil rights
suit, and that his case had been held over until the following term of the federal court, whereas the story in fact
should have referred to the plaintiff's brother. The trial
court instructed the jury that the article was libelous
per se, and that the jury's only task was to determine
damages. After the jury awarded compensatory damages to the plaintiff, the trial court denied the defendant's
motion for a new trial, ruling that since the libelous
article did not relate to the public offices held or sought by
the plaintiff, the case was not governed by the constitutional rule prohibiting a public official from recovering
damages for a defamatory falsehood relating to his official
conduct unless he proved that the statement was made

with actual malice, that is, with knowledge that it was false or with reckless disregard of whether it was false or not. The Florida District Court of Appeal affirmed (221 So 2d 459), and the Supreme Court of Florida refused to review the judgment (231 So 2d 822).

On certiorari, the United States Supreme Court reversed and remanded. In an opinion by **Stewart, J.**, expressing the view of seven members of the court, it was held that the constitutional rule was applicable since a charge of criminal conduct against a public official or a candidate for office, no matter how remote in time or place, was always relevant to his fitness for office for purposes of applying the rule.

White, J., concurring, stated that the constitutional rule, by imposing on libel-and-slander plaintiffs the burden of showing knowing or reckless falsehood in specified situations, would inevitably result in extending constitutional protection to lies and falsehoods which, though neither knowing nor reckless, did severe damage to personal reputation, and that the sole basis for protecting publishers who spread false information was that otherwise the truth would too often be suppressed.

Black, J., joined by **Douglas, J.**, concurred in the judgment, but dissented from permitting the case to be tried again under different jury instructions, expressing the view that the First Amendment was intended to leave the press free from the harassment of libel judgments.

COUNSEL

Harold B. Wahl argued the cause and filed briefs for petitioners.

Wallace Dunn argued the cause and filed a brief for respondent.

GEORGE RAMSEY and Leon Nunley,
dba Leon Nunley Coal Company,
et al., Petitioners,

v

UNITED MINE WORKERS OF AMERICA

401 US 302, 28 L Ed 2d 64, 91 S Ct 658

Argued December 7, 1970. Decided
February 24, 1971.

Decision: Norris-LaGuardia "clear proof" standard held applicable only to union's authorization of, participation in, or ratification of, acts allegedly performed on its behalf, and not to other issues as to union's antitrust liability.

SUMMARY

Several coal mine operators brought a Sherman Act suit against the United Mine Workers in the United States District Court for the Eastern District of Tennessee, alleging that the UMW conspired with various coal producers to drive the plaintiffs out of business by agreeing to impose on all coal mine operators the provisions of the National Bituminous Coal Wage Agreement, knowing that small and nonmechanized operators would be unable to meet the contract's terms. The District Court dismissed the case for failure of proof because there was not "clear proof" of a conspiracy to standardize employment terms throughout the industry aimed at destroying marginal producers (265 F Supp 388). The United States Court of Appeals for the Sixth Circuit affirmed by an equally divided court (416 F2d 655).

On certiorari, the Supreme Court of the United States reversed. In an opinion by **White, J.,** expressing the views of five members of the court, it was held that the "clear proof" standard of § 6 of the Norris-LaGuardia Act (29 USC § 106) applies only to a union's authorization of, participation in, or ratification of, the acts allegedly performed on its behalf, and that otherwise the usual preponderance of evidence rule applies in treble damage antitrust suits against labor unions.

Douglas, J., joined by **Black, Harlan,** and **Marshall, JJ.,** dissented on the ground that the "clear proof" standard governs the quantum of evidence required to prove the occurrence of the alleged unlawful acts.

COUNSEL

John A. Rowntree argued the cause for petitioners. With him on the briefs were Clarence E. Walker, William M. Ables, Jr., Sizer Chambliss, and A. Allan Kelly.

Edward Bennett Williams argued the cause for respondent. With him on the brief were Steven M. Umin, Edward L. Carey, Harrison Combs, Willard P. Owens, E. H. Rayson, and M. E. Boiarsky.

Guy Farmer filed a brief for the Bituminous Coal Operators' Association as amicus curiae urging affirmance.

ZENITH RADIO CORPORATION, Petitioner,

v

HAZELTINE RESEARCH, Inc.

401 US 321, 28 L Ed 2d 77, 91 S Ct 795

Argued November 10, 1970. Decided
February 24, 1971.

Decision: Posttrial limitations and release defenses held
properly found waived; Clayton Act limitations tolling provisions held applicable to nonparty in government proceedings; release of coconspirator held effective only as to parties intended to be released.

SUMMARY

In a patent infringement suit in the United States
District Court for the Northern District of Illinois, the
defendant filed an antitrust counterclaim in 1963 seeking
damages suffered by it in the 1959–1963 period for its
exclusion from the Canadian, British, and Australian
markets by reason of the plaintiff's participation in patent
pools there. The plaintiff claimed that there was no
conspiracy and that the defendant had suffered no damage, but the evidence showed the plaintiff's participation
in an antitrust conspiracy, including participation in a
Canadian patent pool with various other American companies against whom the government had brought a civil
antitrust suit in 1958. The government suit was terminated as to all parties on November 1, 1962. The District Court, sitting without a jury, entered preliminary
findings of fact and conclusions of law that the defendant
had been damaged in stated amounts in all three foreign
markets. The plaintiff then moved to amend its reply
to the defendant's counterclaim, and to reopen the record

[Supreme Ct Sum]

for the taking of additional evidence, seeking to assert
the defenses that (1) part or all of the damages awarded
for the 1959–1963 period were barred by the 4-year
statute of limitations governing antitrust claims (§ 4B
of Clayton Act), in that they resulted from pre-1959
conspiratorial conduct; and (2) the defendant's release
executed in 1957 to certain other American companies,
and their parents and subsidiaries, precluded recovery for
damages resulting from pre-1957 conduct. The District
Court permitted the limitations and release defenses to
be filed, and heard further evidence with respect to the
British and Australian markets, as a result of which it
reduced its damage award for those markets, but it refused to reopen the record for other purposes or to modify
its findings or conclusions as to the Canadian market
(239 F Supp 51). Putting aside other issues, the United
States Court of Appeals for the Seventh Circuit reversed
on the ground that the defendant had failed to prove
injury to its business in any of the three markets (388 F2d
25). The Supreme Court of the United States affirmed
as to the British and Australian markets but reversed as
to the Canadian market (395 US 100, 23 L Ed 2d 129,
89 S Ct 1562). On remand, the Court of Appeals ruled
that the District Court had not rejected the limitations
and release defenses on waiver grounds; that the 4-year
statute of limitations on the counterclaim was not tolled
during the pendency of the government antitrust suit.
because the plaintiff was not a party to that suit; that the
plaintiff was entitled to the benefit of the release because
the defendant had failed to reserve expressly any right
against the plaintiff; and that the trial court should take
further evidence to determine the extent to which damages should be reduced by virtue of these defenses (418
F2d 21).

On certiorari, the Supreme Court of the United States
reversed and remanded with instructions to reinstate the

District Court's judgment with respect to the Canadian market. In an opinion by **White, J.**, expressing the views of seven members of the court, it was held that (1) if the District Court ruled that the limitations and release defenses were waived by the untimeliness of their presentation, it did not abuse its discretion, because allowing those defenses to be litigated would have entitled the defendant to perfect its proof as to damages resulting from pool operations during the 1959–1963 period, and thus would have required a virtual retrial of the damage issue; (2) if the District Court rejected the limitations defense on the merits, it did not err, because (a) the statute of limitations was tolled during the 1958–1963 period, by virtue of the tolling provisions of § 5(b) of the Clayton Act suspending the statute of limitations on private antitrust actions during the pendency of government antitrust proceedings and for one year thereafter, even though the plaintiff was not named by the government as a defendant or as a coconspirator, and (b) damages suffered during the 1959–1963 period as a result of the pre-1954 conduct of the conspiracy were not barred, since the cause of action for such damages had not accrued before 1954; and (3) if the District Court rejected the release defense on the merits, it did not err, because the release of other companies and their parents and subsidiaries was not intended to benefit the plaintiff.

Harlan, J., joined by **Stewart, J.**, concurred in the result on the grounds that the trial judge properly rejected the limitations and release defenses as too belatedly raised, and that it was unnecessary to reach the other issues.

COUNSEL

Thomas C. McConnell argued the cause for petitioner.

With him on the briefs were Philip J. Curtis and Francis J. McConnell.

Victor P. Kayser argued the cause for respondent. With him on the briefs were John T. Chadwell, C. Lee Cook, Jr., Joseph V. Griffin, Robert F. Ward, and Laurence B. Dodds.

———————

ISIAH RELFORD, Petitioner,

v

COMMANDANT, U. S. DISCIPLINARY
BARRACKS, Ft. Leavenworth, Kansas

401 US 355, 28 L Ed 2d 102, 91 S Ct 649

Argued December 15 and 16, 1970.   Decided
February 24, 1971.

Decision: Crimes of variety normally tried in civilian
courts committed by serviceman on military posts,
which violate the security of persons or property on
post, held triable by court-martial.

SUMMARY

In 1961, when petitioner was on active duty in the
United States Army, he was tried and convicted by a
general court-martial of kidnapping and raping two
women.   Each of the women, one of whom was the sister
of a serviceman and the other of whom was a serviceman's wife, was raped on military reservation property.
Petitioner's death sentence was later reduced to hard
labor for 30 years, total forfeitures of all pay and allow-
ances, and a dishonorable discharge, and the Court of
Military Appeals denied a petition for review in 1963.
In 1967, petitioner filed an application for a writ of habeas corpus with the United States District Court for the
District of Kansas, alleging inadequate representation by
counsel in the court-martial, which application was denied.   On appeal, the United States Court of Appeals
for the Tenth Circuit reviewed the petitioner's inadequate
representation claim, and other claims raised for the
first time as well, but affirmed the District Court's denial
of relief (409 F2d 824).   Several weeks thereafter, the

United States Supreme Court decided O'Callahan v Parker (395 US 258, 23 L Ed 2d 291, 89 S Ct 1683), in which case the court held that a court-martial could not try a member of the Armed Forces charged with attempted rape of a civilian, with housebreaking, and with assault with intent to commit rape, when the alleged offenses were committed off-post on American territory, when the soldier was on leave, and when the charges could have been prosecuted in a civilian court, since the alleged crimes were not sufficiently "service-connected."

On certiorari, the United States Supreme Court affirmed the judgment below. In an opinion by **Blackmun, J.**, expressing the unanimous views of the court, it was held that (1) there were significant differences between the instant case and O'Callahan v Parker, in that the petitioner here was not properly absent from the military base when he committed the crimes, the crimes were committed on a military reservation in an area under military control, one of the two victims was engaged in the performance of a duty relating to the military, and the two victims were both properly on the post and were "service-connected" personnel at the times their persons were violated; (2) the crimes with which petitioner was charged were properly triable by a military court; (3) a serviceman who is charged with an offense committed within or at the geographical boundary of a military post, which offense is violative of the security of a person or of property on the post, may be properly tried by a court-martial; and (4) the conclusion that petitioner was properly tried by a court-martial obviated the need for deciding whether O'Callahan v Parker, supra, should be retroactively applied.

COUNSEL

Judson W. Detrick, by appointment of the Court, 397

US 1020, 25 L Ed 2d 529, 90 S Ct 1264, argued the cause and filed briefs for petitioner.

Solicitor General Erwin N. Griswold argued the cause for respondent. With him on the brief were Assistant Attorney General Wilson, Deputy Solicitor General Springer, Beatrice Rosenberg, and Roger A. Pauley.

GLADYS BODDIE et al., Appellants,

v

STATE OF CONNECTICUT et al.

401 US 371, 28 L Ed 2d 113, 91 S Ct 780

Reargued November 17, 1970. Decided
March 2, 1971.

Decision: Connecticut statutes requiring payment of
court fees and costs held unconstitutionally applied
to prevent indigents from suing for divorce.

SUMMARY

In a class action brought on behalf of all female welfare
recipients residing in Connecticut and wishing divorces,
but prevented from bringing divorce suits by Connecticut
statutes requiring payment of court fees and costs for
service of process as a condition precedent to access to
the courts, the plaintiffs sought in the United States District Court for the District of Connecticut a judgment
declaring the statutes invalid as applied to the class, and
an injunction requiring defendants to permit members
of the class to sue for divorce without payment of any
fees and costs. A three-judge court dismissed the complaint for failure to state a claim (286 F Supp 968).

On appeal, the Supreme Court of the United States
reversed. In an opinion by **Harlan, J.**, expressing the
views of six members of the court, it was held that a
state denies due process of law to indigent persons by
refusing to permit them to bring divorce actions except
on payment of court fees and service-of-process costs
which they are unable to pay.

Douglas, J., concurred on the ground that the equal
protection clause rather than the due process clause was
the proper basis of decision.

Brennan, J., concurred on the ground that while denying indigents access to the courts for nonpayment of a fee is a denial of due process, it is also a denial of equal protection of the laws, and no distinction can be drawn between divorce suits and other actions.

Black, J., dissented on the ground that charging practically nominal initial court costs in civil actions does not violate either the due process or equal protection clause.

COUNSEL

Arthur B. LaFrance argued the cause and filed briefs for appellants on the original argument and on the reargument.

Raymond J. Cannon, Assistant Attorney General of Connecticut, argued the cause for appellees on the original argument and on the reargument. With him on the brief were Robert K. Killian, Attorney General, and William S. Kaplan.

Allan Ashman filed a brief for the National Legal Aid and Defender Association as amicus curiae urging reversal.

Briefs of amici curiae urging affirmance were filed by Francis B. Burch, Attorney General of Maryland, and J. Michael McWilliams, Assistant Attorney General, joined by George F. Kugler, Jr., Attorney General of New Jersey, and Stephen Skillman, Assistant Attorney General, and by the following Attorneys General: David P. Buckson of Delaware, Jack P. F. Gremillion of Louisiana, Clarence A. H. Meyer of Nebraska, Harvey Dickerson of Nevada, Helgi Johanneson of North Dakota, and Lee Johnson of Oregon.

PRESTON A. TATE, Petitioner,

v

HERMAN SHORT, Chief of Police, Houston, Texas

401 US 395, 28 L Ed 2d 130, 91 S Ct 668

Argued January 14, 1971. Decided March 2, 1971.

Decision: Imprisonment of indigent for nonpayment of fines for traffic offenses held violative of equal protection clause of Fourteenth Amendment.

SUMMARY

In the Corporation Court of Houston, Texas, the petitioner was convicted of nine traffic offenses which were punishable by fines only, and he was fined a total of $425. He was unable to pay the fines because of indigency, and pursuant to a state statute and municipal ordinance, the Corporation Court ordered him imprisoned for 85 days, each day of imprisonment serving as a substitute for $5 of the fines. His petition for habeas corpus was denied by the County Criminal Court of Harris County, and the Texas Court of Criminal Appeals affirmed, rejecting the petitioner's contention that because he was too poor to pay the fines his imprisonment was unconstitutional (445 SW2d 210).

On certiorari, the United States Supreme Court reversed and remanded the case. In an opinion by **Brennan, J.**, expressing the view of seven members of the court, it was held that imprisonment of the petitioner solely because of his indigency constituted invidious discrimination in violation of the equal protection clause of the Fourteenth Amendment.

Black, J., concurred in the result.

Harlan, J., concurred in the court's judgment, but on the basis of due process rather than equal protection.

Blackmun, J., concurring in the court's opinion, stated that the court's decision might encourage legislatures to eliminate fines and to make jail terms the only punishment for a broad range of traffic offenses.

COUNSEL

Norman Dorsen argued the cause for petitioner. With him on the briefs were Peter Sanchez-Navarro, Jr., and Stanley A. Bass.

Joseph G. Rollins argued the cause for respondent. With him on the brief were Crawford C. Martin, Attorney General of Texas, Nola White, First Assistant Attorney General, Alfred Walker, Executive Assistant Attorney General, and Robert C. Flowers and Gilbert J. Pena, Assistant Attorneys General.

Allan Ashman filed a brief for the National Legal Aid and Defender Association as amicus curiae urging reversal.

CITIZENS TO PRESERVE OVERTON PARK, Inc., et al., Petitioners,

v

JOHN A. VOLPE, Secretary, Department of Transportation, et al.

401 US 402, 28 L Ed 2d 136, 91 S Ct 814

Argued January 11, 1971. Decided March 2, 1971.

Decision: Secretary of Transportation's decision approving routing of proposed interstate highway through public park held, in view of federal statutes restricting use of parklands for such purposes, subject to broad and substantial judicial review.

SUMMARY

In 1956, the Bureau of Public Roads approved a route for construction of an interstate highway in Memphis, Tennessee, which route would have destroyed 26 acres of a 342-acre park located near the center of Memphis and which would have severed that portion of the park containing the zoo from the remainder of the park, which contained a golf course, an art academy, 170 acres of forest, and other recreational areas. This route was again approved in 1966 by the Federal Highway Administrator. However, in 1966, Congress passed the Department of Transportation Act, § 4(f) of which declared it to be the national policy that special effort should be made to preserve, inter alia, public park and recreation lands and which ordered the Secretary of Transportation not to approve any program or project which required the use of any publicly owned land from a public park or recreation area unless (1) there was no feasible and prudent alternative to the use of such land, and (2) there was included in any such program all possible planning to minimize harm to any park or recreational area used for such purposes. The state continued to acquire rights of way on both sides of the park, and, after the Secretary of Transportation announced in 1968 that he concurred in the judgment of local officials that the highway should be built through the park, the state in 1969 acquired the right of way inside the park from the city. Final approval of the route and design for the road was not announced until late in 1969 after Congress had reiterated in § 138 of the Federal-Aid Highway Act of 1968 that highway construction through public parks was to be restricted. The announcements approving the route and design of the highway were not accompanied by formal findings of fact, nor did the Secretary state why he believed there were no feasible and prudent alternative routes or why design changes could not be made to reduce harm to the park. Petitioners, a group of private citizens and local and national conservation organizations, brought suit in the United States District Court for the Western District of Tennessee, seeking to halt construction of the highway through the park and arguing that (1) the Secretary's action in approving the route and design was invalid without formal findings, (2) the Secretary made no independent determination but relied on the judgment of local officials as to the route selected, (3) there were feasible and prudent alternative routes for the highway both north and south of the park, and (4) the design plans did not include "all possible" methods for reducing harm to the park. The District Court held that the statutes did not require the Secretary to file formal findings, and, construing its review powers narrowly, decided that the Secretary had not exceeded his authority in approving the route. Therefore, it granted defendants' motion for summary judgment and dismissed the action (309 F Supp 1189). The United States Court of Appeals for the Sixth Circuit affirmed the judgment of the District Court (432 F2d 1307).

On certiorari, the United States Supreme Court reversed and remanded the case to the United States District Court for the Western District of Tennessee with instructions to review the Secretary of Transportation's decision. In an opinion by **Marshall, J.**, expressing the views of six members of the court, it was held that (1) the Secretary of Transportation was not required to file formal findings, under either § 4(f) of the Department of Transportation Act of 1966 or § 138 of the Federal-Aid Highway Act of 1968, that there were no feasible and prudent alternatives to routing the highway through the park prior to his approving the design and route, (2) judicial review of the Secretary's action was inadequate, however, because it was based solely on litigation affidavits, (3) petitioners were entitled to seek judicial review of the Secretary's action, (4) Congress had not sought to prohibit judicial review nor to restrict judicial review of the Secretary's action, (5) the Secretary's action did not fall within the exception in § 701 of the Administrative Procedure Act prohibiting judicial review of agency actions committed to agency discretion by law, (6) the use of federal funds for the construction of highways through parks was barred, except in the most unusual circumstances, by the language of § 4(f) of the Department of Transportation Act of 1966 and by § 138 of the Federal-Aid Highway Act of 1968, (7) Congress intended by those Acts to give the protection of parklands paramount importance and preference over such other factors as cost and community disruption, (8) although a de novo review was not required, the reviewing court should engage in a substantial inquiry as to whether the Secretary acted within the scope of his authority, whether he considered the relevant factors in reaching his decision, whether there had been a clear error of judgment, and whether the necessary procedural requirements were followed, (9) judicial review should be based on the full administrative record before the Secretary at the time he made his decision, and (10) while inquiry into the mental processes of administrative decisionmakers should usually be avoided, the District Court, on remand, could make such an inquiry if that should prove to be the only way effective judicial review could be had.

Black, J., joined by **Brennan, J.,** filed a separate opinion in which he agreed that the judgment of the Court of Appeals was wrong and should be reversed, but stated that inasmuch as the Secretary of Transportation had failed to comply with the duty imposed on him not to permit the construction of highways through public parks except where no feasible and prudent alternatives exist, the case should be remanded to the Secretary rather than to the District Court so that the Secretary could hold a hearing in the matter in obedience to Congress' command.

Blackmun, J., while joining in the opinion and judgment, filed a separate statement noting that the controversy involving this particular interstate highway spanned a decade and that the imposition by the 1966 and 1968 federal statutes of new standards and conditions upon a situation that already was largely developed undoubtedly accounted for the sketchiness of the record before the court.

Douglas, J., did not participate.

COUNSEL

John W. Vardaman, Jr., argued the cause for petitioners.   With him on the briefs was Edward Bennett Williams.

Solicitor General Erwin N. Griswold argued the cause for respondent Volpe. With him on the brief were Assistant Attorney General Gray, Alan S. Rosenthal, and Daniel Joseph. J. Alan Hanover argued the cause for respondent Speight. With him on the brief were David M. Pack, Attorney General of Tennessee, Lurton C. Goodpasture, Assistant Atorney General, and James B. Jalenak.

Briefs of amici curiae were filed by James M. Manire and Jack Petree for the city of Memphis et al., and by Roberts B. Owen and Gerald P. Norton for the Committee of 100 on the Federal City, Inc., et al.

WILLIE S. GRIGGS et al., Petitioners,

v

DUKE POWER COMPANY

401 US 424, 28 L Ed 2d 158, 91 S Ct 849

Argued December 14 1970. Decided
March 8, 1971.

Decision: High school diploma and satisfactory intelligence test score tending to exclude Negroes and unrelated to successful job performance held improper job requirements under Civil Rights Act.

SUMMARY

Negro employees of a power company brought a class action against their employer in the United States District Court for the Middle District of North Carolina, alleging that the employer violated the Civil Rights Act of 1964 by requiring a high school diploma and a satisfactory intelligence test score for certain jobs previously limited to white employees, so as to preserve the effects of the employer's past racial discrimination. The District Court dismissed their complaint (292 F Supp 243). The United States Court of Appeals for the Fourth Circuit reversed the District Court's holding that residual discrimination arising from past employment practices was insulated from remedial action, but it affirmed the District Court's holding that absent a discriminatory purpose, the diploma and test requirements were proper (420 F2d 1225).

On certiorari, the Supreme Court of the United States reversed. In an opinion by **Burger,** Ch J., expressing the unanimous view of the court, it was held that the Civil Rights Act prohibits an employer from requiring a high school education or passing of a standardized general intelligence test as a condition of employment in or trans-

[Supreme Ct Sum]

fer to jobs when (1) neither standard is shown to be significally related to successful job performance, (2) both requirements operate to disqualify Negroes at a substantially higher rate than white applicants, and (3) the jobs in question formerly had been filled only by white employees as part of a longstanding practice of giving preference to whites.

Brennan, J., did not participate.

COUNSEL

Jack Greenberg argued the cause for petitioners. With him on the briefs were James M. Nabrit III, Norman C. Amaker, William L. Robinson, Conrad O. Pearson, Julius LeVonne Chambers, and Albert J. Rosenthal.

George W. Ferguson, Jr., argued the cause for respondent. With him on the brief were William I. Ward, Jr., and George M. Thorpe.

Lawrence M. Cohen argued the cause for the Chamber of Commerce of the United States as amicus curiae urging affirmance. With him on the brief were Francis V. Lowden, Jr., Gerard C. Smetana, and Milton A. Smith.

Briefs of amici curiae urging reversal were filed by Solicitor General Erwin N. Griswold, Assistant Attorney General Leonard, Deputy Solicitor General Wallace, David L. Rose, Stanley Hebert, and Russell Specter for the United States; by Louis J. Lefkowitz, Attorney General, pro se, Samuel A. Hirshowitz, First Assistant Attorney General, and George D. Zuckerman and Dominick J. Tuminaro, Assistant Attorneys General, for the Attorney General of the State of New York; and by Bernard Kleiman, Elliot Bredhoff, Michael H. Gottesman, and George H. Cohen for the United Steelworkers of America, AFL-CIO.

GUY PORTER GILLETTE, Petitioner,

v

UNITED STATES (No. 85)

LOUIS A. NEGRE, Petitioner,

v

STANLEY R. LARSEN et al. (No. 325)

401 US 437, 28 L Ed 2d 168, 91 S Ct 828

Argued December 9, 1970.   Decided March 8, 1971.

Decision: Conscientious objections to Vietnam War, rather than to all war, held insufficient to warrant exemption from draft or discharge from service; statutory exemption only of objectors to all war held constitutional under religious clauses of First Amendment.

SUMMARY

In the instant cases, one of the questions presented was whether conscientious objection to a particular war, rather than objection to all war, relieved the objector from military service responsibilities under the provision of § 6(j) of the Military Selective Service Act of 1967 exempting registrants "conscientiously opposed to participation in war in any form," and under administrative regulations incorporating the same standards for conscientious-objector discharges of servicemen. Another issue presented was whether limitation of conscientious-objector status only to those who objected to all wars violated the religious clauses of the First Amendment. In No. 85, conscientious-objector status was administratively denied to a draft registrant who, on the basis of a humanist approach to religion and fundamental principles of conscience, objected to participation in the Vietnam war as being unjust, but not to participation in a war of national defense or a war sponsored by the United Nations as a peace-keeping measure. The registrant was subsequently convicted in the United States District Court for the Southern District of New York for wilful failure to report for induction, the District Court having determined that there was a basis in fact to support the denial of the conscientious-objector exemption, since the registrant's objection ran only to a particular war. The United States Court of Appeals for the Second Circuit affirmed the conviction (420 F2d 298). In No. 325, the Army denied an application for a conscientious-objector discharge which had been made by a soldier after completion of basic training and receipt of orders for Vietnam duty, and which was based on objection to the Vietnam war but not to all wars. Such objection was founded on the soldier's duty under the Catholic faith to forswear participation in an "unjust" war. The United States District Court for the Northern District of California denied habeas corpus relief to the soldier, finding a basis in fact for the Army's rejection of the application for discharge, and the United States Court of Appeals for the Ninth Circuit affirmed on the ground that objection to the Vietnam war, but not to all wars, did not qualify the soldier for discharge (418 F2d 908).

On certiorari, the United States Supreme Court affirmed both judgments. In an opinion by **Marshall, J.**, it was held, expressing the view of eight members of the court, that (1) § 6(j) of the Military Selective Service Act of 1967, properly construed, exempted only persons opposed to participation in any and all wars, rather than those opposed to participation in a particular war, even if the latter objection was "religious" in character; and it was held, expressing the view of seven members of the court, that (2) the statute, so construed, did not violate the establishment of religion clause of the First Amendment, since the statute focused on individual conscientious belief and did not discriminate on its face on the basis of religious affiliation or belief, and since limitation of the exemption to conscientious objectors to all war was supported by valid neutral and secular reasons relating to the need for a fair and uniform system of determining entitlement to exemption, and (3) Congress did not violate the free exercise of religion clause of the First Amendment by conscripting persons who objected to a particular war on grounds of conscience and religion, since the conscription laws were not designed to interfere with religious rituals or practice and did not penalize any theological position, and since the impact of the law on objectors to particular wars was justified by substantial government interest in maintaining a fair system for determining exemption eligibility, and in procuring the manpower necessary for military purposes.

Black, J., concurred in the court's judgment and in holding (1), above.

Douglas, J., dissenting in No. 85, expressed the view that there was no doubt that the registrant's objection to service in the Vietnam war was sincere and genuine, as a matter of conscience within the requirement of the statutory exemption; that conscience and belief were the main ingredients of First Amendment rights of free speech and religion; that the statute as written was constitutionally infirm under the First Amendment because of its invidious discrimination; and that if exemption was afforded to persons holding religious or conscientious scruples against all wars, so must it be afforded to those with religious or conscientious objection to participation in particular wars. Dissenting in a separate opinion in No. 325 also, Douglas, J., stated that there was no question as to the sincerity of the serviceman's opposition to participation in the Vietnam war, which opposition was based on his moral duty under the Catholic faith not to participate in wars considered in personal conscience to be unjust, and that therefore the judgment below should be reversed for the reasons expressed in the dissent in No. 85.

COUNSEL

Conrad J. Lynn argued the cause for petitioner in No. 85. With him on the brief were Leon Friedman, Marvin M. Karpatkin, and Melvin L. Wulf. Richard Harrington argued the cause for petitioner in No. 325. With him on the briefs were Leigh Athearn, Stuart J. Land, and John T. Noonan, Jr.

Solicitor General Erwin N. Griswold argued the cause for the United States and for respondents in both cases. With him on the briefs were Assistant Attorney General Wilson and Beatrice Rosenberg.

George T. Altman, pro se, filed a brief as amicus curiae in both cases. Leo Rosen filed a brief for the American Ethical Union as amicus curiae in No. 85. Briefs of amici curiae in No. 325 were filed by Charles H. Tuttle and Thomas A. Shaw, Jr., for the National Council of the Churches of Christ in the U. S. A. et al.; by Peter J. Donnici for the Executive Board of the National Federation of Priests' Councils; by Joseph B. Robison, Ephraim Margolin, Stanley J. Friedman, Seymour Farber, and Edwin J. Lukas for the American Jewish Congress; by Michael N. Pollet and Elsbeth Levy Bothe for Louis P. Font; and by the American Friends Service Committee.

REUBIN ASKEW et al., Appellants,

v

ROBERT H. HARGRAVE et al.

401 US 476, 28 L Ed 2d 196, 91 S Ct 856

Argued February 23 and 24, 1971.
Decided March 8, 1971.

Decision: Federal District Court held to have erred in
refusing to apply abstention doctrine, and in holding,
on motion for summary judgment, that Florida
school tax statute violated equal protection clause
of Fourteenth Amendment.

SUMMARY

A Florida statute, which dealt with the financing of
public education through state appropriations and local
ad valorem taxes assessed by each school district, provided
that to be eligible to receive state funds, a local school district had to limit its ad valorem taxes for school purposes
to not more than 10 mills of assessed valuation. The
plaintiffs filed a class action against state officials in the
United States District Court for the Middle District of
Florida, alleging that the state statute violated the equal
protection clause of the Fourteenth Amendment by dis-
criminating against school children of property-poor
counties, in which 10 mills of ad valorem tax would produce fewer dollars per child for educational purposes
than would 10 mills of ad valorem tax in other counties.
Subsequently to the filing of the plaintiffs' federal action,
an action was filed in a Florida state court attacking the
same statute, but primarily on the state law grounds that
the statute violated the Florida Constitution. The District Court rejected the defendants' argument that the

court should abstain from considering the case in deference to the state court proceeding, and after both sides had moved for summary judgment on the ground that there was no material issue of fact, the District Court, granting the plaintiffs' motion for summary judgment, held the state statute unconstitutional and enjoined the defendants from withholding state funds from any school district by virtue of the provisions of the statute (313 F Supp 944).

On appeal, the United States Supreme Court vacated the judgment below and remanded the case for further proceedings. In a per curiam opinion, it was held in Part I, expressing the view of eight members of the court, that the District Court had erred in refusing to abstain from considering the case; and it was held in Part II, expressing the unanimous view of the court, that the pleadings and an affidavit in support of the plaintiffs' motion for summary judgment were inadequate as a basis for deciding the equal protection claim, which claim should not have been decided without fully developing the factual record at a hearing.

Black, J., concurred in the judgment and in Part II of the opinion.

COUNSEL

Charles E. Miner, Jr., argued the cause for appellants. With him on the briefs were Rivers Buford, Jr., and Stephen Marc Slepin.

Hershel Shanks argued the cause for appellees. With him on the brief were Allan I. Mendelsohn, Robert M. Perce, Jr., Richard H. Frank, and David Rubin.

William H. Adams III filed a brief for the Florida Education Research Foundation as amicus curiae urging reversal.

GEORGE WASHINGTON DURHAM, Petitioner,

v

UNITED STATES

401 US 481, 28 L Ed 2d 200, 91 S Ct 858

March 8, 1971

Decision: Accused's death, pending Supreme Court's direct review of federal conviction, held to abate entire prosecution, so as to require dismissal of indictment.

SUMMARY

After the accused's conviction for possession of a counterfeit $20 bill was affirmed by the United States Court of Appeals for the Ninth Circuit, he filed a timely petition for rehearing and was informed that he would be notified as to the disposition of his petition as soon as the court acted. When several months had passed without any word, he wrote to the Court of Appeals and was informed that his petition for rehearing had been denied about 6 months earlier. Less than 3 weeks later, he petitioned the United States Supreme Court for a writ of certiorari, but he died before the Supreme Court took any action upon his petition.

The Supreme Court granted the accused's motion for leave to proceed in forma pauperis and his petition for certiorari, vacated the judgment below, and remanded the case with directions to dismiss the indictment. In a per curiam opinion, expressing the views of five members of the court, it was held that (1) although the petition for certiorari had not been filed until after the expiration of the time limits prescribed in Supreme Court Rule 22 (2), a waiver of this rule was proper under the circumstances of the instant case, and (2) the accused's death pending direct review of his conviction abated all proceedings had in the prosecution from its inception.

Marshall, J., joined by **Burger, Ch. J.**, and **Stewart, J.**, stated that the petition for certiorari should be dismissed as moot because of the accused's death, and that the Court of Appeals should be directed to note this action on its records.

Blackmun, J., dissented, stating that (1) the petition for certiorari was untimely, and (2) he would merely dismiss the petition for certiorari because of the accused's death, rather than direct the dismissal of the indictment.

HERBERT PHILLIP SCHLANGER, Petitioner,

v

ROBERT C. SEAMANS, Jr., Secretary
of the Air Force, et al.

401 US 487, 28 L Ed 2d 251, 91 S Ct 995

Argued February 22, 1971. Decided
March 23, 1971

Decision: Absence of Air Force enlisted man's commanding officer from territorial jurisdiction of Federal
District Court held fatal to court's jurisdiction to
act upon enlisted man's habeas corpus petition.

SUMMARY

An Air Force enlisted man who had been accepted in
an officer training project and who had been assigned
to an Air Force Base in Ohio "with duty at Arizona State
University" was removed from the program, allegedly
for engaging in civil rights activities on the campus.
While he was seeking administrative relief through command channels, he was reassigned to an Air Force Base in
Georgia to complete the remainder of his re-enlistment
in a noncommissioned status. After exhausting those
remedies, he was given permission by his superiors in
Georgia to attend the same university in Arizona under a
different program and at his own expense. Thereafter
he filed his application for habeas corpus in the District
Court for the District of Arizona, alleging that
his enlistment contract had been breached and that
he was being detained unlawfully. The respondents
to the suit were the Secretary of the Air Force, the
commander of the Georgia Air Force base (who had custody and control over the petitioner), and the com-

mander of the Air Force ROTC program at Arizona
State University, who was the only respondent present in
Arizona, but who concededly had no control over the
petitioner. The District Court denied the application,
and the United States Court of Appeals for the Ninth
Circuit affirmed.

On certiorari, the United States Supreme Court affirmed. In an opinion by **Douglas, J.**, expressing the view
of seven members of the court, it was held that the District Court was without jurisdiction to act on the petition,
because (1) the habeas corpus statute necessarily pre-
supposed that the writ would be directed against the
custodian of the person being detained, (2) the only respondent named in the petition who was within the District Court's jurisdiction was the Air Force ROTC commander at the University, and it was conceded that he had
no control over petitioner, who was not in his chain of
command, and (3) the absence of petitioners' custodian,
the commander of the Georgia Air Force base, from the
territorial jurisdiction of the District Court, was fatal to
the court's jurisdiction.

Harlan, J., concurred in the result.

Stewart, J., dissented without opinion.

COUNSEL

Herbert P. Schlanger, petitioner, argued the cause and
filed a brief pro se.

Solicitor General Erwin N. Griswold argued the cause
for respondents. With him on the brief were Assistant
Attorney General Gray, Morton Hollander, and Robert
E. Kopp.

Melvin L. Wulf filed a brief for the American Civil
Liberties Union as amicus curiae urging reversal.

STATE OF OHIO, Plaintiff,

v

WYANDOTTE CHEMICALS CORPORATION et al.

401 US 493, 28 L Ed 2d 256, 91 S Ct 1005

Argued January 18, 1971. Decided
March 23, 1971.

Decision: Ohio was denied leave to file complaint invoking Supreme Court's original jurisdiction in action alleging pollution of Lake Erie by out-of-state corporations.

SUMMARY

The State of Ohio, seeking to invoke the original jurisdiction of the United States Supreme Court over state actions against citizens of other states or countries under Article III of the Federal Constitution, filed a motion for leave to file a bill of complaint for abatement of a nuisance, alleging that the defendants, two out-of-state domestic corporations and a Canadian corporation owned by one of the domestic corporations, were responsible for contaminating Lake Erie by dumping mercury into its tributaries outside of Ohio. The state, suing on behalf of itself and its citizens, sought a decree declaring the introduction of mercury into Lake Erie's tributaries a public nuisance, perpetually enjoining the defendants from such acts, requiring the defendants either to remove the mercury or to pay the costs of such removal, and directing the defendants to pay monetary damages for the harm done to the lake, its fish, wildlife, and vegetation, and the citizens and inhabitants of Ohio.

The United States Supreme Court denied the state's motion for leave to file its complaint, without prejudice to its right to commence other appropriate judicial proceedings. In an opinion by **Harlan, J.**, expressing the view of eight members of the court, it was held that (1) although the complaint stated a cause of action within the court's original jurisdiction, nevertheless the court had discretion to decline jurisdiction in order to protect itself from abuse of the opportunity to resort to its original jurisdiction in the enforcement by states of claims against citizens of another state or country, and (2) notwithstanding the public importance of elimination of environmental blight, the court would decline to exercise its original jurisdiction in the case at bar, particularly since the action was based on complex factual issues and did not call for resolution of difficult or important problems of federal law.

Douglas, J., dissented, stating that Ohio's complaint to abate a public nuisance presented basically a classic type of case congenial to the court's original jurisdiction.

COUNSEL

Paul W. Brown, Attorney General of Ohio, argued the cause and filed a brief for plaintiff.

John M. Moelmann argued the cause for defendant Wyandotte Chemicals Corp. With him on the briefs were Thomas J. Weithers and Milton F. Mallender. Ian W. Outerbridge, by special leave of Court, argued the cause for defendant Dow Chemical Co. of Canada, Ltd. With him on the briefs was Richard W. Galiher. Harley J. McNeal argued the cause and filed briefs for defendant Dow Chemical Co.

Peter L. Strauss argued the cause for the United States as amicus curiae. With him on the brief were Solicitor General Erwin N. Griswold, Assistant Attorney General Kashiwa, and James R. Moore.

Frank J. Kelley, Attorney General, Robert E. Derengoski, Solicitor General, and M. Robert Carr, Assistant Attorney General, filed a brief for the State of Michigan as amicus curiae.

———————

UNITED STATES, Petitioner,

v

WILLIAM L. RANDALL, Trustee

401 US 513, 28 L Ed 2d 273, 91 S Ct 991

Argued February 22, 1971. Decided
March 24, 1971.

Decision: Despite debtor's disobedience of court order
to deposit withheld taxes into special account for
government, claim for such taxes held not entitled to
priority over administrative expenses of bankruptcy
proceedings.

SUMMARY

In arrangement proceedings under Chapter XI of the
Bankruptcy Act, the debtor was ordered by the United
States District Court for the Northern District of Illinois
to deposit into a special account for the United States
Government the income and social security taxes withheld
from the debtor's employees. The debtor withheld such
taxes from its employees, but failed to deposit them into
the special account. After the debtor was adjudicated
a bankrupt, the government requested that the amount of
the withheld taxes be treated as a trust fund entitled to
priority over claims for the costs and expenses of administration of the bankruptcy proceedings. The referee in
bankruptcy denied the government's request, the District
Court upheld the referee's decision (302 F Supp 614), and
the Court of Appeals for the Seventh Circuit affirmed
(419 F2d 1068).

On certiorari, the United States Supreme Court affirmed. In an opinion by **Douglas, J.**, expressing the view
[Supreme Ct Sum]—11

of five members of the court, it was held that the statutory policy of subordinating taxes to costs and expenses of administration would not be served by creating or enforcing trusts which ate up an estate, leaving little or nothing for creditors and court officers whose goods and services created the assets.

Blackmun, J., joined by **Burger, Ch. J., Black, J.,** and **Stewart, J.,** dissented on the ground that the court should not permit the government's right to a trust for the amount of the withheld taxes to be defeated by the debtor's flagrant disobedience of the order to pay the withheld taxes into a special account.

COUNSEL

Richard B. Stone argued the cause for the United States. With him on the brief were Solicitor General Erwin N. Griswold, Assistant Attorney General Walters, and Crombie J. D. Garrett.

Kevin J. Gillogly argued the cause for respondent. With him on the brief was Daniel C. Ahern.

UNITED STATES, Petitioner,

v

DISTRICT COURT IN AND FOR THE COUNTY OF EAGLE and State of Colorado et al.

401 US 520, 28 L Ed 2d 278, 91 S Ct 998

Argued March 2, 1971. Decided March 24, 1971.

Decision:. United States held to have consented to be sued under 43 USC § 666 in Colorado supplemental water adjudication.

SUMMARY

The United States brought an original proceeding in the Supreme Court of Colorado for a writ prohibiting the District Court for Eagle County from asserting jurisdiction over the United States in a supplemental water adjudication suit notifying all owners and claimants in the Eagle River and its tributaries to file a statement of claim and to appear in regard to all water rights owned or claimed by them. Primarily because of reserved waters for the White River National Forest, the United States was served with such a notice pursuant to 43 USC § 666, which, under certain conditions, gives consent to join the United States as a defendant in any suit for the adjudication of rights to the use of water of a river system or other source or for the administration of such rights where the United States is the owner of or is in the process of acquiring such rights. The Surpeme Court of Colorado discharged a rule to show cause why the requested relief should not be granted (169 Colo 555, 458 P2d 760).

On certiorari, the Supreme Court of the United States affirmed. In an opinion by **Douglas, J.,** expressing the unanimous view of the court, it was held that the Eagle

River and its tributaries constitute a "river system" within the meaning of 43 USC § 666(a), which includes appropriated rights, riparian rights, and reserved rights, and that the supplemental suit was within 43 USC § 666(a) even though the owners of rights decreed in the last adjudication were not before the court.

Harlan, J., while joining in the court's opinion, disclaimed intimating any view as to the existence and scope of the United States' reserved water rights.

COUNSEL

Deputy Assistant Attorney General Kiechel argued the cause for United States. With him on the brief were Solicitor General Erwin N. Griswold, Assistant Attorney General Kashiwa, Francis X. Beytagh, Jr., Edmund B. Clark, and Charles N. Woodruff.

Kenneth Balcomb argued the cause for respondents. With him on the brief were Robert L. McCarty, George L. Zoellner, Don H. Sherwood, and Raphael J. Moses.

Briefs of amici curiae were filed by Gary K. Nelson, Attorney General, and Irving A. Jennings for the State of Arizona et al; by Thomas C. Lynch, Attorney General, Walter S. Rountree, Assistant Attorney General, and David B. Stanton, Deputy Attorney General, for the State of California; by Duke W. Dunbar, Attorney General of Colorado, Lee Johnson, Attorney General of Oregon, Harvey Dickerson, Attorney General of Nevada, Robert M. Robson, Attorney General of Idaho, Robert L. Woodahl, Attorney General of Montana, and G. Kent Edwards, Attorney General of Alaska, for the States of Colorado et al.; by G. T. Blankenship, Attorney General, and W. Howard O'Bryan, Jr., Assistant Attorney General for the State of Oklahoma; by Vernon B. Romney, Attorney General, Robert B. Hansen, Deputy Attorney General, and Dallin W. Jensen Assistant Attorney General, for the State of Utah; by Slade Gorton, Attorney General, and Charles B. Roe, Jr., and Henry W. Ipsen, Assistant Attorneys General, for the State of Washington; and by James E. Barrett, Attorney General, Sterling A. Case, Deputy Attorney General, and Jack R. Gage, Special Attorney General, for the State of Wyoming.

UNITED STATES, Petitioner,

v

DISTRICT COURT IN AND FOR WATER
DIVISION NO. 5, State
of Colorado, et al.

401 US 527, 28 L Ed 2d 284, 91 S Ct 1003

Argued March 2, 1971.   Decided March 24, 1971.

Decision: Suit against United States under Colorado
Water Right Determination and Administration Act
of 1969 held within consent-to-be-sued provision of
43 USC § 666.

SUMMARY

In an original suit in the Supreme Court of Colorado,
the United States sought a writ of prohibition precluding
the District Court for Water Division No. 5 from asserting jurisdiction over the United States in a suit under the
Colorado Water Right Determination and Administration Act of 1969.   The Supreme Court of Colorado
denied the writ.

On certiorari, the Supreme Court of the United States
affirmed.   In an opinion by **Douglas, J.**, expressing the
unanimous view of the court, it was held that a suit under
the Colorado statute is a suit for a general adjudication
with the scope of the consent-to-be-sued provision of 43
USC § 666, which gives consent to join the United States
as a defendant in any suit for the adjudication of rights
to the use of water of a river system or other source
where the United States is the owner of or is in the process
of acquiring such rights, even though the Colorado statute contemplates monthly proceedings before a water

referee for which an application has been filed within a particular month.

Harlan, J., while joining in the court's opinion, disclaimed intimating any view as to the existence and scope of the United States' reserved water rights.

COUNSEL

Deputy Assistant Attorney General Kiechel argued the cause for the United States. With him on the briefs were Solicitor General Erwin N. Griswold, Assistant Attorney General Kashiwa, Samuel Huntington, and Edmund B. Clark.

Kenneth Balcomb argued the cause for respondents. With him on the brief was Robert L. McCarty.

LOU BERTHA LABINE, Natural Tutrix
of Minor Child, Rita Nell Vincent,
Appellant,

v

SIMON VINCENT, Administrator of the
Succession of Ezra Vincent

401 US 532, 28 L Ed 2d 288, 91 S Ct 1017

Argued January 19, 1971. Decided
March 29, 1971.

Decision: Louisiana statutes barring acknowledged illegitimate child from sharing in intestate father's estate with legitimate heirs, held not violative of due process or equal protection.

SUMMARY

The guardian of an illegitimate child, who had been acknowledged but not legitimated by her father, petitioned a Louisiana state court for appointment of an administrator for the estate of the father, who had died intestate, for a declaration that the child was the sole heir, and for an order directing the administrator to pay support and maintenance for the child. Collateral relatives of the decedent asserted that they were entitled to the whole estate under Louisiana statutes providing that an illegitimate child who had been acknowledged but not legitimated by the father could not claim the rights of a legitimate child and could take the father's property only to the exclusion of the state when the father left no descendants, ascendants, collateral relations, or surviving wife. Other statutory provisions gave legitimate and legitimated children a right of forced heirship in the father's estate. The trial court ruled in favor of the collateral relatives, and the Louisiana Court of Appeal, Third Circuit, affirmed (229 So 2d 449). The Supreme Court of Louisiana denied a petition for writ of certiorari (255 La 480, 231 So 2d 395).

On appeal, the United States Supreme Court affirmed. In an opinion by **Black, J.**, expressing the view of five members of the court, it was held that (1) the state's statutory scheme, barring an illegitimate child who had been acknowledged but not legitimated from sharing equally with legitimate heirs in the father's estate, had a rational basis in view of the state's interest in promoting family life and of directing the disposition of property left within the state, and (2) such statutory scheme did not constitute an invidious discrimination against illegitimate children in violation of the due process and equal protection clauses.

Harlan, J., concurring, stated that there was no denial of equal protection in the constitutional sense, since it was reasonable for the state to provide that a man who entered into a marital relationship thereby undertook obligations to any resulting offspring beyond those which he owed to the products of a casual liaison, whether or not he admitted fatherhood in the latter case.

Brennan, J., joined by **Douglas, White,** and **Marshall, JJ.**, dissented, expressing the view that the state's intestate succession laws, insofar as they treated illegitimate children whose fathers had publicly acknowledged them differently from legitimate children, plainly violated the equal protection cause of the Fourteenth Amendment, there being no rational basis for the distinction made by the state.

COUNSEL

James J. Cox argued the cause and filed a brief for appellant.

James A. Leithead argued the cause for appellee. With him on the brief was Norman F. Anderson.

Briefs of amici curiae urging reversal were filed by Harry D. Krause, Norman Dorsen, and Melvin L. Wulf for the American Civil Liberties Union, and by Jonathan Weiss and Davaid Gilman for the Center on Social Welfare Policy and Law.

Briefs of amici curiae urging affirmance were filed by Jack P. F. Gremillion, Attorney General for the State of Louisiana, and by A. Leon Hebert and E. Drew Mc-Kinnis for the Buras Heirs et al.

HAROLD WHITELEY, Petitioner,

v

WARDEN OF WYOMING STATE PENITENTIARY

401 US 560, 28 L Ed 2d 306, 91 S Ct 1031

Argued January 13, 1971. Decided
March 29, 1971.

Decision: Probable cause for arrest held lacking where information on police radio bulletin was based on uncorroborated informer's tip.

SUMMARY

After learning from a view of the scene that some business buildings had been broken into during the previous night, a sheriff, acting on an unnamed informer's tip, signed a complaint naming the petitioner and another person as those who had unlawfully broken into the buildings. After receiving this complaint, a justice of the peace issued a warrant for the arrest of the petitioner and the other person. The sheriff sent out a police radio bulletin describing the petitioner, the other person, the car which they were probably driving, and items which had been taken from the buildings. An officer in another part of the state stopped a car which met the description on the radio bulletin and which had two men in it. The officer observed that one of the men, the petitioner, met the description on the radio bulletin, and the officer learned that the petitioner had given the officer a false name. The officer was aware, from his personal knowledge, that the other occupant of the car was the other person named on the radio bulletin. The officer arrested both occupants and searched the car. Items which had been taken from one of the buildings and described on the radio bulletin were found in the interior of the car, and burglar's tools were found in the trunk. In the District Court, Second Judicial Circuit, Carbon County, Wyoming, the petitioner was prosecuted for breaking and entering, and his motion to suppress evidence on the ground that the search of the car was illegal was overruled. His conviction for breaking and entering was affirmed by the Supreme Court of Wyoming (418 P2d 164). His petition for habeas corpus was denied by the United States District Court for the District of Wyoming (292 F Supp 381), and the Court of Appeals for the Tenth Circuit affirmed (416 F2d 36).

On certiorari, the United States Supreme Court reversed and remanded with directions to issue the writ of habeas corpus unless the state makes appropriate arrangements to retry the petitioner. In an opinion by **Harlan, J.**, expressing the views of six members of the court, it was held that since the complaint on which the warrant issued could not support a finding of probable cause, and since the arresting officer did not possess any factual data tending to corroborate the informer's tip that the petitioner and the other person had committed the crime, the petitioner's arrest violated his constitutional rights under the Fourth and Fourteenth Amendments, and the evidence secured as an incident to the arrest should have been excluded from his trial.

Black, J., joined by **Burger, Ch. J.**, dissented on the grounds that there was probable cause to arrest the petitioner and that the search of the car was lawful.

Blackmun, J., dissenting, stated that he agreed with much that was said by Black, J.

COUNSEL

William J. Knudsen, Jr., argued the cause for petitioner. With him on the briefs was Richard A. Mullens.

Jack Speight, Assistant Attorney General of Wyoming, argued the cause for respondent. With him on the brief was James E. Barrett, Attorney General.

———————

UNITED TRANSPORTATION UNION,
Petitioner,

v

THE STATE BAR OF MICHIGAN

401 US 576, 28 L Ed 2d 339, 91 S Ct 1076

Argued January 20, 1971. Decided
April 5, 1971.

Decision: Michigan state court injunction against union's furnishing legal advice to members and controlling legal fees by agreement with lawyers held unconstitutional.

SUMMARY

The Michigan State Bar sued in the Circuit Court of Jackson County, Michigan, to enjoin the members of a railroad union from violating a Michigan statute making it a misdemeanor to "solicit" damage suits. An injunction against the union's activities was reversed and remanded by the Michigan Supreme Court (374 Mich 152, 132 NW2d 78). The Circuit Court then entered a decree enjoining the union from giving or furnishing legal advice to its members or to their families; furnishing to any attorney the names of injured members or information relating to their injuries; accepting or receiving compensation of any kind, directly or indirectly, for the solicitation of legal employment for any lawyer, whether by way of salary, commission, or otherwise; sharing in the legal fees of any lawyer; controlling the fees charged by any lawyer; or stating or suggesting that a recommended lawyer would defray expenses of any kind or make advances for any purpose to such injured persons or their families pending settlement of their claim. The Michigan Supreme Court affirmed (383 Mich 201, 174 NW2d 811).

On certiorari, the United States Supreme Court reversed. In an opinion by **Black, J.**, expressing the views of five members of the court, it was held that the provision of the decree barring the union from controlling legal fees and the provision precluding the union from stating that a recommended lawyer would defray expenses or make advances violated the First Amendment right to act collectively to obtain affordable and effective legal representation; that the decree also violated First Amendment rights in enjoining giving or furnishing legal advice to union members or their families, furnishing to any attorney the names of injured members or information relating to their injuries, or accepting compensation of any kind for the solicitation of legal employment for any lawyer; and that the decree provision forbidding sharing fees or recoveries was unjustified as not supported by the complaint or the record.

Harlan, J., concurring in part and dissenting in part, agreed that the prohibition on controlling legal fees was unconstitutional, but declared that the other decree provisions were valid.

White, J., joined by **Blackmun, J.**, concurring in part and dissenting in part, stated that the decree was valid except for the provision prohibiting the union from giving or furnishing legal advice to its members or their families and forbidding the setting of fees by union-lawyer agreement.

Stewart, J., did not participate.

COUNSEL

John J. Naughton argued the cause and filed a brief for petitioner.

A. D. Ruegsegger argued the cause for respondent. With him on the brief were Phillip C. Kelly and Louis Rosenzweig.

J. Albert Woll, Laurence Gold, and Thomas E. Harris filed a brief for the American Federation of Labor and Congress of Industrial Organizations as amicus curiae urging reversal.

UNITED STATES, Appellant,

v

DONALD FREED and Shirley Jean Sutherland

401 US 601, 28 L Ed 2d 356, 91 S Ct 1112

Argued January 11, 1971. Decided
April 5, 1971.

Decision: Registration provisions of amended National
Firearms Act held not violative of privilege against
self-incrimination, and not to require allegation of
scienter in prosecution for unlawful possession of
unregistered handgrenades.

SUMMARY

The defendants were indicted for possession of and
conspiracy to possess unregistered handgrenades in violation of the amended National Firearms Act, which makes
it unlawful for any person to possess a firearm that has
not been registered to him by the transferor thereof, and
which requires that registration be made only by the
transferor and that the application for the transfer and
registration of the firearm to the transferee must be supported by the transferee's photograph and fingerprints.
The United States District Court for the Central District of California granted the defendants' motion to
dismiss on the grounds that the amended Act violated the
self-incrimination clause of the Fifth Amendment, and
that the indictment failed to allege scienter.

On direct appeal, the United States Supreme Court reversed. In an opinion by **Douglas, J.**, it was held (1) expressing the unanimous view of the court, that the amended National Firearms Act did not violate the self-incrimi-

nation clause of the Fifth Amendment, since the Act bars use of registration data in a prosecution for prior or concurrent offenses, and since, as a matter of practice, registration data was not made available to local, state, or other federal authorities, and (2) expressing the view of eight members of the court, that the Act, being a regulatory measure in the interest of the public safety, did not require specific intent or knowledge that the handgrenades were unregistered.

Brennan, J., concurred in holding (1) above, and in the conclusion that the Act did not require proof of knowledge of the unregistered status of the handgrenades, stating that such proof was not required since the case law under earlier provisions of the Act dispensed with proof of intent in connection with such element of the offense, and since the Act covered major weapons involving so great a likelihood of governmental regulation that anyone must be presumed to be aware of it.

COUNSEL

Matthew J. Zinn argued the cause for the United States.   On the brief were Solicitor General Erwin N. Griswold, Assistant Attorney General Wilson, Peter L. Strauss, Beatrice Rosenberg, and Mervyn Hamburg.

Luke McKissack argued the cause and filed a brief for appellees.

INVESTMENT COMPANY INSTITUTE
et al., Petitioners,

v

WILLIAM B. CAMP, Comptroller of the
Currency, et al. (No. 61)

NATIONAL ASSOCIATION OF SECURITIES
DEALERS, Inc., Petitioner,

v

SECURITIES AND EXCHANGE COMMISSION
et al. (No. 59)

401 US 617, 28 L Ed 2d 367, 91 S Ct 1091

Argued December 14 and 15, 1970. Decided
April 5, 1971.

Decision: Investment companies and association thereof
held to have standing to challenge Comptroller's
regulation authorizing banks to operate collective
investment funds; regulation held invalid insofar as
it authorized competition with mutual fund industry.

SUMMARY

The right of a national bank to operate a mutual investment fund was challenged in two separate proceedings. In No. 61, several open-end investment companies
and an association of such companies instituted an action
in the United States District Court for the District of
Columbia, attacking the validity of a regulation of the
Comptroller of the Currency which authorized national
banks to operate collective investment funds, as well as
the validity of the Comptroller's approval of an applica-

tion of the First National City Bank of New York for permission to operate a fund whereby investors were issued redeemable and transferable units of participation in a stock fund which was created and managed by the bank as investment advisor pursuant to managing agency agreements. The plaintiffs contended that such activities were prohibited by various provisions of the Glass-Steagall Banking Act of 1933 as amended, including § 16 of the Act, prohibiting a national bank from underwriting any issue of securities or stock and from purchasing for its own account any shares of stock of any corporation, and § 21 of the Act, prohibiting a national bank from engaging in the business of issuing, underwriting, selling, or distributing stocks or securities. The District Court entered judgment for the plaintiffs (274 F Supp 624). The United States Court of Appeals for the District of Columbia consolidated the appeal in No. 61 with No. 59, which was a petition filed in the Court of Appeals by the National Association of Securities Dealers for review of an order of the Securities and Exchange Commission that partially exempted the collective investment fund of the First National City Bank of New York from various provisions of the Investment Company Act of 1940. The Court of Appeals, holding that the actions of both the Securities and Exchange Commission and the Comptroller were valid, affirmed the Commission's order in No. 59, and reversed the District Court's judgment in No. 61 (420 F2d 83).

On certiorari, the United States Supreme Court reversed the judgment in No. 61, and vacated the judgment in No. 59, finding it unnecessary to consider the propriety of the action of the Securities and Exchange Commission. In an opinion by **Stewart, J.**, expressing the view of six members of the court, it was held that (1) the plaintiffs in No. 61 had standing to seek review of the Comptroller's regulation authorizing operation of collective investment funds by national banks, (2) the operation of the fund involved in the case at bar, which was in direct competition with the mutual fund industry and which was distinguishable from the mere pooling of trust assets by the bank or its purchase of stock for the account of its customers, violated §§ 16 and 21 of the Glass-Steagall Act, and (3) the Comptroller's regulation was thus invalid insofar as it authorized the sale of interests in an investment fund of the type involved.

Harlan, J., dissented on the grounds that (1) the plaintiffs lacked standing to sue in No. 61, thus rendering it unnecessary to reach the merits, and (2) the Securities and Exchange Commission had not abused its discretion in No. 59.

Blackmun, J., dissenting, expressed the view that (1) the Glass-Steagall Act prohibited a national bank from engaging in investment banking or in issuing or acquiring speculative securities for its own account, but did not preclude operation of mutual investment funds, thus requiring affirmance of the Court of Appeals' judgment in No. 61, and (2) the Securities and Exchange Commission had not acted arbitrarily or exceeded its statutory authority in No. 59.

Burger, Ch. J., did not participate.

COUNSEL

G. Duane Vieth argued the cause for petitioners in No. 61. With him on the briefs were James F. Fitzpatrick, Melvin Spaeth, and Robert Augenblick. Joseph B. Levin argued the cause for petitioner in No. 59. With him on the briefs was Lloyd J. Derrickson.

Deputy Solicitor General Friedman argued the cause for respondent Camp, Comptroller of the Currency, in

No. 61.   With him on the brief were Solicitor General
Erwin N. Griswold, Assistant Attorney General Ruckel-
shaus, Richard B. Stone, Alan S. Rosenthal, Leonard
Schaitman, and C. Westbrook Murphy.   Mr. Friedman,
by special leave of court, argued the cause for the United
States as amicus curiae urging affirmance in No. 59.
With him on the brief were Solicitor General Erwin N.
Griswold and Mr. Stone.   Archibald Cox argued the
cause for respondent First National City Bank in both
cases.   With him on the brief was Stephen Ailes.

Robert L. Stern filed a brief for Corporate Fiduciaries
Association of Chicago as amicus curiae urging affirmance in both cases.

CLARENCE WILLIAMS, Petitioner,

v

UNITED STATES (No. 81)

JOSEPH ELKANICH, Petitioner,

v

UNITED STATES (No. 82)

401 US 646, 28 L Ed 2d 388, 91 S Ct 1148

Argued October 21, 1970. Decided April 5, 1971.

Decision: Constitutional principles announced in Chimel v California, narrowing permissible scope of search incident to arrest, held not retroactively applicable.

SUMMARY

The instant cases, Nos. 81 and 82, involve the question whether the constitutional principles announced by the United States Supreme Court in Chimel v California (1969) 395 US 752, 23 L Ed 2d 685, 89 S Ct 2034, should be applied retroactively. In the Chimel Case, decided on June 23, 1969, the Supreme Court (1) overruling Harris v United States (1947) 331 US 145, 91 L Ed 1399, 67 S Ct 1089, and United States v Rabinowitz (1950) 339 US 56, 94 L Ed 653, 70 S Ct 430, announced constitutional standards which had the effect of narrowing the permissible scope of a search incident to an arrest, and (2) without discussing the issue of retroactivity, reversed Chimel's conviction, thereby retroactively applying the new standards to a search which had been conducted in Chimel's house.

In No. 81, the accused was arrested in 1967 in the living room of his house. The entire house was then searched by officers for about an hour and 45 minutes, and some heroin was found in a container on a closet shelf in a bedroom. The heroin was admitted in evidence at the accused's trial in the United States District Court for the District of Arizona, and the accused was convicted of concealing illegally imported heroin. The Court of Appeals for the Ninth Circuit affirmed, holding (1) that although the search of the accused's home was illegal under the Chimel Case, the decision in the Chimel Case was not retroactive and did not apply to searches carried out prior to June 23, 1969, and (2) that the search was valid under the pre-Chimel standards stated in the Harris and Rabinowitz Cases (418 F2d 159).

In No. 82, the accused was arrested in 1962 in his apartment. The apartment was then searched by officers, and evidence connecting the accused with the sale of heroin was found. This evidence was admitted at the accused's trial in the United States District Court for the Northern District of California, and the accused was convicted of selling heroin. In 1964, the Court of Appeals for the Ninth Circuit affirmed the conviction and upheld the validity of the search of the apartment (327 F2d 417), and the Supreme Court denied certiorari (377 US 917, 12 L Ed 2d 186, 84 S Ct 1182). The accused later applied unsuccessfully to the District Court for postconviction relief under 28 USC § 2255. Although the Chimel Case was decided while the accused's appeal from the denial of his § 2255 application was pending, the Court of Appeals affirmed.

On certiorari, the Supreme Court affirmed the Court of Appeals' judgments in Nos. 81 and 82. Though not agreeing on an opinion, a majority of the court reached the conclusion that (except for the retroactive application which had already occurred in the Chimel Case itself) the principles announced in the Chimel Case were not retroactively applicable to searches conducted prior to June 23, 1969.

Announcing the judgment of the court, **White, J.,** joined by **Burger,** Ch. J., **Stewart, J.,** and **Blackmun, J.,** expressed the view that regardless of whether a conviction was challenged on direct review or in collateral proceedings, the Chimel Case was not retroactively applicable.

Stewart, J., besides joining in the opinion by **White, J.,** would affirm the judgment in No. 82 on the alternative ground that the issue presented was not one cognizable in a § 2255 proceeding.

Brennan, J., concurring, agreed that the Chimel standards were not retroactively applicable to searches conducted before June 23, 1969.

Black, J., concurred in the result on the ground that the Chimel Case was wrongly decided.

Harlan, J., and **Marshall, J.,** each in a separate opinion, concurring in part and dissenting in part, would affirm the judgment in No. 82 on the ground that the Chimel standards were not retroactively applicable on collateral review of a conviction which had become final prior to the date of the Chimel decision, but would reverse the judgment in No. 81 on the ground that the Chimel standards were retroactively applicable on direct review of a conviction.

Douglas, J., did not participate.

COUNSEL

Henry J. Florence argued the cause for petitioner in No. 81. With him on the brief was Philip M. Haggerty. Charles A. Miller, by appointment of the Court, 396 US

1065, 25 L Ed 2d 82, 90 S Ct 762, argued the cause and filed briefs for petitioner in No. 82.

James van R. Springer argued the cause for the United States in both cases. On the brief in No. 81 were Solicitor General Erwin N. Griswold, Assistant Attorney General Wilson, Francis X. Beytagh, Jr., Richard B. Stone, and Beatrice Rosenberg. On the brief in No. 82 were Solicitor General Erwin N. Griswold, Assistant Attorney General Wilson, Mr. Beytagh, and Miss Rosenberg.

FRED T. MACKEY, Petitioner,

v

UNITED STATES

401 US 667, 28 L Ed 2d 404, 91 S Ct 1160

Argued October 21, 1970. Decided April 5, 1971.

Decision: Supreme Court decisions invalidating federal wagering tax statutes held not retroactively applicable on collateral review of conviction for income tax evasion.

SUMMARY

In 1964, following a trial in which the government introduced as part of its case numerous monthly wagering excise tax returns which had been filed by the accused, a jury in the United States District Court for the Northern District of Indiana found the accused guilty of income tax evasion. In 1965, the Court of Appeals for the Seventh Circuit affirmed his conviction (345 F2d 499) and the United States Supreme Court denied certiorari (382 US 824, 15 L Ed 2d 69, 86 S Ct 54). On January 29, 1968, the Supreme Court, overruling earlier decisions, held in Marchetti v United States, 390 US 39, 19 L Ed 2d 889, 88 S Ct 697, and Grosso v United States, 390 US 62, 19 L Ed 2d 906, 88 S Ct 709, that the Fifth Amendment privilege against self-incrimination was a valid defense to a prosecution for failure to register as a gambler and to pay wagering excise taxes. A few days later, the accused filed a motion under 28 USC § 2255 to vacate his sentence and set aside his conviction on the basis of the Marchetti and Grosso decisions. The District Court, holding that the Marchetti and Grosso decisions were not retroactively applicable, denied the § 2255 motion, and the Court of Appeals affirmed (411 F2d 504).

On certiorari, the United States Supreme Court affirmed. Though not agreeing on an opinion, a majority of the court reached the conclusion that under the circumstances of the instant case, the principles announced in the Marchetti and Grosso Cases were not retroactively applicable to the accused's conviction.

Announcing the judgment of the Court, **White, J.,** joined by **Burger, Ch. J., Stewart, J.,** and **Blackmun, J.,** expressed the view that under the Marchetti and Grosso Cases, the registration and excise tax returns filed in response to statutory command were compelled statements within the meaning of the Fifth Amendment and accordingly were inadmissible in evidence as part of the prosecution's case in chief, but that the principles announced in those cases should not (except insofar as those principles were already applied in the Marchetti and Grosso Cases themselves) be applied retroactively to any trials which occurred prior to the date of the Marchetti and Grosso decisions.

Harlan, J., would affirm the judgment below on the ground that the Marchetti and Grosso decisions were not retroactively applicable on collateral review of a conviction which had become final prior to the date of such decisions.

Brennan, J., joined by **Marshall, J.,** concurred in the affirmance on the ground that even if the Marchetti and Grosso decisions were retroactively applicable, those decisions were distinguishable from the instant case, and the Fifth Amendment did not preclude the admission in evidence of wagering excise tax returns in a criminal prosecution for income tax evasion.

Douglas, J., joined by **Black, J.,** dissented on the ground that since the defendants in the Marchetti and Grosso Cases were given the benefit of the new rule announced therein, such rule should be applied retroactively so that all victims of the old, unconstitutional rule will be treated equally.

COUNSEL

William M. Ward argued the cause and filed briefs for petitioner.

Matthew J. Zinn argued the cause for the United States. With him on the brief were Solicitor General Erwin N. Griswold, Assistant Attorney General Wilson, Francis X. Beytagh, Jr., Beatrice Rosenberg, and Mervyn Hamburg.

UNITED STATES, Petitioner,

v

UNITED STATES COIN AND CURRENCY, etc.

401 US 715, 28 L Ed 2d 434, 91 S Ct 1041

Argued February 25 and 26, 1969. Reargued
October 20, 1970. Decided April 5, 1971.

Decision: Supreme Court decisions invalidating federal
wagering tax statutes as violative of privilege against
self-incrimination held retroactively applicable on
direct review of forfeiture proceedings.

SUMMARY

After a person had been convicted for violating federal
gambling registration and tax statutes, forfeiture proceedings involving money which the government had
seized from the person's possession at the time of his
arrest were instituted in the United States District Court
for the Northern District of Illinois. The District Court
ordered the money forfeited pursuant to 26 USC § 7302,
which authorized the forfeiture of property used in
violation of the internal revenue laws. The Court of
Appeals for the Seventh Circuit affirmed (379 F2d 946).
Subsequently, on January 29, 1968, the United States
Supreme Court, overruling earlier cases, held in Marchetti v United States, 390 US 39, 19 L Ed 2d 889,
88 S Ct 697, and Grosso v United States, 390 US 62, 19
L Ed 2d 906, 88 S Ct 709, that the Fifth Amendment
privilege against self-incrimination was a valid defense
to a prosecution for failure to comply with the federal
gambling registration and tax statutes. A few weeks
later the Supreme Court granted certiorari in the instant case and remanded the case for further consideration

in light of the Marchetti and Grosso decisions (390 US 204, 19 L Ed 2d 1035, 88 S Ct 899). Upon remand, the Court of Appeals, holding that the privilege against self-incrimination could properly be asserted in forfeiture proceedings, ordered the government to return the seized money (393 F2d 499).

On certiorari, the Supreme Court affirmed. In an opinion by **Harlan, J.**, expressing the views of five members of the court, it was held that the privilege against self-incrimination could properly be invoked in forfeiture proceedings under § 7302, and that the Marchetti and Grosso decisions could properly be applied retroactively to seizures of property which had occurred before the date of such decisions.

Black, J., concurred in the court's opinion as far as it went, but stated that he would go further and overrule cases which had limited the retroactive effect of Supreme Court decisions.

Brennan, J., concurring, joined the court's opinion and offered some additional reasons for rejecting the views expressed in the dissenting opinion.

White, J., joined by **Burger, Ch J., Stewart, J.**, and **Blackmun, J.**, dissented on the ground that the Marchetti and Grosso decisions should not be given retroactive application.

COUNSEL

Jerome M. Feit argued the cause for the United States on the reargument. Philip A. Lacovara argued the cause for the United States, pro hac vice, on the original argument. On the brief were Solicitor General Erwin N. Griswold, Assistant Attorney General Vinson, Francis

X. Beytagh, Jr., Beatrice Rosenberg, and Lawrence P. Cohen.

Anna R. Lavin reargued the cause for respondent. With her on the briefs was Edward J. Calihan, Jr.

Charles Alan Wright, Marvin K. Collie, and Harry M. Reasoner filed a brief for Joseph P. Lucia as amicus curiae on the reargument.

UNITED STATES, Petitioner,

v

JAMES A. WHITE

401 US 745, 28 L Ed 2d 453, 91 S Ct 1122

Argued November 10, 1969. Reargued October 20, 1970. Decided April 5, 1971.

Decision: Police electronic monitoring of conversation between accused and informant, by means of radio transmitter concealed on informant's person, held not violative of Fourth Amendment.

SUMMARY

During a narcotics prosecution in the United States District Court for the Northern District of Illinois, the court overruled the accused's objections to testimony by government agents regarding conversations in 1965 and 1966 between the accused and an informant which the agents overheard by monitoring the frequency of a radio transmitter concealed on the informant's person. The prosecution was unable to locate and produce the informant at the trial. The United States Court of Appeals for the Seventh Circuit reversed the convictions, on the ground that the evidence was inadmissible under the holding in Katz v United States (1967) 389 US 347, 19 L Ed 2d 576, 88 S Ct 507, that the Fourth Amendment makes inadmissible the recordings of conversations made by government agents by means of a listening device attached to the outside of a public telephone booth (405 F2d 838).

On certiorari, the United States Supreme Court reversed. Five members of the court, although not agree-

[Supreme Ct Sum]—13

ing on an opinion, agreed that the Katz decision was improperly given retroactive effect.

White, J., announced the judgment of the court, and in an opinion joined by **Burger, Ch. J., Stewart, J.**, and **Blackmun, J.**, expressed the view that (1) eavesdropping on conversations between an accused and an informant by means of a radio transmitter concealed on the informant's person does not violate the Fourth Amendment any more than does an informant's reporting on or secretly recording the conversations, neither of which is an unlawful search and seizure; (2) no different result should obtain by reason of the informant's disappearance and unavailability at trial; and (3) the Katz decision applies only to electronic surveillances occurring subsequent to its date, December 18, 1967.

Black, J., concurred on the ground that eavesdropping carried on by electronic means does not constitute a "search" or "seizure" within the meaning of the Fourth Amendment.

Brennan, J., concurring in the result, agreed that the Katz decision was improperly given retroactive effect but stated that the Fourth Amendment interposes a warrant requirement both where an informant secretly records his conversations with an accused and where he secretly transmits them to the police by means of an electronic monitoring device.

Douglas, J., dissented on the grounds that electronic surveillance violates the Fourth Amendment, whether by a recording device or a radio transmitter concealed on an informant's person, and that the Katz decision should be given retroactive effect.

Harlan, J., dissenting, seriously questioned whether an informant's secretly recording his conversations with an accused comports with the Fourth Amendment, and declared that third-party electronic monitoring violates the Fourth Amendment and that the Katz decision should be applied retroactively.

Marshall, J., dissented on the grounds that electronic surveillance violates the Fourth Amendment and that the Katz decision should be applied retroactively.

COUNSEL

Assistant Attorney General Wilson argued the cause for the United States on the original argument and on the reargument. With him on the briefs were Solicitor General Erwin N. Griswold, Joseph J. Connolly, John S. Martin, Jr., Jerome M. Feit, Beatrice Rosenberg, and Sidney M. Glazer.

John L. Boeger argued the cause for respondent on the original argument and on the reargument. With him on the brief were Morris A. Shenker and Chauncey Eskridge.

Abraham Glasser and Maurice Edelbaum filed a brief for John G. Broady et al. as amici curiae urging affirmance.

ARCHIE WILLIAM HILL, Jr., Petitioner,

v

STATE OF CALIFORNIA

401 US 797, 28 L Ed 2d 484, 91 S Ct 1106

Argued January 19, 1970. Reargued October
21, 1970. Decided April 5, 1971.

Decision: Constitutional principles announced in Chimel
v California, narrowing permissible scope of search
incident to arrest, held not retroactively applicable,
and search unheld despite mistaken identity of person
arrested.

SUMMARY

In 1966, police officers, after arresting for possession
of narcotics two men who were driving the defendant's
car, found in the car some property which had been stolen
in a recent robbery. The two men admitted taking part
in the robbery, implicated the defendant, told the police
where the defendant's apartment was, and stated that
some stolen property and the guns used in the robbery
were in the apartment. Some officers, having received a
description of the defendant and having gone to the
apartment to arrest him, knocked on the door, and it
was opened by a man who met the defendant's description. Th officers arrested this man, but he denied that
he was the defendant, and he produced identification
showing who he was. Nevertheless, the officers, mistakenly believing that the arrestee was the defendant,
proceeded to search the entire apartment and found a
revolver and masks, property stolen in the robbery, and
two pages of the defendant's diary containing a full con-

fession of his participation in the robbery. The evidence found in the apartment was admitted at the defendant's trial in a California state court, the trial judge concluding that the officers had believed in good faith that the arrestee was the defendant. The defendant was convicted of robbery, and the California Supreme Court, affirming the conviction, held that the arrest at the apartment was valid, and that neither the defendant's absence nor the arrestee's lack of control of the premises vitiated the search, since the officers had a reasonable and good-faith belief that the arrestee was the defendant and that the arrestee controlled the premises (69 Cal 2d 550, 72 Cal Rptr 641, 446 P2d 521).

On certiorari, the United States Supreme Court affirmed. In an opinion by **White, J.**, it was held (1) expressing the view of five members of the court, that although Chimel v California (1969) 395 US 752, 23 L Ed 2d 685, 89 S Ct 2034, decided after the California Supreme Court's affirmance of the defendant's conviction, narrowed the permissible scope of a search incident to an arrest, the Chimel Case was not retroactively applicable to searches occurring before the date of the Chimel decision, (2) expressing the view of seven members of the court, that the arrest in the apartment was valid, and the police were entitled to search incident to the arrest and to seize evidence of the crime which they had probable cause to believe the defendant had committed, and (3) expressing the view of seven members of the court, that since a Fifth Amendment issue relating to the admission in evidence of pages of the defendant's diary had not been raised in the lower courts or in the petition for certiorari, this issue was not properly before the Supreme Court.

Black, J., concurred in the result.

Harlan and **Stewart, JJ.**, concurred as to holdings (2) and (3) above, but dissented from holding (1) on the ground that the Chimel Case should be applied retroactively on direct review of a conviction.

Douglas, J., did not participate.

COUNSEL

Joseph Amato, by appointment of the Court, 396 US 999, 24 L Ed 2d 491, 90 S Ct 566, argued the cause and filed briefs for petitioner on the original argument and on the reargument.

Ronald M. George, Deputy Attorney General of California, argued the cause for respondent on the original argument and on the reargument. With him on the brief were Thomas C. Lynch, Attorney General, and William E. James, Assistant Attorney General.

Keith C. Monroe filed a brief for the Orange County Criminal Courts Bar Association et al. as amici curiae urging reversal. Duke W. Dunbar, Attorney General, pro se, and John P. Moore, Deputy Attorney General, filed a brief for the Attorney General of Colorado et al. as amici curiae.

JAMES WINTFORED REWIS and
Mary Lee Williams, Petitioners,

v

UNITED STATES

401 US 808, 28 L Ed 2d 493, 91 S Ct 1056

Argued January 19, 1971. Decided
April 5, 1971.

Decision: Travel Act held not violated by interstate
travel to place bets or by conducting gambling operation frequented by out-of-state bettors.

SUMMARY

Two Georgia residents who traveled to Yulee, Florida,
to place bets at a lottery or numbers operation there, and
the two numbers operators, who were Florida residents
and did not cross state lines in connection with the operation of their lottery, were convicted in the United States
District Court for the Middle District of Georgia of violating the Travel Act (18 USC § 1952), which prohibits
interstate travel in furtherance of certain criminal activity, under jury instructions that the bettors violated the
Travel Act if they traveled interstate for the purpose of
gambling, and that a defendant could be found guilty
under the aiding and abetting statute (18 USC § 2)
without proof that he personally performed every act
constituting the charged offense. The United States
Court of Appeals for the Fifth Circuit reversed the bettors' conviction on the ground that the Travel Act does
not outlaw crossing a state line for the purpose of placing
a bet, but it affirmed the numbers operators' convictions
on the ground that gambling establishment operators are

responsible for their customers' interstate travel (418 F2d 1218).

On certiorari, the United States Supreme Court reversed. In an opinion by **Marshall, J.,** expressing the unanimous view of the court, it was held that the Travel Act does not outlaw either interstate travel by gambling-establishment customers or conducting a gambling operation frequented by out-of-state bettors, even though the operator can reasonably foresee the customers will cross state lines for the purpose of patronizing the operation; and that while a gambling operator's actively seeking to attract out-of-state business might violate the Travel Act, the government's failure to introduce evidence of such solicitation and the trial court's failure to instruct the jury with respect to solicitation precluded affirmance of the operators' convictions on that ground.

White, J., did not participate.

COUNSEL

Albert J. Datz argued the cause and filed briefs for petitioners.

Sidney M. Glazer argued the cause for the United States. With him on the brief were Solicitor General Erwin N. Griswold, Assistant Attorney General Wilson, Beatrice Rosenberg, and Michael G. Kelly.

WILLIAM P. ROGERS, Secretary of State,
Appellant,

v

ALDO MARIO BELLEI

401 US 815, 28 L Ed 2d 499, 91 S Ct 1060

Argued January 15, 1970. Reargued
November 12, 1970. Decided
April 5, 1971.

Decision: Section 301 (b) of Immigration and Nationality Act of 1952 held constitutional in providing for loss of citizenship by foreign-born child of an American parent unless he is present here continuously for 5 years between ages 14 and 28.

SUMMARY

The Italian-born son of an alien father and a United States citizen mother, having been advised of the loss of his citizenship by virtue of § 301 (b) of the Immigration and Nationality Act, sued the Secretary of State in the United States District Court for the Southern District of New York for an injunction against the enforcement of § 301 (b) and a judgment declaring it unconstitutional in its provision that one who is a citizen by virtue of being born abroad of parents one of whom is an alien and the other a United States citizen who has met specified residence conditions in this country shall lose his citizenship unless between the ages of 14 and 28 he is physically present in the United States continuously for 5 years. The case was transferred to the District of Columbia because the New York venue was improper, and a three-judge United States District Court for the District of

Columbia granted the plaintiff's motion for summary judgment (296 F Supp 1247).

On direct appeal, the United States Supreme Court reversed. In an opinion by **Blackmun, J.**, expressing the views of five members of the court, it was held that (1) the plaintiff, not having been born or naturalized in or subject to the jurisdiction of the United States, was outside the Fourteenth Amendment's constitutional definition of citizenship; (2) the plaintiff's claim of citizenship was therefore necessarily subject to proper congressional action; and (3) § 301(b) had no constitutional infirmity in its application to him.

Black, J., joined by **Douglas** and **Marshall, JJ.**, dissented on the grounds that one born abroad of an American parent is "naturalized in the United States" within the meaning of the Fourteenth Amendment.

Brennan, J., joined by **Douglas, J.**, dissented on a similar ground in a separate opinion.

COUNSEL

Solicitor General Erwin N. Griswold argued the cause for appellant on the reargument. With him on the brief were Assistant Attorney General Wilson and Charles Gordon. Joseph J. Connolly argued the cause for appellant on the original argument.

O. John Roggee argued the cause and filed a brief for appellee on the original argument and on the reargument.

Richard N. Gardner argued the cause on the reargument for the Association of American Wives of Europeans et al. as amici curiae urging affirmance. With him on the brief were Alexis C. Coudert, Eugene L. Girden, Joseph H. Gordon, David M. Gooder, and Arlene Tuck Ulman.

James Sinclair, pro se, filed a brief as amicus curiae urging reversal.

Donald L. Ungar filed a brief for Vicente Gonzalez-Gomez as amicus curiae urging affirmance.

———————

JAMES MELVIN KITCHENS, Petitioner,

v

S. LAMONT SMITH, Warden

401 US 847, 28 L Ed 2d 519, 91 S Ct 1089

April 5, 1971

Decision: Rule of Gideon v Wainwright requiring appointment of counsel for indigent criminal defendants held fully retroactive and not dependent on request for counsel.

SUMMARY

An accused who pleaded guilty to robbery in a Georgia state court in 1944, when he was not represented by counsel, who escaped while serving his sentence, and who was returned to Georgia in 1969 to finish his sentence, brought a habeas corpus action in a Georgia county court, alleging that his conviction was void under Gideon v Wainwright, 372 US 335, 9 L Ed 2d 799, 83 S Ct 792, 93 ALR2d 733, since he was not provided with counsel at the time of his conviction although he was too poor to hire a lawyer. At his habeas corpus hearing, his uncontradicted testimony was that at the time of his conviction "I was a lot younger and I didn't have any money and I didn't have a lawyer." The county court denied relief on the ground that the Gideon decision is not retroactive. The Georgia Supreme Court affirmed on the ground that the accused did not testify at the habeas corpus hearing that at the time of his conviction he wanted a lawyer, asked for one, or was unable to hire a lawyer because of his poverty.

On certiorari, the United States Supreme Court reversed. In a per curiam opinion expressing the unanimous view of the court, it was held that (1) the Gideon decision is fully retroactive, (2) the right to counsel, whether on a guilty plea or at a trial, does not depend on a request for counsel, and (3) the accused proved that he was without counsel due to indigency at the time of his conviction.

JAMES E. SWANN et al., Petitioners,

v

CHARLOTTE-MECKLENBURG BOARD
OF EDUCATION et al. (No. 281)

CHARLOTTE-MECKLENBURG BOARD
OF EDUCATION et al., Petitioners,

v

JAMES E. SWANN et al. (No. 349)

402 US 1, 28 L Ed 2d 554, 91 S Ct 1267

Argued October 12, 1970. Decided
April 20, 1971.

Decision: Federal court orders requiring North Carolina
county school board to adopt plans for desegregating
dual school system affirmed where plans included
provisions for desegregation of faculty, new attendance zones, and busing of students.

SUMMARY

In the United States District Court for the Western District of North Carolina, an action was brought for the
purpose of requiring the defendant, a North Carolina
county school board, to cease maintaining a racially segregated, dual public school system. The District Court
approved a desegration plan at the commencement of
the action, but after the passage of several years, the
school system, which included approximately 29 percent
Negro students and 71 percent white students, remained
substantially segregated. The District Court found the
school board's further proposals for desegregation inadequate and appointed an expert who provided additional

desegregation proposals. The District Court ordered, among other things (1) that faculty members be reassigned in such a manner as to result in the ratio of Negro and white faculty members in each school being approximately the same as the ratio of Negro and white faculty members throughout the school system; (2) that in accordance with the school board's plan, as modified by the expert's plan, new attendance zones be created for secondary schools, and some inner-city Negroes be transported to outlying, predominantly white schools, so that the percentage of Negroes would range from about 17 percent to less than 36 percent in each high school and would range from about 9 percent to about 33 percent in each junior high school; and (3) that in accordance with the expert's plan, new attendance zones and pairing and grouping of schools be used for elementary schools, and the amount of busing of elementary school students be substantially increased, so that the percentage of Negroes in each elementary school would range from about 9 percent to about 38 percent (311 F Supp 265). The Court of Appeals for the Fifth Circuit affirmed the orders pertaining to faculty desegregation and secondary school rezoning and busing, but vacated the order pertaining to elementary school students on the ground that the amount of additional busing would be unnecessarily extensive (431 F2d 138). On remand from the Court of Appeals, the District Court requested the school board to adopt a new plan for elementary school students, but after the school board failed to do so, the District Court reinstated the expert's plan.

On certiorari, the United States Supreme Court affirmed the Court of Appeals' judgment to the extent that the Court of Appeals had affirmed the District Court's judgment, and the Supreme Court affirmed the District Court's order reinstating the expert's plan for elementary school students. In an opinion by **Burger**, Ch. J., express-

ing the unanimous views of the court, it was held that (1)
in default by school authorities of their obligation to prof-
fer acceptable remedies, the District Court had broad
power to fashion a remedy which would assure a unitary
school system, and such power was not restricted by public
education provisions of the Federal Civil Rights Act of
1964 (42 USC §§ 2000c(b), 2000c-6); (2) the District
Court's order reassigning teachers in order to achieve
faculty desegregation was proper; (3) although the constitutional command to desegregate schools did not mean
that the number of students in every school in every community always had to reflect the racial composition of the
school system as a whole, the use of racial ratios as a
starting point in the process of shaping a remedy was
within the District Court's equitable discretion; (4) in
order to achieve truly nondiscriminatory assignments of
students, the District Court could properly take affirmative action in the form of remedial altering of attendance
zones, including pairing or grouping of schools and use
of noncompact or noncontiguous zones; and (5) under the
circumstances of the instant case, the District Court's
orders requiring additional busing of elementary and
secondary school students as a means of school desegregation were within the court's power to provide equitable
relief.

COUNSEL

Julius LeVonne Chambers and James M. Nabrit III
argued the cause for petitioners in No. 281 and respondents in No. 349. With them on the briefs were Jack Greenberg, Norman J. Chachkin, C. O. Pearson, and Anthony
G. Amsterdam.

William J. Wagonner and Benjamin S. Horack argued
the cause and filed briefs for respondents in No. 281 and
petitioners in No. 349.

Solicitor General Erwin N. Griswold argued the cause for the United States as amicus curiae in both cases. With him on the brief was Assistant Attorney General Leonard.

Briefs of amici curiae in No. 281 were filed by Earl Faircloth, Attorney General, Robert J. Kelly, Deputy Attorney General, Ronald W. Sabo, Assistant Attorney General, and Rivers Buford for the State of Florida; by Andrew P. Miller, Attorney General, William G. Broaddus and Theodore J. Markow, Assistant Attorneys General, Lewis F. Powell, Jr., John W. Riely, and Guy K. Tower for the Commonwealth of Virginia; by Claude R. Kirk, Jr., pro se, and Gerald Mager for Claude R. Kirk, Jr., Governor of Florida; by W. F. Womble for the Winston-Salem/Forsyth County Board of Education; by Raymond B. Witt, Jr., and Eugene N. Collins for the Chattanooga Board of Education; by Kenneth W. Cleary for the School Board of Manatee County, Florida; by W. Crosby Few and John M. Allison for the School Board of Hillsborough County, Florida; by Sam J. Ervin, Jr., Charles R. Jonas, and Ernest F. Hollings for the Classroom Teachers Association of the Charlotte-Mecklenburg School System, Inc.; by Mark Wells White, Jr., for Mrs. H. W. Cullen et al., members of the Board of Education of the Houston Independent School District; by Jack Petree for the Board of Education of Memphis City Schools; by Sherwood W. Wise for the Jackson Chamber of Commerce, Inc., et al; by Stephen J. Pollak, Benjamin W. Boley, and David Rubin for the National Education Association; by William L. Taylor, Richard B. Sobol, and Joseph L. Rauh, Jr., for the United Negro College Fund, Inc., et al.; by Owen H. Page for Concerned Citizens Association, Inc.; by Charles S. Conley, Floyd B. McKissick, and Charles S. Scott for the Congress of Racial Equality; by the Tennessee Federation for Constitutional

[Supreme Ct Sum]—14

Government et al.; by William C. Cramer, pro se, and Richard B. Peet, joined by Albert W. Watson et al., for William C. Cramer; by Charles E. Bennett, pro se, James C. Rinaman, Jr., and Yardley D. Buckman for Charles E. Bennett; by Calvin H. Childress and M. T. Bohannon, Jr., for David E. Allgood et al.; by William B. Spong, Jr., and by Newton Collier Estes.

BIRDIE MAE DAVIS et al., Petitioners,

v

BOARD OF SCHOOL COMMISSIONERS OF
MOBILE COUNTY et al.

402 US 33, 28 L Ed 2d 577, 91 S Ct 1289

Argued October 13 and 14, 1970. Decided
April 20, 1971.

Decision: Federal court order requiring Alabama county
school board to desegregrate faculty and staff affirmed, but case remanded for further consideration
as to changes in student attendance zones.

SUMMARY

In the United States District Court for the Southern
District of Alabama, an action was brought for the purpose of requiring the defendant, an Alabama county
school board, to cease maintaining a racially segregated,
dual public school system, which included approximately
42 percent Negro students and 58 percent white students.
The metropolitan area of the county was divided by a
major north-south highway, and most of the Negro
elementary school students in the metropolitan area lived
on the east side of the highway and attended all-Negro or
nearly all-Negro schools. A desegregation plan was approved by the District Court, but the Court of Appeals for
the Fifth Circuit, holding the District Court's plan de-
ficient in faculty and staff desegregation and in student
assignment, (1) directed that faculty and staff members
be reassigned in such a manner that the ratio of Negro and
white faculty and staff members in each school would be
substantially the same as that for the entire school system,
and (2) required additional desegregation of students, but
treated the eastern part of the county's metropolitan area

in isolation from the rest of the school system and required
no bus transportation of students for purposes of desegregation, with the result that more than 90 percent of the
students in each of nine elementary schools in the eastern
part of the metropolitan area would be Negro (430 F2d
883; 430 F2d 889).

On certiorari, the United States Supreme Court affirmed in part, reversed in part, and remanded the case.
In an opinion by **Burger, Ch. J.**, expressing the unanimous
views of the court, it was held that the Court of Appeals
had properly directed faculty and staff desegregation, but
had improperly felt constrained to treat the eastern part
of the metropolitan area in isolation from the rest of the
school system and had given inadequate consideration
to the possible use of bus transportation and split zoning.

COUNSEL

Jack Greenberg argued the cause for petitioners. With
him on the briefs were James M. Nabrit III, Michael
Davidson, Norman J. Chachkin, and Anthony G. Amsterdam.

Abram L. Philips, Jr., argued the cause for respondents
Board of School Commissioners of Mobile County et al.
With him on the brief were George F. Wood, John J.
Sparkman, James B. Allen, and Jack Edwards. Samuel
L. Stockman argued the cause for respondents Mobile
County Council Parent-Teacher Associations et al. With
him on the brief were W. A. Kimbrough, Jr., and John
W. Adams, Jr.

Solicitor General Erwin N. Griswold argued the cause
for the United States as amicus curiae. With him on the
brief was Assistant Attorney General Leonard.

Briefs of amici curiae were filed by Albert P. Brewer,
Governor, MacDonald Gallion, Attorney General, and

Joseph D. Phelps, Special Assistant Attorney General, for the State of Alabama; by A. F. Summer, Attorney General, and Semmes Luckett, Special Assistant Attorney General, for the State of Mississippi; by Robert V. Light and Herschel H. Friday for the Little Rock School District et al., and by William L. Taylor, Richard B. Sobol, and Joseph L. Rauh, Jr., for the United Negro College Fund, Inc., et al.

CHARLES McDANIEL, Superintendent
of Schools, et al., Petitioners,

v

JOSEPH BARRESI, Jr., et al.

402 US 39, 28 L Ed 2d 582, 91 S Ct 1287

Argued October 13, 1970. Decided
April 20, 1971.

Decision: Georgia county school board, in desegregating
dual school system, held not precluded by equal
protection clause or by federal civil rights legislation from considering students' race in assigning them
to new attendance zones.

SUMMARY

In the Superior Court of Clarke County, Georgia, an
injunction was sought against the operation of a Georgia
county school board's desegregation plan for the county's
public elementary schools. Approximately one-third of
the elementary school students were Negro, and under
the school board's plan, which created new attendance
zones and required busing of students, the percentage of
Negroes in each elementary school would range from
about 20 percent to 50 percent. The Superior Court denied injunctive relief against the operation of the desegregation plan, but the Georgia Supreme Court reversed
(226 Ga 456, 175 SE2d 649), holding that (1) in attempting to achieve a predetermined racial balance in the
elementary schools by treating students differently because of their race, the county school board violated the
equal protection clause of the Fourteenth Amendment,
and (2) the plan violated federal civil rights legislation
pertaining to the assignment of students to overcome

racial imbalance (42 USC § 2000c(b)) and the transportation of students to achieve racial balance (42 USC § 2000c–6(a)).

On certiorari, the United States Supreme Court reversed. In an opinion by **Burger,** Ch. J., expressing the unanimous views of the court, it was held that (1) the county school board, as part of its affirmative duty to disestablish a dual school system, properly took into account the race of its elementary schoolchildren in drawing attendance lines, and (2) 42 USC §§ 2000c(b) and 2000c–6 did not restrict state school authorities in the exercise of their discretionary powers to assign students within their school systems.

COUNSEL

Eugene A. Epting argued the cause and filed a brief for petitioners.

E. Freeman Leverett argued the cause and filed a brief for respondents.

Briefs of amici curiae were filed by Solicitor General Erwin N. Griswold and Assistant Attorney General Leonard for the United States, and by Arthur K. Bolton, Attorney General, Harold N. Hill, Jr., Executive Assistant Attorney General, and Alfred L. Evans, Jr., and J. Lee Perry, Assistant Attorneys General, for the State of Georgia.

NORTH CAROLINA STATE BOARD OF EDUCATION et al., Appellants,

v

JAMES E. SWANN et al.

402 US 43, 28 L Ed 2d 586, 91 S Ct 1284

Argued October 13, 1970. Decided
April 20, 1971.

Decision: North Carolina statute prohibiting assignment or busing of students on basis of race or for purpose of creating racial balance or ratio held unconstitutional.

SUMMARY

The North Carolina legislature enacted a statute providing that no student shall be assigned to attend any school on account of race or for the purpose of creating a racial balance or ratio, and that involuntary busing in contravention of this provision was prohibited. A three-judge United States District Court for the Western District of North Carolina held this statute unconstitutional (312 F Supp 503) and enjoined its enforcement.

On appeal, the United States Supreme Court affirmed. In an opinion by **Burger,** Ch. J., expressing the unanimous view of the court, it was held that the statute's absolute prohibition against the assignment or busing of students on the basis of race or for the purpose of creating a racial balance or ratio was unconstitutional, since the prohibition would hamper the ability of local school authorities to effectively fulfil their constitutional obligation to eliminate racially segregated, dual school systems.

COUNSEL

Andrew A. Vanore, Jr., Assistant Attorney General of North Carolina, argued the cause for appellants. With him on the brief were Robert B. Morgan, Attorney General, and Ralph Moody, Deputy Attorney General.

James M. Nabrit III argued the cause for appellees. With him on the brief were Jack Greenberg, Norman J. Chachkin, J. LeVonne Chambers, C. O. Pearson, and Anthony G. Amsterdam.

Solicitor General Erwin N. Griswold and Assistant Attorney General Leonard filed a brief for the United States as amicus curiae.

MRS. ROBERT LEE MOORE et al.,
Appellants,

v

CHARLOTTE-MECKLENBURG BOARD
OF EDUCATION et al.

402 US 47, 28 L Ed 2d 590, 91 S Ct 1292

Argued October 13, 1970. Decided
April 20, 1971.

Decision: Appeal from three-judge District Court decision declaring portion of North Carolina antibusing
statute unconstitutional, dismissed for lack of jurisdiction.

SUMMARY

In proceedings in the United States District Court for
the Western District of North Carolina to desegregate a
North Carolina school system, which proceedings included
cases that had been removed from state courts and consolidated for hearing, a three-judge court was convened to
consider the constitutionality of the North Carolina antibusing statute. Both parties in the instant case argued
to the three-judge panel that the statute was constitutional. The District Court entered a judgment declaring
a portion of the antibusing statute unconstitutional, and
enjoining its enforcement (312 F Supp 503).

The United States Supreme Court dismissed the appeal. In a per curiam opinion, expressing the unanimous
view of the court, it was held that the Supreme Court
lacked jurisdiction, since (1) there was no case or controversy, both litigants having sought a holding that the
antibusing statute was constitutional, and (2) no direct
appeal was available under 28 USC § 1253, the appeal

not being one from a civil action required to be heard by a three-judge District Court because neither party had sought an injunction to restrain enforcement of a state statute alleged to be unconstitutional.

COUNSEL

Whiteford S. Blakeney argued the cause for appellants. With him on the brief was William H. Booe.

William J. Waggoner argued the cause for appellees. With him on the brief was Benjamin S. Horack.

Solicitor General Erwin N. Griswold and Assistant Attorney General Leonard filed a brief for the United States as amicus curiae.

GEORGE K. ROSENBERG, District Director,
Immigration and Naturalization Service,
Petitioner,

v

YEE CHIEN WOO

402 US 49, 28 L Ed 2d 592, 91 S Ct 1312

Argued February 23, 1971. Decided
April 21, 1971

Decision: Alien's firm resettlement in third country following flight held bar to refugee status under § 203 (a)(7) of Immigration and Nationality Act of 1952.

SUMMARY

This case involves § 203(a)(7)(A) of the Immigration and Nationality Act of 1952 (8 USC § 1153(a)(7)(A)), which allows conditional entry to "aliens who satisfy an Immigration and Naturalization Service officer at an examination in any non-Communist or non-Communist-dominated country, (A) that (i) because of persecution or fear of persecution on account of race, religion, or political opinion they have fled (I) from any Communist or Communist-dominated country or area, or (II) from any country within the general area of the Middle East, and (ii) are unable or unwilling to return to such country or area on account of race, religion, or political opinion, and (iii) are not nationals of the countries or areas in which their application for conditional entry is made." A native of mainland China who had fled that country in 1953 and sought refuge in Hong Kong, where he lived until 1959, came to this country for trade fairs in 1959 and again in 1960, remaining from 1960 until 1966, when he applied for an immigrant visa under § 203(a)(7)(A).

The District Director of the Immigration and Naturalization Service denied the application on the ground that his presence in the United States was not a consequence of his flight in search of refuge from the Chinese mainland. The Regional Commissioner affirmed, but the United States District Court for the Southern District of California reversed, finding as a fact that the applicant had never firmly resettled in Hong Kong (295 F Supp 1370). The United States Court of Appeals for the Ninth Circuit affirmed on the ground that the "firmly resettled" concept was irrelevant, and that the "firmly resettled" concept was displaced by the "not nationals" requirement of § 203(a)(7)(A)(iii) (419 F2d 252).

On certiorari, the United States Supreme Court reversed and remanded to the Court of Appeals for a review of the District Court's finding that the applicant had never firmly resettled in Hong Kong. In an opinion by **Black, J.**, expressing the view of five members of the court, it was held that (1) the statute requires that the alien's physical presence here be a consequence of his flight in search of refuge, reasonably proximate to the flight, and not following a flight remote in point of time or intervening residence in a third country reasonably constituting a termination of the original flight in search of refuge; and (2) the "not nationals" requirement does not apply to applications for immigrant visas but only to applications for conditional entry made to Immigration and Naturalization officers authorized to accept such applications at points outside the United States.

Stewart, J., joined by **Douglas, Brennan,** and **Marshall, JJ.**, dissented on the ground that resettlement following flight is no bar to refugee status under the statute.

COUNSEL

Charles Gordon argued the cause for petitioner. With

him on the briefs were Solicitor General Erwin N. Griswold, Assistant Attorney General Wilson, Jerome M. Feit, Beatrice Rosenberg, Paul C. Summitt, and George W. Masterton.

Gordon G. Dale argued the cause and filed a brief for respondent.

———————

UNITED STATES, Appellant,

v

MILAN VUITCH

402 US 62, 28 L Ed 2d 601, 91 S Ct 1294

Argued January 12, 1971. Decided
April 21, 1971.

Decision: Supreme Court held to have jurisdiction of
government's appeal from District Court dismissal
of prosecution under District of Columbia abortion
statute; abortion statute held not unconstitutionally
vague.

SUMMARY

A licensed physician was indicted for producing and
attempting to produce abortions in violation of a provision
of the District of Columbia Code which makes criminal
the performance or attempted performance of an abortion
unless "done as necessary for the preservation of the
mother's life or health" and under the direction of a
licensed physician. The United States District Court
for the District of Columbia dismissed the indictment on
the ground that the abortion statute was unconstitutionally vague since there was no indication whether the
term "health" included mental as well as physical health,
and since the burden was on the defendant to show that
an abortion was necessary to the preservation of the
mother's life or health (305 F Supp 1032).

On appeal, the United States Supreme Court reversed
and remanded. In an opinion by **Black, J.**, expressing the
views of five members of the court, it was held that (1)
the Supreme Court had jurisdiction over the government's
appeal under the provision of the Criminal Appeals Act

giving the court jurisdiction over direct appeals from District Court judgments "in all criminal cases" dismissing any indictment on the basis of the invalidity of "the statute" upon which the indictment was founded, and (2) the District of Columbia abortion statute was not unconstitutionally vague in violation of the due process clause of the Constitution, since the statute, properly construed, permitted abortions for both physical and mental health reasons, and since, under the statute, the burden was on the prosecution to plead and prove that the abortion was not "necessary for the preservation of the mother's life or health."

White, J., concurring, stated that the statute was not vague on its face, since it put everyone on adequate notice that the health of the mother, whatever that phrase meant, was the governing standard, and since no one of average intelligence could believe that under the statute abortions not dictated by health considerations were legal.

Douglas, J., dissenting in part, agreed with holding (1) above, but expressed the view that the abortion statute did not meet procedural due process requirements, since a physician's judgment as to whether an abortion was necessary for the "preservation of the mother's life or health" was highly subjective and could differ from another physician's judgment, and since the jury was free to create its own standards in each case, based on personal predilections or religious prejudices.

Harlan, J., joined by **Brennan, Marshall,** and **Blackmun, JJ.**, dissented from holding (1) above, stating that the provision of the Criminal Appeals Act authorizing appeal to the Supreme Court from a District Court's dismissal of an indictment based on the invalidity of the "statute" upon which the indictment was founded should be construed as including only cases involving statutes of nationwide applicability, not statutes applicable only in the District of Columbia. Speaking only for himself, **Harlan, J.**, stated that notwithstanding his view on the lack of appellate jurisdiction, it was appropriate to consider the merits and he concurred in holding (2) above.

Stewart, J., dissenting in part, agreed with holding (1) above, but was of the opinion that under the abortion statute, properly construed, a licensed physician, exercising his judgment in favor of performing an abortion as necessary to preserve a patient's life or health, did not violate the statute and was immune from prosecution.

Blackmun, J., although disagreeing with holding (1) above, stated that since a majority of the court upheld appellate jurisdiction but could not agree as to the constitutionality of the abortion statute, it was appropriate for him to consider the merits, and he concurred in holding (2) above.

COUNSEL

Samuel Huntington argued the cause for the United States. With him on the brief were Solicitor General Erwin N. Griswold, Assistant Attorney General Wilson, Jerome M. Feit, and Roger A. Pauley.

Joseph L. Nellis and Norman Dorsen argued the cause for appellee. With Mr. Nellis on the brief was Joseph Sitnick.

Briefs of amici curiae were filed by David W. Louisell for Dr. Bart Heffernan; by Alfred L. Scanlan, Thomas J. Ford, and Gary R. Alexander for Dr. William F. Colliton, Jr., et al.; by Robert E. Dunne for Robert L. Sassone; by Marilyn G. Rose for the National Legal Program on Health Problems of the Poor; by Sylvia S. Ellison for

Human Rights for Women, Inc.; by Lola Boswell for the Joint Washington Office for Social Concern et al.; and by Ralph Temple, Melvin L. Wulf, and Norma G. Zarky for the American Civil Liberties Union et al.

WILLIAM WARD EHLERT, Petitioner,

v

UNITED STATES

402 US 99, 28 L Ed 2d 625, 91 S Ct 1319

Argued January 13, 1971. Decided
April 21, 1971.

Decision: Draft registrant asserting conscientious objector claim after receipt of induction notice but before induction held not entitled to preinduction determination of claim by draft board, but held required to submit claim to postinduction determination by military review board.

SUMMARY

The petitioner, a draft registrant, made no claim to conscientious objector status until after he received his induction notice; but prior to the induction date, he wrote to his local board and asked to be allowed to present his claim, representing that his views had matured only after the induction notice had made immediate the prospect of military service. The petitioner's local board notified him that it had declined to reopen his classification in view of a Selective Service regulation which required for postinduction notice reopenings that there be a "change in the registrant's status resulting from circumstances over which the registrant had no control." The petitioner was subsequently convicted for refusal to submit to induction upon trial in the United States District Court for the Northern District of California, which court held that ripening of conscientious objector views could not be a circumstance over which a registrant had no control; and the conviction was affirmed by the United States Court of Appeals for the Ninth Circuit (422 F2d 332).

On certiorari, the United States Surpeme Court affirmed. In an opinion by **Stewart, J.**, expressing the views of six members of the court, it was held that (1) a regulation explicitly providing that no conscientious objector claim could be considered by a local board unless filed before the mailing of an induction notice would be perfectly valid, provided that no inductee could be ordered to combatant training or service before a prompt, fair, and proper in-service determination of his claim; and (2) the requiring of in-service presentation of postnotice conscientious objector status claims deprived no registrant of any legal right and did not leave a "no man's land" time period in which a claim then arising could not be presented in any forum, because both the government and military authorities had assured the court that present practice not only allowed the presentation of such claims, but prohibited persons who had requested discharge or noncombatant service as conscientious objectors from being required to train in the study, use, or handling of arms or weapons and from being required to perform duties in conflict with their asserted beliefs, and further because there was a military review board which heard and determined such claims.

Douglas, J., dissented on the ground that since in-service processing of postinduction conscientious objector claims by the military was not required by the Military Selective Service Act of 1967 or the Selective Service regulation, any ambiguities should be resolved in favor of determination of such claims by civilian rather than military personnel, as the procedure most protective of the rights of conscience.

Brennan, J., joined by **Marshall, J.**, dissented on the ground that the crystallization of a registrant's conscientious objection to war after receipt of his induction notice but before before his induction was "a change in the registrant's status resulting from circumstances over which the registrant had no control" within the meaning of the pertinent regulation, which thus required the local board to reopen the registrant's classification for further processing by civilian rather than by military personnel.

COUNSEL

Paul N. Halvonik argued the cause for petitioner. With him on the briefs were Stanley J. Friedman, Mortimer H. Herzstein, and Marvin M. Karpatkin.

Assistant Attorney General Rehnquist argued the cause for the United States. On the brief were Solicitor General Erwin N. Griswold, Assisting Attorney General Wilson, Beatrice Rosenberg, and Marshall Tamor Golding.

Norman Leonard filed a brief for the Lawyers' Selective Service Panel of San Francisco as amicus curiae urging reversal.

CALIFORNIA DEPARTMENT OF HUMAN
RESOURCES DEVELOPMENT et al., Appellants,

v

JUDITH JAVA et al.

402 US 121, 28 L Ed 2d 666, 91 S Ct 1347

Argued February 24, 1971. Decided April 26, 1971.

Decision: California's denial of unemployment benefits
pending employer's appeal from award held violative
of Social Security Act.

SUMMARY

Two California unemployment compensation claimants
who were ruled eligible for benefits as a result of an
eligibility interview, but whose payments were stopped,
pending their former employer's appeal, pursuant to
§ 1335 of the California Unemployment Insurance Code,
brought a class action in United States District Court for
the Northern District of California, seeking an order enjoining the operation of § 1335 and a declaration that it
was unconstitutional and inconsistent with the requirement of § 303(a)(1) of the Social Security Act that a
state receiving federal unemployment compensation assistance make payment of benefits "when due." A three-
judge court concluded that § 1335 was defective on both
constitutional and statutory grounds (317 F Supp 875).

On direct appeal, the United States Supreme Court
affirmed. In an opinion by **Burger,** Ch. J., expressing the
unanimous view of the court, it was held that the "when
due" provision of the Social Security Act requires payment of unemployment compensation promptly after an
initial determination of eligibility as a result of a hearing
of which both parties have notice and at which they are

permitted to present their respective positions. The constitutional issue was pretermitted.

Douglas, J., while joining in the court's opinion, filed a concurring opinion declaring that since a former employer in California is not charged with any benefits paid to his former employee if the employer wins on appeal from the award of benefits, immediate payment of benefits does not deny due process to the employer.

COUNSEL

Asher Rubin, Deputy Attorney General of California, argued the cause for appellants. With him on the brief was Thomas C. Lynch, Attorney General.

Stephen P. Berzon argued the cause for appellees pro hac vice. With him on the brief was Kenneth F. Phillips.

Briefs of amici curiae urging reversal were filed by Solicitor General Erwin N. Griswold, Assistant Attorney General Gray, Robert V. Zener, and Peter G. Nash for the United States; by Duke W. Dunbar, Attorney General, John P. Moore, Deputy Attorney General, and Robert L. Harris, Assistant Attorney General, for the State of Colorado; by Robert M. Robson, Attorney General, and R. LaVar Marsh, Assistant Attorney General, for the State of Idaho; by Francis B. Burch, Attorney General, and Louis B. Price, Special Assistant Attorney General, for the State of Maryland, joined by the State of Illinois; by Warren B. Rudman, Attorney General, and William F. Cann, Deputy Attorney General, for the State of New Hampshire, joined by David M. Pack, Attorney General, and Lance D. Evans, Assistant Attorney General, for the State of Tennessee; by Louis J. Lefkowitz, Attorney General, Samuel A. Hirshowitz, First Assistant Attorney General, and Brenda Soloff, Assistant Attorney General, for the State of New York; by Paul W. Brown,

Attorney General, and Franklin R. Wright, Assistant Attorney General, for the State of Ohio; and by Willard Z. Carr, Jr., for the Southern California Edison Co. et al.
Briefs of amici curiae urging affirmance were filed by C. Lyonel Jones, Ed J. Polk, Don B. Kates, Jr., and Joseph A. Matera for California Rural Legal Assistance et al.; by J. Albert Woll, Laurence Gold, and Thomas E. Harris for American Federation of Labor and Congress of Industrial Organizations; by Stephen I. Schlossberg, John A. Fillion, and Jordan Rossen for the International Union, UAW; and by the Employment Project, Center on Social Welfare Policy and Law.

RONALD JAMES et al., Appellants,

v

ANITA VALTIERRA et al., Appellees (No. 154)

VIRGINIA C. SHAFFER, Appellant,

v

ANITA VALTIERRA et al., Appellees (No. 226)

402 US 137, 28 L Ed 2d 678, 91 S Ct 1331

Argued March 3 and 4, 1971. Decided
April 26, 1971.

Decision: Federal Constitution held not violated by
California constitutional provision requiring each
low-income housing project to be approved by
majority vote in local referendum.

SUMMARY

Article 34 of the California Constitution provides that
no low-income housing project shall be developed, con-
structed, or acquired in any manner by a state public
body until the project is approved by a majority vote
in a city, town, or county referendum. After low-income
housing proposals were defeated in local referendums,
some low-income persons who desired such housing
brought suit in the United States District Court for the
Northern District of California, alleging that Article 34
was unconstitutional because its referendum requirement
violated the Federal Constitution's supremacy clause,
privileges and immunities clause, and equal protection
clause. A three-judge District Court held that Article
34 violated the equal protection clause (313 F Supp 1).

On appeal, the United States Supreme Court reversed. In an opinion by **Black, J.**, expressing the views of five members of the court, it was held that (1) Article 34 did not violate the supremacy clause or the privileges and immunities clause, (2) since Article 34 did not rest upon distinctions based on race, the Article did not constitute racial discrimination in violation of the equal protection clause, and (3) since the referendum was a procedure for democratic decision-making, and since low-income persons who desired public housing were not singled out for mandatory referendums which no other group had to face, Article 34 did not deny such persons equal protection.

Marshall, J., joined by **Brennan** and **Blackmun, JJ.**, dissented from holding (3) above, on the grounds that (1) Article 34 explicitly singled out low-income persons to bear its burden; (2) publicly assisted housing developments designed to accommodate the aged, veterans, state employees, persons of moderate income, or any class of citizens other than the poor, were not required to be approved by prior referendums; and (3) by singling out the poor to bear a burden not placed on any other class of citizens, Article 34 constituted invidious discrimination in violation of the equal protection clause.

Douglas, J., did not participate.

COUNSEL

Donald C. Atkinson argued the cause and filed a brief for appellants in No. 154. Moses Lasky argued the cause for appellant in No. 226. With him on the briefs was Malcolm T. Dungan.

Archibald Cox argued the cause for appellees in both cases. On the brief were Lois P. Sheinfeld and Anthony G. Amsterdam. Warren Christopher and Donald M.

Wessling filed a brief for appellee Housing Authority of the city of San Jose in both cases.

Briefs of amici curiae urging affirmance in both cases were filed by Solicitor General Erwin N. Griswold, Assistant Attorney General Leonard, and Lawrence G. Wallace for the United States, and by Louis J. Lefkowitz, Attorney General, pro se, Samuel A. Hirshowitz, First Assistant Attorney General, and George D. Zuckerman, Dominick J. Tuminaro, and Lloyd G. Milliken, Assistant Attorneys General, for the Attorney General of the State of New York.

ALCIDES PEREZ, Petitioner,

v

UNITED STATES

402 US 146, 28 L Ed 2d 686, 91 S Ct 1357

Argued March 22, 1971. Decided April 26, 1971.

Decision: Loan shark provisions of Consumer Credit Protection Act, prohibiting extortionate credit transactions, held constitutional, under commerce clause.

SUMMARY

The petitioner, in intrastate transactions, made loans to a businessman, increased the borrower's weekly payments on several occasions, and, upon the borrower's objections to the increased payments, made threats of violence against the borrower and his family. Upon jury trial in the United States District Court for the Eastern District of New York, the petitioner was convicted of using extortionate means to collect or attempt to collect extensions of credit in violation of Title II of the Consumer Credit Protection Act, the District Court having overruled the petitioner's motion to dismiss the indictment on the ground that the Act was unconstitutional. On appeal, the United States Court of Appeals for the Second Circuit held the Act constitutional and affirmed the petitioner's conviction (426 F2d 1073).

On certiorari, the United States Supreme Court affirmed. In an opinion by **Douglas, J.**, expressing the views of eight members of the court, it was held that (1) the findings by Congress contained in § 201 of Public Law 90–321 in enacting Title II of the Consumer Credit Protection Act that extortionate credit transctions, though purely intrastate, adversely affect interstate commerce, and that there is a connection between local "loan sharks" and interstate crime, were sufficient to sustain the regulation and prohibition by Congress of such activities, and (2) Title II of the Act, as applied to the petitioner, was a permissible exercise by Congress of its powers under the commerce clause of the United States Constitution to regulate interstate commerce.

Stewart, J., dissented on the ground that Congress did not have the authority to define as a crime and to order the prosecution of such a wholly local activity as loan sharking through the enactment of federal criminal laws.

COUNSEL

Albert J. Krieger argued the cause for petitioner. With him on the briefs was Joel M. Finkelstein.

Solicitor General Erwin N. Griswold argued the cause for the United States. With him on the brief were Assistant Attorney General Wilson, Beatrice Rosenberg, and Marshall Tamor Golding.

UNITED STATES, Petitioner,

v

SOUTHERN UTE TRIBE OR BAND OF INDIANS

402 US 159, 28 L Ed 2d 695, 91 S Ct 1336

Argued March 1, 1971.   Decided April 26, 1971.

Decision: Indian tribe's claim against United States for compensation for former Indian lands, held res judicata under consent judgment in earlier suit.

SUMMARY

The Southern Ute Tribe or Band of Indians asserted a claim against the United States before the Indian Claims Commission, based on the government's alleged failure to comply with its fiduciary duties under 1880 and 1895 Acts whereby proceeds from the government's disposition of certain Colorado lands ceded by the tribe to the government were to be held for the tribe's benefit. The government asserted the defense of res judicata by reason of a consent judgment entered in an earlier action against the United States by the Confederated Bands of Utes, including the claimant tribe, which judgment recited that it was res judicata as to any Colorado lands formerly owned or claimed by the plaintiffs therein and ceded to the government under the 1880 Act. The Indian Claims Commission rejected the defense on the ground that the lands involved in the instant claim had not been ceded to the government by the 1880 Act (21 Ind Cl Comm 268), and the Court of Claims affirmed (423 F2d 346, 191 Ct Cl 1).

On certiorari, the United States Supreme Court reversed. In an opinion by **Brennan, J.**, expressing the view of eight members of the court, it was held that the claim in the case at bar was res judicata under the judgment in the earlier action, since (1) the 1880 Act, on its face, included the lands involved in the instant claim, and (2) the record did not support the conclusion that such lands were not intended to be ceded to the government under the Act, or that the plain words of the Act had been varied under the doctrines of estoppel or waiver by governmental action after the 1880 Act.

Douglas, J., dissented on the grounds that the question presented was one of fact, or, at best, a mixed question of law and fact, thus making the lower court's determination binding if supported by substantial evidence, and that the record clearly supported the determination below.

COUNSEL

Lawrence G. Wallace argued the cause for the United States. On the briefs were Solicitor General Erwin N. Griswold, Assistant Attorney General Kashiwa, Peter L. Strauss, and Edmund B. Clark.

Glen A. Wilkinson argued the cause for respondent. With him on the brief was Richard A. Baenen.

DENNIS COUNCLE McGAUTHA, Petitioner,

v

STATE OF CALIFORNIA (No. 203)

JAMES EDWARD CRAMPTON, Petitioner,

v

STATE OF OHIO (No. 204)

402 US 183, 28 L Ed 2d 711, 91 S Ct 1454

Argued November 9, 1970. Decided May 3, 1971.

Decision: Absence of standards to guide jury's determination in capital cases as to whether death penalty should be imposed, and single-verdict procedure for determining guilty and penalty, held constitutional.

SUMMARY

The constitutional issue of a jury's fixing the death penalty without any guidelines as to when the death penalty should be imposed was presented in two cases: No. 203, wherein the accused was convicted of first degree murder in the Superior Court of Los Angeles County, California, and was sentenced to death after a separate penalty trial, and on automatic appeal his conviction was affirmed by the California Supreme Court (70 Cal 2d 770, 76 Cal Rptr 434, 452 P2d 650); and No. 204, wherein the accused was convicted of first degree murder, with no recommendation for mercy, and sentenced to death, after a trial in Lucas County, Ohio, and his conviction was affirmed by the Lucas County Court of Appeals, which was affirmed by the Supreme Court of Ohio (18 Ohio St 2d 182, 47 Ohio Ops 2d 394, 248 NE2d 614).

On certiorari, the United States Supreme Court affirmed. In an opinion by **Harlan, J.**, expressing the view of five members of the court, it was held that (1) as to both cases, the absence of standards to guide the jury's discretion in determining whether to impose or withhold the death penalty did not violate due process; and (2) as to No. 204, Ohio's single-verdict procedure for determining guilt and punishment in capital cases was not unconstitutional.

Black, J., concurred specially, declaring his agreement with substantially all of the court's opinion, and adding that the Eighth Amendment's prohibition of cruel and unusual punishments does not outlaw capital punishment.

Douglas, J., joined by **Brennan,** and **Marshall, JJ.**, dissented in No. 204 on the ground that Ohio's single-verdict procedure violates due process.

Brennan, J., joined by **Douglas** and **Marshall, JJ.**, dissented in both cases on the ground that a jury's unguided exercise of its discretion to impose the death penalty violates due process.

COUNSEL

Herman F. Selvin, by appointment of the Court, 400 US 885, 27 L Ed 2d 137, 91 S Ct 136, argued the cause and filed briefs for petitioner in No. 203. John J. Callahan, by appointment of the Court, 399 US 924, 26 L Ed 2d 789, 90 S Ct 2246, argued the cause for petitioner in No. 204. With him on the brief were Dan H. McCullough, William T. Burgess, William D. Driscoll, and Gerald S. Lubitsky.

Ronald M. George, Deputy Attorney General of California, argued the cause for respondent in No. 203.

With him on the brief were Thomas C. Lynch, Attorney General, and William E. James, Assistant Attorney General. Melvin L. Resnick argued the cause for respondent in No. 204. With him on the brief were Harry Friberg and Alice L. Robie Resnick.

Solicitor General Erwin N. Griswold argued the cause for the United States as amicus curiae urging affirmance in both cases. With him on the brief was Philip A. Lacovara.

Jack Greenberg, James M. Nabrit III, Michael Meltsner, and Anthony G. Amsterdam filed a brief for the NAACP Legal Defense and Educational Fund, Inc., et al. as amici curiae in both cases. Luke McKissack filed a brief as amicus curiae in No. 203. Briefs of amici curiae in No. 204 were filed by Richard F. Stevens for the Attorney General of Ohio; by Elmer Gertz and Willard J. Lassers for the American Civil Liberties Union, Illinois Division, et al.; and by Willard J. Lassers, Elmer Gertz, Alex Elson, and Marvin Braiterman for the American Friends Service Committee et al.

BLONDER-TONGUE LABORATORIES,
Inc., Petitioner,

v

UNIVERSITY OF ILLINOIS FOUNDATION et al.

402 US 313, 28 L Ed 2d 788, 91 S Ct 1434

Argued January 14, 1971. Decided May 3, 1971.

Decision: Determination of invalidity of patent in patentee's suit against alleged infringer held basis for pleading defense of collateral estoppel in patentee's suit against different alleged infringer.

SUMMARY

In a patent assignee's suit alleging patent infringement, the United States District Court for the Southern District of Iowa held that because a radio and television antenna covered by the patent would have been obvious to one ordinarily skilled in the art, the patent was invalid; judgment was accordingly entered in favor of the alleged infringer and against the patent assignee, and this judgment was affirmed by the Court of Appeals for the Eighth Circuit. In a suit by the same patent assignee alleging infringement of the same patent by a different defendant, the United States District Court for the Northern District of Illinois, relying upon the United States Supreme Court's decision in Triplett v Lowell, 297 US 638, 80 L Ed 949, 56 S Ct 645, concluded that it was not bound by the prior determination of the patent's invalidity, and the District Court proceeded to hold that the antenna was nonobvious and that the patent was valid and had been infringed by the defendant. The Court of Appeals for the Seventh Circuit, also relying on Triplett v Lowell, held that the prior determination of the patent's invalidity was not binding, and the Court of Appeals affirmed the District Court's holdings that the patent was valid and had been infringed by the defendant (422 F2d 769).

On certiorari, the United States Supreme Court vacated the judgment below and remanded the case. In an opinion by **White, J.**, expressing the unanimous views of the court, it was held, overruling Triplett v Lowell, that (1) regardless of whether there would be mutuality of estoppel, a patentee whose patent is held invalid in his suit against one alleged infringer may be precluded, under the doctrine of collateral estoppel, from asserting the validity of the patent in a suit against a different alleged infringer, and (2) the defendant in the instant case should be allowed to amend its pleadings in the District Court to assert a plea of collateral estoppel.

COUNSEL

Robert H. Rines argued the cause for petitioner.   With him on the brief were Richard S. Phillips, Paul J. Foley, and Nelson H. Shapiro.

William A. Marshall argued the cause for respondent University of Illinois Foundation.   With him on the brief were Charles J. Merriam and Basil P. Mann.   Sidney G. Faber argued the cause for respondent JFD Electronics Corp.   With him on the brief were Jerome M. Berliner, Robert C. Faber, and Myron C. Cass.

Assistant Attorney General McLaren argued the cause for the United States as amicus curiae urging reversal. With him on the brief were Solicitor General Erwin N. Griswold, Assistant Attorney General Gray, Peter L. Strauss, Howard E. Shapiro, and Walter H. Fleischer.

Briefs of amici curiae were filed by Donald R. Dunner, James B. Gambrell, and W. Grown Morton, Jr., for the

American Patent Law Association; by Theodore W. Anderson for the Automatic Electric Co.; by Harold F. McNenny, John F. Pearne, and Walther E. Wyss for the Finney Co.; and by Joseph B. Brennan and Richard D. Mason for the Kawneer Co., Inc.

———————

UNITED STATES, Appellant,

v

NORMAN GEORGE REIDEL

402 US 351, 28 L Ed 2d 813, 91 S Ct 1400

Argued January 20, 1971.   Decided May 3, 1971.

Decision: 18 USC § 1461, prohibiting use of mails for delivery of obscene matter, held constitutional as applied to distribution of such matter to willing, adult recipients.

SUMMARY

The defendant, who had mailed allegedly obscene material to recipients who responded to a newspaper advertisement which required that the recipient state that he was 21 years of age, was indicted for violating 18 USC § 1461, which prohibits knowing use of the mails for the delivery of obscene matter.   The United States District Court for the Central District of California granted the defendant's motion to dismiss the indictment, holding that § 1461 was unconstitutional as applied to the defendant, since the Constitution protected a person's right to receive and possess obscene material, and since the material involved was not directed at children or at an unwilling public.

On appeal, the United States Supreme Court reversed. In an opinion by **White, J.**, expressing the views of six members of the court, it was held that (1) 18 USC § 1461 was constitutional as applied to the distribution of obscene materials to willing recipients who stated that they were adults, and (2) the constitutional right of a person to possess obscene material in the privacy of his own home did not confer on another a First Amendment right to sell and deliver such material.

Harlan, J., concurred, stating that the right to private possession of obscene materials, which right was based on freedom of thought, did not afford First Amendment protection of obscenity for its content, and that the right to receive obscene materials for private possession was not a right to the existence of commercial modes of distribution of obscenity.

Marshall, J., concurred in the judgment, on the grounds that (1) while obscene matter could not be outlawed merely because antisocial conduct might thereby somehow be encouraged, regulatory action could be validly taken to protect children and unwilling adults from exposure to obscene materials, and (2) the mail-order distribution in the case at bar did not have sufficient safeguards against receipt of materials by minors, the defendant's conduct thus not being beyond a constitutionally valid construction of the federal statute.

Black, J., joined by **Douglas, J.**, dissented, expressing the view that the First Amendment's literal command that Congress shall make no law abridging freedom of speech or of the press denied Congress the power to act as censor to determine what books citizens might read.

COUNSEL

Solicitor General Erwin N. Griswold argued the cause for the United States. With him on the brief were Assistant Attorney General Wilson and Roger A. Pauley.

Sam Rosenwein argued the cause for appellee. With him on the brief was Stanley Fleishman.

UNITED STATES, Appellant,

v

THIRTY-SEVEN (37) PHOTOGRAPHS,
Milton Luros, Claimant

402 US 363, 28 L Ed 2d 822, 91 S Ct 1400

Argued January 20, 1971. Decided May 3, 1971.

Decision: Specific time limits read into 19 USC § 1305(a)
as to institution and completion of judicial proceedings for forfeiture of obscene materials seized by
customs officials; application of statute to importer
of pictures for commercial use held valid.

SUMMARY

Acting pursuant to 19 USC § 1305(a), which authorizes seizure of obscene materials by customs collectors
and provides for institution of forfeiture proceedings in
a Federal District Court, but which fails to prescribe time
limits for institution and completion of such forfeiture
proceedings, customs agents seized allegedly obscene
photographs from the luggage of a person returning to
the United States from Europe. Thirteen days later,
forfeiture proceedings were instituted in the United States
District Court for the Central District of California, and
the owner, as claimant, challenged the constitutionality
of § 1305(a). A three-judge court was convened as de-
manded by the claimant, who stipulated that some or
all of the photographs were to be used in a book for
commercial distribution. The District Court declared
§ 1305(a) unconstitutional on the grounds that it failed
to specify procedural time limits for judicial determination of obscenity as required under the First Amendment,
and that the statute's prohibition of importation of ob-

scenity for private as well as commercial use was unconstitutional, since the First Amendment protected the right to receive and possess obscene material for private use in one's own home (309 F Supp 36).

On appeal, the United States Supreme Court reversed and remanded. In an opinion by **White, J.**, announcing the judgment of the court, it was held, expressing the views of six members of the court, that (1) in order to avoid decision of constitutional questions and in order to give the statute a saving construction, § 1305(a) was to be construed as requiring that judicial forfeiture proceedings be instituted no more than 14 days after seizure of allegedly obscene materials, and as requiring that final decision in the District Court be reached no more than 60 days after the filing of the action, unless delays were caused by the claimant or, as in the case at bar, by a three-judge court's consideration of constitutional issues, and (2) the statute, so construed, was constitutionally applied in the instant action, in view of the intended use of the photographs for commercial rather than private purposes.

White, J., also expressed the view, joined in by **Burger, Ch. J.**, **Brennan, J.**, and **Blackmun, J.**, that regardless of the right to receive and possess obscene material for private use in one's home, the government could properly prevent importation of obscene materials, even when intended for private use.

Harlan, J., concurred in holdings (1) and (2) above, stating that the claimant, who admitted importation of the pictures for commercial purposes, lacked standing to attack the statute as being overbroad because of its apparent prohibition of importation for private use.

Stewart, J., concurring in holdings (1) and (2) above, expressed the view that the case was not a proper one for deciding the question whether the government could lawfully seize literary material intended for the purely private use of the importer.

Black, J., joined by **Douglas, J.,** dissented on the grounds that (1) the First Amendment denied Congress the power to act as censor of books and pictures, (2) in any event, the recognized right to possession of "obscene" material in the privacy of one's home should be considered as including the right to carry such material privately in one's luggage when entering the country, and (3) the court had no power to rewrite § 1305(a) by adding specific time limitations, but should instead affirm the lower court's determination of unconstitutionality.

Marshall, J., dissented, expressing the view that although regulatory action could be taken to protect children and unwilling adults from exposure to obscene materials upon public or commercial distribution, nevertheless the government had ample opportunity to protect its valid interest if and when the claimant affected commercial distribution of the material.

COUNSEL

Solicitor General Erwin N. Griswold argued the cause for the United States. With him on the brief were Assistant Attorney General Wilson and Roger A. Pauley.

Stanley Fleishman argued the cause for appellees. With him on the brief was Sam Rosenwein.

ELLIOT L. RICHARDSON, Secretary
of Health, Education, and Welfare,
Petitioner,

v

PEDRO PERALES

402 US 389, 28 L Ed 2d 842, 91 S Ct 1420

Argued January 13, 1971. Decided
May 3, 1971.

Decision: Written reports adverse to social security disability claimant prepared by licensed physicians not
appearing at administrative hearing held admissible
and sufficient to sustain finding of nondisability.

SUMMARY

At administrative proceedings to determine a social
security disability claim arising from the claimant's work-
related back injury, the hearing examiner admitted in
evidence the written reports of some licensed physicians
who had examined the claimant, which reports set forth
findings within the physicians' areas of competence and
which were generally unfavorable to the claimant. These
physicians were not present and did not testify at the
hearing. The examiner also admitted testimony of a physician, selected as the examiner's medical adviser, which
testimony was based on the other medical evidence rather
than on an examination of the claimant. The claimant's
objections to the admission of such testimony and the
medical reports, based on hearsay and denial of the right
to cross-examine the physicians who had prepared the
reports, were overruled by the examiner, who concluded
that the claimant had not met his burden of proving entitlement to disability benefits, notwithstanding the tes-

timony of the claimant and the physician who had treated him to the effect that the claimant was totally and permanently disabled. The examiner's conclusion was affirmed by the Appeals Council. On review, the United States District Court for the Western District of Texas remanded the case for a new hearing before a different examiner, concluding that admission of the reports denied the claimant the opportunity to cross-examine the witnesses (288 F Supp 313). On appeal, the Court of Appeals for the Fifth Circuit held that the claimant's failure to request subpoenas precluded his complaint about inability to cross-examine, and that the reports, although hearsay evidence, were admissible in administrative hearings. However, the Court of Appeals affirmed the District Court's judgment because of its conclusion that the reports did not constitute "substantial evidence," as required by § 205(g) of the Act (42 USC § 405(g)), that would support the hearing examiner's findings in view of the objections made to it and its contradiction by evidence from the only live witnesses (412 F2d 44, petition for rehearing denied, 416 F2d 1250).

On certiorari, the United States Surpeme Court reversed and remanded. In an opinion by **Blackmun, J.**, expressing the views of six members of the court, it was held that (1) a written report by a licensed physician who had examined a social security disability claimant and who set forth in his report his medical findings in his area of competence could be received as evidence in a disability hearing and, despite its hearsay character and an absence of cross-examination, and despite the presence of opposing direct medical testimony and testimony by the claimant himself, could constitute substantial evidence supportive of a finding by the hearing examiner adverse to the claimant, when the claimant had not exercised his right to subpoena the reporting physician and thereby provide himself with the opportunity to cross-examine the physician; (2) hearsay being admissible up to the point of relevancy in such administrative proceedings, the admission of such reports, subject to the reports being material and to the claimant's timely use of the subpoena and consequent cross-examination of the physicians who prepared them, did not violate procedural due process; and (3) the presence at such hearings of medical advisers for the purpose of explaining medical problems in complex cases in terms understandable to the hearing examiner was not unconstitutional or improper.

Douglas, J., with whom **Black** and **Brennan, JJ.,** concurred, dissented on the ground that while the hearsay medical reports were properly received in evidence, such uncorroborated hearsay untested by cross-examination did not by itself constitute "substantial evidence" and could not by itself be the basis for a ruling adverse to a social security disability claimant.

COUNSEL

Deputy Solicitor General Friedman argued the cause for petitioner. With him on the briefs were Solicitor General Erwin N. Griswold, Assistant Attorney General Ruckelshaus, Assistant Attorney General Gray, Lawrence G. Wallace, Kathryn H. Baldwin, and Michael C. Farrar.

Richard Tinsman, by appointment of the Court, 398 US 902, 26 L Ed 2d 60, 90 S Ct 1689, argued the cause and filed a brief for respondent.

Briefs of amici curiae were filed by Franklin M. Schultz and John T. Miller, Jr., for the American Bar Association; by Frank P. Christian, Harry B. Adams III, and Melvin N. Eichelbaum for the Bexar County Legal Aid Association; and by Jonathan Weiss for the Appalachian Research and Defense Fund et al.

ORGANIZATION FOR A BETTER AUSTIN
et al., Petitioners,

v

JEROME M. KEEFE

402 US 415, 29 L Ed 2d 1, 91 S Ct 1575

Argued January 20, 1917. Decided
May 17, 1971.

Decision: Injunction against distribution of literature,
where leaflets had accused real-estate broker of
"panic peddling" activities, held unconstitutional as
prior restraint on First Amendment rights.

SUMMARY

The office and business activities of the plaintiff, a real-
estate broker, were in an urban neighborhood, but his
home was in a suburb 7 miles away. The defendants,
who were from a racially integrated community organization in the urban neighborhood, distributed in the suburb
leaflets accusing the plaintiff of engaging in "panic peddling" activities. The distribution of leaflets was peaceful,
did not disrupt pedestrian or vehicular traffic, and did
not precipitate any fights, disturbances, or other breaches
of the peace. The Circuit Court of Cook County, Illinois, granted a temporary injunction against the defendants' distribution of pamphlets, leaflets, or literature of
any kind anywhere in the suburb. The Appellate Court
of Illinois, First District, affirmed, holding that the defendants' activities in the suburb had invaded the plaintiff's right of privacy, that the defendants' activities were
coercive, and that the defendants' right of free speech
was not involved (115 Ill App 2d 236, 253 NE2d 76).
On certiorari, the United States Supreme Court reversed. In an opinion by **Burger, Ch. J.,** expressing the

views of eight members of the court, it was held (1) that the Supreme Court had jurisdiction under 28 USC § 1257 even though the state courts had referred to the injunction as a "temporary" injunction, and (2) that the injunction, operating not to redress alleged private wrongs, but to suppress, on the basis of previous publications, distribution of literature of any kind in the suburb, was unconstitutional as a prior restraint on the defendants' First Amendment rights.

Harlan, J., dissented from holding (1) above.

COUNSEL

David C. Long argued the cause for petitioners. With him on the briefs was Williard J. Lassers.

Thomas W. McNamara argued the cause for respondent. With him on the brief was John C. Tucker.

CALIFORNIA, Petitioner,

v

JONATHAN TODD BYERS

402 US 424, 29 L Ed 2d 9, 91 S Ct 1535

Argued December 8, 1970. Decided
May 17, 1971.

Decision: California statute requiring motorist to stop
and identify himself after being involved in property
damage accident held not violative of privilege
against self-incrimination.

SUMMARY

The first count of a criminal complaint charged a motorist with violation of the California Vehicle Code's
provision against passing another vehicle without maintaining a safe distance, and the second count of the
complaint charged him with failing to comply with the
provisions of the "hit and run" statute, requiring the
driver of a motor vehicle involved in an accident resulting
in damage to any property to stop at the scene and give
his name and address. Both charges arose out of the same
accident, and the defendant's demurrer to the second
count, asserting violation of his privilege against self-
incrimination, was overruled by a California Justice
Court. The defendant then sought a writ of prohibition
from the Superior Court of Mendocino County, California, to restrain prosecution of the second count. The
Superior Court issued the writ, and the Supreme Court
of California ultimately affirmed, holding that the privilege against self-incrimination was applicable to a motorist, such as the defendant, who reasonably believed that
compliance with the statute would result in a substantial

risk of self-incrimination. The California Supreme Court also held that in the case of such a motorist, the hit-and-run statute should be limited by a restriction preventing use in subsequent criminal prosecutions, arising from the motorist's conduct, of information disclosed under the statute, and the fruits of such information, but the court concluded that it would be unfair to punish the defendant for failure to comply with the statute, since he could have had no knowledge that use restrictions would be imposed by the courts (71 Cal 2d 1039, 80 Cal Rptr 553, 458 P2d 465).

On certiorari, the United States Supreme Court vacated the judgment and remanded the case. Five members of the court, although not agreeing upon an opinion, agreed that the California hit-and-run statute did not violate the constitutional privilege against compulsory self-incrimination.

Burger, Ch. J., announced the judgment of the court, and in an opinion joined by **Stewart, White,** and **Blackmun, JJ.,** expressed the views that (1) the privilege against self-incrimination was not infringed by the hit-and-run statute, since a substantial risk of self-incrimination did not result from complying with the statute, which was essentially regulatory, promoting satisfaction of civil liabilities for automobile accidents, rather than criminal, and which was directed at the public at large, rather than at a highly selective group inherently suspect of criminal activities, and (2) even if the statutory reporting requirement was viewed as incriminating in the traditional sense, nevertheless it was not testimonial in the Fifth Amendment sense.

Harlan, J., concurring in the judgment, stated that (1) the presence of a "real" and not "imaginary" risk of self-incrimination was not a sufficient predicate for extending

[Supreme Ct Sum]—17

the privilege against self-incrimination to regulatory schemes, such as the one in the case at bar, for collection of data for purposes essentially unrelated to criminal prosecutions, (2) it was the Supreme Court's task continually to seek that line of accommodation which would render the uncertain mandate of the self-incrimination clause relevant to contemporary conditions, and (3) the purposes of the Fifth Amendment did not warrant imposition of a restriction on the subsequent prosecutorial use of information and its fruits obtained under the hit-and-run statute, in view of the noncriminal governmental purpose in securing the information, the necessity for self-reporting as a means of securing the information, and the nature of the disclosures involved as the minimal requirement essential to the state's nonprosecutorial goal of assuring personal financial responsibility for automobile accidents, the state continuing to have the burden of establishing any criminal aspect of the driving behavior of a motorist who complied with the hit-and-run statute.

Black, J., joined by **Douglas** and **Brennan, JJ.**, dissented, expressing the views that (1) the defendant would have subjected himself to a substantial risk of self-incrimination by complying with the statute, which was directed at a group "suspect" of illegal activities, that is, drivers who were involved in accidents causing property damage, (2) even assuming that the Fifth Amendment prohibited the state only from compelling a man to produce "testimonial" evidence against himself, a man's statement that he was a person involved in an automobile accident inflicting property damage must be considered to be "testimonial," (3) the scope of the privilege against self-incrimination should not be subject to a balancing by the court of the importance of a defendant's right not to be forced to help convict himself against the government's interest in forcing him to do so, and (4) the decision of

[Supreme Ct Sum]

the Supreme Court of California should be affirmed, since it allowed the state to require compliance with the hit-and-run statute, but denied use of the fruits of such compelled testimony in criminal proceedings.

Brennan, J., joined by **Douglas** and **Marshall, JJ.**, dissented, stating that (1) under the facts obtaining in the case at bar, the defendant, confronted with a substantial hazard of self-incrimination, was entitled to rely on the privilege as a defense to prosecution for failure to stop and report his involvement in the accident, and (2) in any event, the hit-and-run statute could properly be enforced only if those reporting their involvement in an accident likely to result in criminal prosecution under California traffic laws were given immunity from prosecution.

COUNSEL

Louise H. Renne, Deputy Attorney General of California, argued the cause for petitioner. With her on the briefs were Thomas C. Lynch, Attorney General, and Albert W. Harris, Jr., Assistant Attorney General.

John W. Poulos, by appointment of the Court, 400 US 813, 27 L Ed 2d 40, 91 S Ct 32, argued the cause and filed a brief for respondent.

VINCENT FRANCIS McGEE, Jr.,
Petitioner,

v

UNITED STATES

402 US 479, 29 L Ed 2d 47, 91 S Ct 1565

Argued February 23, 1971. Decided
May 17, 1971.

Decision: Draft registrant's failure to take administrative
appeal from denial of conscientious objector claim
held to preclude his raising claim in prosecution for
refusing induction.

SUMMARY

One convicted in the United States District Court for
the Southern District of New York of failing to submit
to induction and of other draft law violations appealed
to the United States Court of Appeals for the Second
Circuit on the ground that his I–A classification, and the
rejection of his conscientious objector claim, were unlawful. The Second Circuit affirmed, ruling that this defense
was barred because the accused, when his conscientious
objector claim was denied by his local board, failed to
appear before the local board or to take an administrative
appeal to contest the denial (426 F2d 691).

On certiorari, the United States Supreme Court affirmed. In an opinion by **Marshall, J.,** expressing the
views of eight members of the court, it was held that the
defense was barred because the accused's failure to ex-
haust his administrative remedies denied the Selective
Service System the opportunity to supplement the record
of relevant facts and denied the appeal board an opportunity to exercise its expertise.

Douglas, J., dissented on the ground that the accused was entitled to raise the conscientious objector claim in court because the local board never considered it.

COUNSEL

Alan H. Levine argued the cause for petitioner. With him on the briefs were Marvin M. Karpatkin and Melvin L. Wulf.

William Bradford Reynolds argued the cause for the United States pro hac vice. With him on the brief were Solicitor General Erwin N. Griswold and Assistant Attorney General Wilson.

Marvin B. Haiken filed briefs for Richard Kenneth LeGrande as amicus curiae.

IB OTTO ASTRUP, Petitioner,

v

IMMIGRATION AND NATURALIZATION
SERVICE

402 US 509, 29 L Ed 2d 68, 91 S Ct 1583

Argued April 20, 1971. Decided May 24, 1971.

Decision: Alien who once claimed draft exemption on ground of alienage held not thereby debarred from citizenship when later drafted but found physically unfit.

SUMMARY

An alien lawfully admitted to the United States for permanent residence on February 20, 1950, was called for the draft and passed his preinduction medical examination on October 11, 1950. On November 14, 1950, he requested an exemption from military service on the ground of alienage. Effective June 19, 1951, Congress withdrew such exemptions from permanent resident aliens. The alien was again called for the draft but was found to be physically unfit. Several years later his petition for naturalization was denied by the United States District Court for the Northern District of California on the ground that he was debarred from citizenship, and the United States Court of Appeals for the Ninth Circuit affirmed (432 F2d 438).

On certiorari, the United States Supreme Court reversed. In an opinion by **Black, J.**, expressing the unanimous view of the court, it was held that an alien relieved from military service on his claim of alienage but later reclassified for service which he never performs because of physical unfitness is not barred from citizenship by reason of having once claimed exemption on the ground of alienage.

COUNSEL

Paul N. Halvonik argued the cause for petitioner. With him on the brief was Marshall W. Krause.

Richard B. Stone argued the cause for respondent. With him on the brief were Solicitor General Erwin N. Griswold, Assistant Attorney General Wilson, and Charles Gordon.

GAINESVILLE UTILITIES DEPARTMENT
et al., Petitioners,

v

FLORIDA POWER CORPORATION
(No. 464)

FEDERAL POWER COMMISION,
Petitioner,

v

FLORIDA POWER CORPORATION
(No. 469)

402 US 515, 29 L Ed 2d 74, 91 S Ct 1592

Argued February 24, 1971. Decided
May 24, 1971.

Decision: Federal Power Commission's order for inter-connection of two Florida electric utility companies held supported by record.

SUMMARY

A small Florida electric utility sought an order from the Federal Power Commission to direct a large Florida electric utility to interconnect its transmission facilities with those of the small utility pursuant to § 202(b) of the Federal Power Act, which authorizes the Federal Power Commission, upon finding such action to be in the public interest, to direct interconnection of a utility's transmission facilities with those of another utility, and to prescribe the terms of such arrangement, including the apportionment of cost and the compensation or reimbursement reasonably due to either utility. After hear-

ings, the Commission entered an order requiring the interconnection to be made, directing the small utility to pay
the entire cost of the interconnection and to maintain
specified generating capacity resources, and specifying
rates to be paid by each utility for actual emergency
energy transfers across the interconnection made by the
other utility on an "as available" basis. Rejecting the
large utility's contention that since only the small utility
would benefit from the interconnection, it should be required to pay an annual fee to the large utility for the
emergency backup service provided by the interconnection, the Commission concluded that appropriate analysis
under the statute should focus on responsibilities shared
by the interconnected operations rather than on respective
gains to be realized by the parties, but that in any event,
the large utility would obtain benefits from the interconnection, including increased reliability of service to
certain of its customers, availability of additional reserve
capacity during certain periods, and savings from coordi-
nated planning as to efficient use of generating equip-
ment (40 FPC 1227; 41 FPC 4). However, the United
States Court of Appeals for the Fifth Circuit, in proceedings to review the Commission's order, denied enforcement insofar as no provision was made for reasonable
compensation of the large utility by way of a requirement
that the small utility pay an annual standby fee, the Court
of Appeals concluding that whereas the small utility
would receive high benefits and no real obligations under
the interconnection, the large utility would receive no
benefits and would incur real responsibilities (425 F2d
1196).

On certiorari, the United States Supreme Court reversed and remanded for entry of a judgment enforcing
the Commission's order. In an opinion by **Brennan, J.**,
expressing the unanimous view of the court, it was held
that the Commission's order, denying imposition of an

annual standby fee, was valid, and that the Court of Appeals erred in not deferring to the Commission's expert judgment and in denying enforcement of its order, since substantial evidence supported the Commission's findings as to benefits which would accrue to the large utility from the interconnection, § 313(b) of the Federal Power Act providing that the Commission's finding as to facts shall be conclusive if supported by substantial evidence.

Blackmun, J., did not participate.

COUNSEL

George Spiegel argued the cause for petitioners in No. 464. With him on the briefs was Melvin Richter. Gordon Gooch argued the cause for petitioner in No. 469. With him on the brief were Solicitor General Erwin N. Griswold, Samuel Huntington, Peter H. Schiff, and Leonard D. Eesley.

Richard W. Emory argued the cause for respondent in both cases. With him on the brief were Robert A. Shelton and S. A. Brandimore.

Northcutt Ely filed a brief for the American Public Power Association as amicus curiae urging reversal.

Thomas M. Debevoise filed a brief for the American Electric Power Service Corp. et al. as amici curiae urging affirmance.

UNITED STATES, Petitioner,

v

RAYMOND J. RYAN

402 US 530, 29 L Ed 2d 85, 91 S Ct 1580

Argued April 26, 1971. Decided May 24, 1971.

Decision: Federal District Court order refusing to quash grand jury subpoena duces tecum, and directing attempted compliance with Kenya law requiring official consent for removal of corporate records, held not appealable.

SUMMARY

The respondent was served with a subpoena duces tecum commanding him to produce before a federal grand jury all books, records, and documents of five named companies doing business in Kenya. Claiming that Kenya law forbade the removal of books of account, minute books, and lists of members from the country without consent of the Kenyan Registrar of Companies, the respondent moved to quash the subpoena. Denying the motion to quash, the United States District Court for the Central District of California ordered the respondent to attempt to obtain the necessary consent to remove such documents from Kenya to the United States, and further ordered him, if such consent was not obtained, to make such documents available for inspection in Kenya by agents of the United States government. Holding that the District Court, as a result of its direction to the respondent to make application to the Kenyan official, had in effect granted a mandatory injunction which was appealable under 28 USC § 1292(a)(1), the Court of Appeals for the Ninth Circuit, reaching the merits, reversed on the ground that the order was oppressive and overly broad (430 F2d 658).

On certiorari, the United States Supreme Court reversed. In an opinion by **Brennan, J.**, expressing the unanimous views of the court, it was held that (1) the District Court's order was not appealable, the respondent having the option of refusing to comply with the subpoena, litigating the propriety of the subpoena if contempt or similar proceedings were brought against him, and appealing if his contentions were rejected in such proceedings, and (2) the inclusion in the District Court's order of the provisions as to seeking permission for removal of the records from Kenya, and if permission was denied, making the records available for inspection in Kenya, did not render the order an appealable injunctive order under the provisions of 28 USC § 1292(a)(1), which confers jurisdiction on Courts of Appeals of appeals from interlocutory injunctive orders of District Courts.

COUNSEL

Jerome M. Feit argued the cause for the United States. With him on the briefs were Solicitor General Erwin N. Griswold, Assistant Attorney General Wilson, and Philip R. Monahan.

Herbert J. Miller, Jr., argued the cause for respondent. With him on the brief were Raymond G. Larroca and Nathan Lewin.

PAUL J. BELL, Jr., Petitioner,

v

R. H. BURSON, Director, Georgia Department of Public Safety

402 US 535, 29 L Ed 2d 90, 91 S Ct 1586

Argued March 23, 1971. Decided
May 24, 1971.

Decision: Due process clause of Fourteenth Amendment held violated by Georgia procedure for suspension of license and registration of uninsured motorist who was involved in accident and who did not post security.

SUMMARY

Under Georgia's motor vehicle safety responsibility statute, an uninsured motorist's motor vehicle registration and driver's license are subject to suspension if he is involved in an accident and he fails to post security to cover the amount of damages claimed by aggrieved parties. The petitioner, an uninsured motorist, was involved in an accident when a girl rode her bicycle into the side of his automobile. He did not post security for the damages claimed to have been suffered by the girl. At an administrative hearing, his offer to prove that he was not liable for the accident was rejected, and he was given 30 days to post security or to have his license and registration suspended. The administrative decision was upheld by the Georgia Court of Appeals (121 Ga App 418, 174 SE2d 235), and the Georgia Surpeme Court denied review.

On certiorari, the United States Supreme Court reversed and remanded the case. In an opinion by **Brennan, J.**, expressing the view of six members of the court, it was held that before the state could suspend the petitioner's license and registration, procedural due process required a determination whether there was a reasonable possibility of a judgment being rendered against him as a result of the accident, since liability, in the sense of an ultimate judicial determination of responsibility, played a crucial role under the state's statutory scheme for motor vehicle safety responsibility.

Burger, Ch. J., and Black and Blackmun, JJ., concurred in the result.

COUNSEL

Elizabeth Roediger Rindskopf argued the cause for petitioner pro hac vice. With her on the brief was Howard Moore, Jr.

Dorothy T. Beasley, Assistant Attorney General of Georgia, argued the cause for respondent. With her on the brief were Arthur K. Bolton, Attorney General, Harold N. Hill, Jr., Executive Assistant Attorney General, and Courtney Wilder Stanton, Assistant Attorney General.

JAMES PALMER, Appellant,

v

CITY OF EUCLID, Ohio

402 US 544, 29 L Ed 2d 98, 91 S Ct 1563

Argued January 11, 1971. Decided
May 24, 1971.

Decision: Euclid, Ohio, "suspicious person ordinance"
held unconstitutionally vague as applied to parked
motorist talking on two-way radio late at night.

SUMMARY

An unarmed man who let a female out of his car late
at night in a parking lot in Euclid, Ohio, after which she
entered an adjoining apartment house; who then pulled
onto the street, parked with his lights on, and used a
two-way radio; and who, when arrested, gave three different addresses for himself and denied knowing who the
female was or where she was going, was convicted by a
jury of violating Euclid's "suspicious person ordinance,"
under which it was a crime to be a person who wanders
about the streets or other public ways or who is found
abroad at late or unusual hours in the night without any
visible or lawful business and who does not give a satisfactory account of himself. The County Court of Appeals
affirmed and an appeal to the Supreme Court of Ohio was
dismissed for lack of a substantial constitutional question.

On appeal, the United States Supreme Court reversed.
In a per curiam opinion, expressing the views of six members of the court, it was held that the ordinance was unconstitutionally vague as applied, because it gave insufficient notice to the average person that discharging a
friend at an apartment house and then talking on a two-

way radio while parked in the street was "without visible or lawful business."

Harlan, J., concurred in the result.

Stewart, J., joined by Douglas, J., agreed that the ordinance was unconstitutionally vague as applied but declared that it was also unconstitutionally vague on its face.

COUNSEL

Niki Z. Schwartz argued the cause for appellant. With him on the brief was Joshua J. Kancelbaum.

David J. Lombardo argued the cause for appellee. With on the brief was William T. Monroe.

JAMES HERMAN BOSTIC, Petitioner,

v

UNITED STATES

402 US 547, 29 L Ed 2d 102, 91 S Ct 2174

Argued April 21, 1971. Decided
May 24, 1971.

Decision: Certiorari granted on mistaken representation
dismissed as improvidently granted.

SUMMARY

After granting certiorari to determine whether the
United States Court of Appeals for the Sixth Circuit had
erred in affirming (424 F2d 951) the petitioner's conviction in the United States District Court for the Middle
District of Tennessee of conspiracy to commit murder to
avoid apprehension for the robbery of a federally insured
bank, the United States Supreme Court determined that
the record showed that the petitioner was neither charged
with nor convicted of conspiracy to commit murder, and
it dismissed the writ as improvidently granted.

COUNSEL

Thomas C. Binkley argued the cause for petitioner.
With him on the brief was Philip M. Carden.

Beatrice Rosenberg argued the cause for the United
States. With her on the brief were Solicitor General
Erwin N. Griswold, Assistant Attorney General Wilson,
and Jerome M. Feit.

UNITED STATES, Appellant,

v

GREATER BUFFALO PRESS, Inc., et al.

402 US 549, 29 L Ed 2d 170, 91 S Ct 1692

Argued April 19, 1971. Decided
June 1, 1971.

Decision: Acquisition by company engaged in printing
and sale of color comic supplements for newspapers,
of another company engaged only in printing such
supplements for comic feature syndicate selling to
newspapers, held violative of § 7 of Clayton Act.

SUMMARY

The United States instituted a civil antitrust suit in
the United States District Court for the Western District
of New York, alleging principally that the acquisition by
a company engaged in printing and selling color comic
supplements for newpapers which did not print their
own supplements, of all the stock of a second company
engaged only in printing such supplements for a
comic feature syndicate, which sold to newspapers,
violated the prohibition of § 7 of the Clayton Act
against such an acquisition where the effect thereof
may be substantially to lessen competition in any line of
commerce in any section of the country. After the acquisition was effected, the acquiring company controlled
approximately 75 percent of independent color comic
supplement printing, and the comic feature syndicate became dependent on the acquiring company for most of the
printing of supplements, which the syndicate sold in
competition with the acquiring company. After entry of
a consent decree with regard to the comic feature syndi-

cate's involvement in an alleged conspiracy to restrain the sale to newspapers of the printing of comic supplements, and after a full trial on the Clayton Act charge, the District Court dismissed the complaint, holding that (1) in considering the effects of the acquisition on competition in the comic supplement industry, the significant lines of commerce should be divided into the category of printing of supplements for papers which did not print their own, and the separate category of printing of supplements for syndicates engaged in selling copyrighted features to papers, (2) the acquisition did not result in substantial lessening of competition in the color comic supplement industry in violation of § 7 of the Clayton Act, (3) the acquisition came within the "failing company" exception to § 7, and (4) even if there had been a violation of § 7, an order for divestiture would not be warranted, since 15 years had passed after the acquisition was effected.

On appeal, the United States Supreme Court reversed and remanded. In an opinion by **Douglas, J.**, expressing the unanimous views of the court, it was held that (1) in determining whether the acquisition violated § 7 of the Clayton Act, the significant line of commerce consisted of both the printing and the sale or distribution of color comic supplements, and the "area of effective competition" comprised the business of both the printing companies and the comic feature syndicate, (2) the record established a violation of § 7, (3) the "failing company" exception to § 7 was not applicable, since the acquired company had been actively pursuing expansion plans and continuing to pay dividends to its owners, and it had shown a substantial increase in profits in the year of the sale, and since numerous smaller comic supplement printers, other than the acquiring company, had never been approached as prospective purchasers, (4) the mere passage of time was no barrier to ordering divestiture, and

(5) the nature of the decree to be fashioned should be initially considered by the District Court.

COUNSEL

Deputy Solicitor General Friedman argued the cause for the United States. With him on the brief were Solicitor General Erwin N. Griswold, Assistant Attorney General McLaren, Samuel Huntington, and Elliot H. Feldman.

Frank G. Raichle argued the cause and filed a brief for appellees.

UNITED STATES, Appellant,

v

INTERNATIONAL MINERALS & CHEMICAL
CORP.

402 US 558, 29 L Ed 2d 178, 91 S Ct 1697

Argued April 26, 1971. Decided June 1, 1971.

Decision: Proof of defendant's knowledge of regulation
held not required under federal statute imposing
criminal sanctions for whoever "knowingly" violates
administrative regulation pertaining to transportation of dangerous articles.

SUMMARY

Under 18 USC § 834, the Department of Transportation is granted power to formulate regulations for the safe
transportation of corrosive liquids and other dangerous
articles, and criminal sanctions are provided for whoever
"knowingly violates any such regulation." In a criminal
proceeding in the United States District Court for the
ant with "knowingly" violating the regulation, the District Court dismissed the information. The government
appealed to the Court of Appeals for the Sixth Circuit,
Southern District of Ohio, the information charged the
acid in interstate commerce and with knowingly failing
defendant with shipping sulfuric acid and hydrofluosilicic
quiring that the classification of certain hazardous materials appear on the shipping papers for such materials.
Holding that the information did not charge the defend-
to show on the shipping papers the classification of the
shipment as corrosive liquid, in violation of 49 CFR §
173.427, a Department of Transportation regulation re-

and the Court of Appeals certified the case to the United States Supreme Court.

On certified appeal, the United States Supreme Court reversed. In an opinion by **Douglas, J.**, expressing the views of six members of the court, it was held (1) that although knowledge of the shipment of dangerous materials was required under 18 USC § 834, knowledge of the regulation was not required, § 834 not having been intended as an exception to the general rule that ignorance of the law is no excuse; and (2) that where, as in the present case, dangerous or deleterious devices or products or obnoxious waste materials were involved, the probability of regulation was so great that anyone who was aware that he was in possession of them or dealing with them had to be presumed to be aware of the regulation.

Stewart, J., joined by **Harlan** and **Brennan, JJ.**, dissented on the grounds that the court was effectively deleting the word "knowingly" from § 834 and was totally disregarding plain statutory language, established judicial precedent, and explicit legislative history.

COUNSEL

John F. Dienelt argued the cause for the United States pro hac vice. With him on the briefs were Solicitor General Erwin N. Griswold, Assistant Attorney General Wilson, and Beatrice Rosenberg.

Harold E. Spencer argued the cause for appellee. With him on the brief was Charles J. McCarthy.

CHICAGO AND NORTH WESTERN
RAILWAY COMPANY, Petitioner,

v

UNITED TRANSPORTATION UNION

402 US 570, 29 L Ed 2d 187, 91 S Ct 1731

Argued January 18, 1971. Decided June 1, 1971.

Decision: Railway strike after exhaustion of Railway
Labor Act procedures held enjoinable for union's
failure to make reasonable effort to reach agreement.

SUMMARY

The Chicago and North Western Railway Company
sued the United Transportation Union in the United
States District Court for the Northern District of Illinois,
seeking injunctive relief against the union's threatened
strike, on the ground that the union had failed to perform its obligation under § 2 First of the Railway Labor
Act to exert every reasonable effort to make and maintain agreements concerning rates of pay, rules, and working conditions. The trial court concluded that the question was not justiciable, and that the Norris-LaGuardia
Act deprived it of jurisdiction to enjoin the strike. The
United States Court of Appeals for the Seventh Circuit
affirmed (422 F2d 979).

On certiorari, the United States Supreme Court reversed. In an opinion by **Harlan, J.**, expressing the view
of five members of the court, it was held that (1) § 2 First
is more than a mere statement of policy or exhortation,
but creates a judicially enforceable obligation; (2) the
obligation precludes a union's going through the motions
of complying with the formal procedures of the Act with
a desire not to reach an agreement; and (3) the Norris-

LaGuardia Act does not prevent a federal court from enjoining a railway strike when an injunction is the only practical, effective means of enforcing § 2 First.

Brennan, J., joined by **Black, Douglas,** and **White, JJ.,** dissented on the ground that after the completion of the statutory procedures, a District Court may not enjoin a strike on the ground that the union has violated § 2 First.

COUNSEL

William H. Dempsey, Jr., argued the cause for petitioner.   With him on the briefs were David Booth Beers and Richard M. Freeman.

John H. Haley, Jr., argued the cause for respondent. With him on the brief was John J. Naughton.

J. Albert Woll, Laurence Gold, and Thomas E. Harris filed a brief for the American Federation of Labor and Congress of Industrial Organizations as amicus curiae urging affirmance.

NATIONAL LABOR RELATIONS
BOARD, Petitioner,

v

THE NATURAL GAS UTILITY DISTRICT
OF HAWKINS COUNTY, Tennessee

402 US 600, 29 L Ed 2d 206, 91 S Ct 1746

Argued April 20, 1971. Decided June 1, 1971.

Decision: Tennessee gas utility district held "political subdivision" exempt from Labor-Management Relations Act.

SUMMARY

The National Labor Relations Board ordered a representation election among the pipefitters of a Tennessee natural gas utility district over the district's objection that it was exempt from the Labor-Management Relations Act as a political subdivision of the state (167 NLRB 691). The union won the election and was certified by the NLRB as the pipefitters' collective bargaining representative, but the district refused to bargain with it. The NLRB issued a cease and desist order (170 NLRB No. 156) and sought enforcement in the United States Court of Appeals for the Sixth Circuit. The court refused enforcement, holding that the district was a "political subdivision" (427 F2d 312).

On certiorari, the United States Supreme Court affirmed. In an opinion by **Brennan, J.**, expressing the view of eight members of the court, it was held that the district was a political subdivision because it was administered by a board of commissioners appointed by an elected county judge but subject to removal from office for misfeasance or nonfeasance, had the power of eminent domain, and was a political subdivision under federal income tax and social security laws.

Stewart, J., dissented on the ground that the court should not weigh the facts de novo and displace the NLRB's reasoned decision.

COUNSEL

Dominick L. Manoli argued the cause for petitioner. With him on the brief were Solicitor General Erwin N. Griswold, Peter L. Strauss, Arnold Ordman, and Norton J. Come.

Eugene Greener, Jr., argued the cause and filed a brief for respondent.

Charles F. Wheatley, Jr., and Jerome C. Muys filed a brief for the American Public Gas Association as amicus curiae urging affirmance.

———————————

DENNIS COATES et al., Appellants,

v

CITY OF CINCINNATI

402 US 611, 29 L Ed 2d 214, 91 S Ct 1686

Argued January 11, 1971. Decided
June 1, 1971.

Decision: Cincinnati ordinance punishing sidewalk assemblies "annoying" to passerby held unconstitutional on its face.

SUMMARY

A student demonstrator and four labor pickets were convicted in the Hamilton County Municipal Court, Ohio, of violating a Cincinnati ordinance making it a criminal offense for three or more persons to assemble on a sidewalk "and there conduct themselves in a manner annoying to persons passing by." The Hamilton County Court of Appeals affirmed, and the Supreme Court of Ohio affirmed (21 Ohio St 2d 66, 50 Ohio Ops 2d 161, 255 NE2d 247).

On appeal, the United States Supreme Court reversed. In an opinion by **Stewart, J.**, expressing the view of five members of the court, it was held that the ordinance was unconstitutional on its face as violating both the due process standard of vagueness and the right of free assembly and association.

Black, J., filed a separate opinion stating that he would vacate the judgment and remand the case so that the record could be supplemented to show the conduct actually punished.

White, J., joined by **Burger, Ch. J.**, and **Blackmun, J.**, dissented on the ground that the ordinance was not unconstitutionally vague on its face, and in the state of the record, the court could not judge the ordinance as applied.

COUNSEL

Robert R. Lavercombe argued the cause and filed a brief for appellants.

A. David Nichols argued the cause for appellee. With him on the brief was William A. McClain.

LOUIS S. NELSON, Warden, Petitioner,

v

JOE J. B. O'NEIL

402 US 622, 29 L Ed 2d 222, 91 S Ct 1723

Argued March 24, 1971. Decided June 1, 1971.

Decision: Admission in state prosecution of codefendant's alleged out-of-court statement implicating other defendant at joint trial held not violative of other defendant's Sixth and Fourteenth Amendment rights where codefendant takes stand, denies making statement, is available for cross-examination, and testifies favorably as to other defendants.

SUMMARY

At their joint trial in a California state court on charges of kidnapping, robbery, and vehicle theft, a police officer testified that after the arrest of the respondent and his codefendant, the codefendant had made an unsworn oral statement admitting the crimes and implicating the respondent as his confederate. The trial judge ruled the officer's testimony admissible against the codefendant, but instructed the jury that they could not consider it against the respondent. On direct examination, the codefendant denied having made the statement, asserted that the substance of the statement was false, and stuck to his story in every particular even though he was intensively cross-examined by the prosecutor. The respondent's counsel chose not to cross-examine the codefendant. After the jury convicted both defendants, unsuccessful efforts were made to set aside the conviction in the California courts. During the pendency of a habeas corpus petition in the United States District Court for the Northern District of California, the United States Supreme Court decided Bruton v United States (1968) 391 US 123, 20 L Ed 2d 476, 88 S Ct 1620, holding that under certain circumstances the confrontation clause of the Sixth Amendment was violated when a codefendant's confession implicating another defendant was placed before the jury at their joint trial, and Roberts v Russell (1968) 392 US 293, 20 L Ed 2d 1100, 88 S Ct 1921, making the rule expressed in the Bruton case retroactive without limitation. On the basis of those two cases, the District Court ruled that the respondent's conviction must be set aside, and the Court of Appeals for the Ninth Circuit affirmed (422 F2d 319).

On certiorari, the United States Supreme Court reversed and remanded. In an opinion by **Stewart, J.**, expressing the views of six members of the court, it was held that (1) unlike the Bruton case, wherein the confessing codefendant did not take the witness stand and was not subject to cross-examination by the other defendant who was inculpated in the confessor's statement, where a codefendant takes the stand in his own defense, denies making an alleged out-of-court statement implicating the other defendant in a joint trial, and proceeds to give testimony favorable to the latter concerning the underlying facts, then the other defendant has been denied no rights protected by the Sixth and Fourteenth Amendments, and (2) the respondent was not denied either the opportunity or the benefit of full and effective cross-examination of the codefendant.

Harlan, J., while joining in the opinion and judgment of the court, stated that because respondent's conviction became final before the decision in the Bruton case, he should not have been allowed to avail himself of that new rule in subsequent federal habeas corpus proceedings.

Brennan, J., joined by **Douglas** and **Marshall, JJ.**, dissented on the ground that the state, having made the judgment that although the codefendant took the stand, his extrajudicial statements could not be considered by the jury as evidence against the respondent, could not subvert its own judgment by presenting the inadmissible evidence to the jury and then telling the jury to disregard it, since the inevitable result of such a procedure would be the application of different rules of evidence to different defendants, depending solely upon whether they were jointly or separately tried.

Marshall, J., further dissented, noting that the case illustrated the need for the adoption of new rules regulating the use of joint trials.

COUNSEL

Charles R. B. Kirk, Deputy Attorney General of California, argued the cause for petitioner. With him on the brief were Evelle J. Younger, Attorney General, Albert W. Harris, Jr., Assistant Attorney General, and John T. Murphy, Deputy Attorney General.

James S. Campbell, by appointment of the Court, 400 US 955, 27 L Ed 2d 264, 91 S Ct 352, argued the cause and filed a brief for respondent.

ADOLFO PEREZ et ux., Petitioners,

v

DAVID H. CAMPBELL, Superintendent, Motor
Vehicle Division, Arizona Highway
Department, et al.

402 US 637, 29 L Ed 2d 233, 91 S Ct 1704

Argued January 19, 1971. Decided
June 1, 1971.

Decision: Suspension of bankrupt motorist's license because of failure to satisfy automobile accident judgment held unconstitutional as conflicting with Bankruptcy Act.

SUMMARY

After an uninsured motorist was involved in an accident
while driving an automobile registered in his own name,
he and his wife were sued in an Arizona state court for
personal injuries and property damage sustained in the
accident. The husband and wife confessed judgment, and
a judgment for over $2,400 was entered against them.
The husband and wife filed petitions in bankruptcy and
listed this judgment among their debts, and the bankruptcy court discharged the husband and wife from all of
their debts, including this judgment. Under § 28-1163
(B) of Arizona's motor vehicle safety responsibility statute, the fact that a judgment against a motorist remained
unsatisfied for 60 days was a ground for suspending the
motorist's license and registration, even if the motorist
received a discharge in bankruptcy following the rendering of such judgment. Pursuant to these statutory provisions, the husband's registration and the husband's and
wife's licenses were suspended. The husband and wife
then sought declaratory and injunctive relief in the Unit-

ed States District Court for the District of Arizona, contending that § 28–1163(B) was in conflict with the Bankruptcy Act and was thus violative of the supremacy clause of the Federal Constitution. In support of their complaint, the husband and wife filed affidavits stating that the suspension of the registration and licenses worked both physical and financial hardship upon them and their children. Relying upon Kesler v Department of Public Safety (1962) 369 US 153, 7 L Ed 2d 641, 82 S Ct 807, and Reitz v Mealey (1941) 314 US 33, 86 L Ed 21, 62 S Ct 24, the District Court rejected the contention that § 28–1163(B) was in conflict with the Bankruptcy Act, and dismissed the complaint. Relying on the same two decisions, the Court of Appeals for the Ninth Circuit affirmed (421 F2d 619).

On certiorari, the United States Supreme Court reversed and remanded the case. In an opinion by **White, J.**, expressing the views of five members of the court, the Kesler and Reitz Cases were overruled in part and distinguished in part, and it was held that § 28–1163(B) had the effect and purpose of frustrating federal law under the Bankruptcy Act and was thus invalid under the supremacy clause.

Blackmun, J., joined by **Burger, Ch. J.**, **Harlan, J.**, and **Stewart, J.**, concurred in the result as to the wife on the ground that the suspension of her license interfered with the paramount federal interest in her bankruptcy discharge and violated the supremacy clause, but dissented as to the husband on the ground that § 28–1163(B), despite its tangential effect upon bankruptcy, did not operate in derogation of the Bankruptcy Act or conflict with it to the extent that it could rightly be said to violate the supremacy clause.

COUNSEL

Anthony B. Ching argued the cause and filed a brief for petitioners.

Robert H. Schlosser argued the cause for respondents. With him on the brief was Gary K. Nelson, Attorney General of Arizona.

Briefs of amici curiae were filed by David A. Binder, Raine Eisler, and Paul L. McKaskle for the Western Center on Law and Poverty et al., and by William D. Browning for the National Organization for Women.

UNITED STATES, Appellant,

v

ARMOUR & CO. and Greyhound Corporation

402 US 673, 29 L Ed 2d 256, 91 S Ct 1752

Argued April 19, 1971. Decided
June 1, 1971.

Decision: 1920 consent decree in antitrust action forbidding meatpackers from engaging in retail food business held not to preclude company engaged in such business from acquiring controlling interest in meatpacking company.

SUMMARY

The United States sought a determination by the United States District Court for the Northern District of Illinois that a regulated motor carrier company, which through subsidiary companies was also engaged in the retail food business, had violated the provisions of a 1920 consent decree entered by a Federal District Court in an antitrust action, by acquiring the majority of the stock of a meatpacking company covered by the 1920 decree. The consent decree, which was entered in the government's antitrust action against the nation's largest meatpackers and their stockholders, expressly prohibited the corporate defendants from directly or indirectly engaging in, or owning any stock or interest in any firm dealing in, the retail food business, and expressly prohibited the individual defendants from acquiring a half interest or more in a retail food firm. The consent decree did not, however, expressly prohibit a meatpacker from selling an interest to a retail food firm. The government asserted that the challenged acquisition of the meatpacking company's stock circumvented the consent decree's purported purpose of separating the meatpackers from the retail food business and resulted in the same kind of anticompetitive evils sought to be prevented by the 1920 suit. The District Court held that the 1920 consent decree did not prohibit the challenged acquisition.

On appeal, the United States Supreme Court affirmed. In an opinion by **Marshall, J.**, expressing the view of four of the seven participating members of the court, it was held that the challenged acquisition of a majority of the meatpacker's stock did not, in itself and without any evidentiary showing as to the consequences, violate the consent decree, which, construed in its natural sense, barred only active conduct by the meatpacker with regard to engaging in the retail food business, and did not preclude all ownership or economic relationships with retail food firms, the case involving only the construction of the consent decree, since the government had not sought modification thereof for additional relief.

Douglas, J., joined by **Brennan** and **White, JJ.**, dissented on the ground that the 1920 consent decree, which was designed to rectify the evils of combining of meatpackers with companies in other food product areas, should be read as prohibiting any combination of a meatpacking company with companies dealing in various food lines.

Black and **Blackmun, JJ.**, did not participate.

COUNSEL

Deputy Solicitor General Springer argued the cause for the United States. With him on the brief were Solicitor General Erwin N. Griswold, Deputy Assistant Attorney General Comegys, and Howard E. Shapiro.

Edward L. Foote argued the cause for appellee Greyhound Corp. With him on the brief was Robert J. Bernard.

———————

PEGGY J. CONNOR et al.

v

PAUL B. JOHNSON et al.

402 US 690, 29 L Ed 2d 268, 91 S Ct 1760
June 3, 1971.

Decision: Three-judge District Court decree creating large multimember state legislative district stayed with instructions to devise single-district apportionment plan.

SUMMARY

A three-judge United States District Court for the Southern District of Mississippi, having invalidated a Mississippi legislative reapportionment statute, issued its own reapportionment plan constituting Hinds County, Mississippi, as a multimember district.

On application for stay pending direct appeal, the United States Supreme Court stayed the District Court's decree for 11 days with instructions to devise and put into effect a single-member district plan for Hinds County by that date, absent insurmountable difficulties. In a per curiam opinion expressing the views of six members of the court, it was held that single-member districts are preferable and that, given the census information apparently available and the dispatch with which the appellants devised suggested apportionment plans, the District Court could have devised single-member districts for Hinds County in the 17 days then available, and could devise and put into effect such a plan in an 11-day period.

Black, J., joined by **Burger**, Ch. J., and **Harlan, J.**, dissented on the ground that the time was insufficient to fairly administer the election process.

A. T. GORDON et al., Petitioners,

v

GRANVILLE H. LANCE et al.

403 US 1, 29 L Ed 2d 273, 91 S Ct 1889

Argued January 18, 1971. Decided
June 7, 1971.

Decision: West Virginia constitutional and statutory provisions requiring 60-percent vote before political subdivisions can issue bonds or raise tax rates held valid.

SUMMARY

West Virginia constitutional and statutory provisions that the state's political subdivisions can neither incur bonded indebtedness nor increase tax rates except by approval of 60 percent of the voters in a referendum election were challenged in declaratory judgment actions in the Circuit Court of Roane County, West Virginia, which dismissed the complaints. The Supreme Court of Appeals of West Virginia reversed, holding that, by diluting the votes of proponents of such revenue measures, the provisions violated the one-man, one-vote rule of the equal protection clause of the Fourteenth Amendment (— W Va —, 170 SE2d 783).

On certiorari, the United States Supreme Court reversed. In an opinion by **Burger**, Ch. J., expressing the views of six members of the court, it was held that a state's requiring more than a simple majority on tax and revenue measures is constitutional as long as it does not discriminate against any identifiable class.

Harlan, J., concurred in the result, on the ground that the federal courts cannot restructure state electoral processes.

Brennan and **Marshall, JJ.,** stated that they would affirm for the reasons expressed by the West Virginia Court of Appeals.

COUNSEL

George M. Scott argued the cause and filed briefs for petitioners.

Charles C. Wise, Jr., argued the cause for respondents. With him on the brief was J. Henry Francis, Jr.

Briefs of amici curiae urging reversal were filed by Slade Gorton, Attorney General of Washington, and Philip H. Austin, Assistant Attorney General, for the State of Washington et al.; by Thomas M. O'Connor for the City and County of San Francisco; by Francis R. Kirkham and Francis N. Marshall for the California Taxpayers' Association; and by George E. Svoboda for Hayes Smith.

Briefs of amici curiae urging affirmance were filed by James R. Ellis for Seattle School District No. 1; by Stephen J. Pollak, William H. Dempsey, Jr., Ralph J. Moore, Jr., and Robert H. Chanin for the National Education Association et al.; by August W. Steinhilber and Robert G. Dixon, Jr., for the National School Boards Association; by David R. Hardy and Robert E. Northup for the Missouri State Teachers Association; by William B. Beebe, Hershel Shanks, and Allan I. Mendelsohn for the American Association of School Administrators et al.; by Melvin L. Wulf for the American Civil Liberties Union et al.; and by Paul W. Preisler for the Committee for the Equal Weighting of Votes.

Briefs of amici curiae were filed by John W. Witt and Joseph Kase, Jr., for the City of San Diego et al., and by Chas. Claflin Allen, pro se.

STATE OF UTAH, Plaintiff,

v

UNITED STATES

403 US 9, 29 L Ed 2d 279, 91 S Ct 1775

Argued April 26, 1971. Decided
June 7, 1971.

Decision: Ownership of shorelands around Great Salt
Lake held to be in state of Utah rather than United
States.

SUMMARY

The state of Utah instituted original proceedings in the
United States Supreme Court to resolve conflicting claims
between it and the United States with regard to ownership of shorelands around the Great Salt Lake. Utah's
claim was premised on the navigability of the lake on
January 4, 1896, the date of Utah's statehood. A Special
Master, appointed by the court, presented a report finding that the lake was navigable at such date, based on
evidence showing that numerous boats had been used on
the lake, particularly during the 1880s, and that the lake
was still physically capable of being used for navigation
in 1896. The Master also submitted a proposed decree
enjoining the United States from asserting against Utah
any claim of right, title, and interest with regard to the
lands involved.

The United States Supreme Court approved the
Master's finding, and invited the parties to address themselves to the Master's proposed decree for possible agreement upon the issues settled. In an opinion by **Douglas,**
J., expressing the unanimous view of the court, it was held
that (1) the test of navigability of watercourses was wheth-

er they were navigable in fact, (2) watercourses were navigable in fact when they were used, or were susceptible of being used, in their ordinary conditions, as highways for commerce, over which trade and travel were or might be conducted in the customary modes of trade and travel on water, and (3) the Special Master's finding that the Great Salt Lake was navigable in 1896 was sustained by sufficient evidence, entitling Utah to the decree sought by it.

Marshall, J., did not participate.

COUNSEL

Dallin W. Jensen, Assistant Attorney General of Utah, argued for plaintiff in support of the Report of the Special Master. With him on the briefs were Vernon B. Romney, Attorney General, Robert B. Hansen, Deputy Attorney General, Paul E. Reimann, Assistant Attorney General, and Clifford L. Ashton and Edward W. Clyde, Special Assistant Attorneys General.

Peter L. Strauss argued for the United States on exceptions to the Report of the Special Master. On the brief were Solicitor General Erwin N. Griswold, Assistant Attorney General Kashiwa, Louis F. Claiborne, and Martin Green.

PAUL ROBERT COHEN, Appellant,

v

CALIFORNIA

403 US 15, 29 L Ed 2d 284, 91 S Ct 1780

Argued February 22, 1971. Decided June 7, 1971.

Decision: Conviction for disturbing peace by wearing jacket bearing words "Fuck the Draft" held violative of First and Fourteenth Amendments

SUMMARY

The defendant, while in the corridor of a county courthouse, was wearing a jacket bearing the plainly visible words "Fuck the Draft." On the basis of his having done this, he was convicted by a California municipal court for disturbing the peace by offensive conduct. The California Court of Appeal, Second Appellate District, affirmed the conviction and rejected the defendant's contention that the conviction violated his federal constitutional right of free speech (1 Cal App 3d 94, 81 Cal Rptr 503), and the California Supreme Court declined review.

On appeal, the United States Supreme Court reversed. In an opinion by **Harlan, J.,** expressing the views of five members of the court, it was held (1) that the conviction rested solely upon speech; (2) that the defendant's vulgar allusion to the Selective Service System did not constitute obscene expression; (3) that the words used by the defendant did not fall within the constitutional principle authorizing the state to proscribe the use of "fighting words"; (4) that California could not excise, as offensive conduct, one particular scurrilous epithet from the public discourse, either upon the theory that its use was inherently likely to cause violent reaction or upon a more general assertion that the states, acting as guardians of public morality, could properly remove this offensive word from the public vocabulary; and (5) that absent a more particularized and compelling reason for its actions, the state could not, consistently with the First and Fourteenth Amendments, make the defendant's simple public display of this single four-letter expletive a criminal offense.

Blackmun, joined by **Burger,** Ch. J., and **Black,** J., dissented, expressing (in Paragraph 1) disagreement with holdings (1) and (3) above, and stating (in Paragraph 2) that the case should be remanded for reconsideration in the light of a California Supreme Court decision rendered subsequently to the state court decisions in the present case.

White, J., concurred in Paragraph 2 of the dissenting opinion by **Blackmun,** J.

COUNSEL

Melville B. Nimmer argued the cause for appellant. With him on the brief was Laurence R. Sperber.

Michael T. Sauer argued the cause for appellee. With him on the brief was Roger Arnebergh.

Anthony G. Amsterdam filed a brief for the American Civil Liberties Union of Northern California as amicus curiae urging reversal.

GEORGE A. ROSENBLOOM, Petitioner,

v

METROMEDIA, Inc.

403 US 29, 29 L Ed 2d 296, 91 S Ct 1811

Argued December 7 and 8, 1970. Decided
June 7, 1971.

Decision: Recovery in diversity libel action based on
radio news reports referring to private person's arrest for possession of "obscene" materials, and to
subsequent suit by "girlie book peddlers" to protect
"the smut literature racket," held precluded under
constitutional guaranties of free speech and press,
absent showing of knowing or reckless falsity.

SUMMARY

A distributor of nudist magazines in the Philadelphia
area instituted a diversity libel action in the United States
District Court for the Eastern District of Pennsylvania
against a local radio station, based on the first two broadcasts in a series of eight broadcasts, which two broadcasts,
in referring to the distributor's arrest by the police for possession of obscene literature, failed at one point to describe the seized books as "allegedly" or "reportedly"
obscene, such omission having been corrected in the
subsequent broadcasts in the series. The action was
also based on a second, later series of 13 broadcasts which,
without mentioning the distributor's name, referred to
a pending court action for injunctive relief against local
officials and certain local news media, in which action
the distributor was one of the plaintiffs, as an action
by "smut distributors" or "girlie book peddlers" seeking
to force the defendants to "lay off the smut literature

racket." After the broadcasts involved, and before institution of the libel action, the distributor was acquitted of state obscenity charges on a finding that the books involved were not obscene as a matter of law. The District Court in the libel action held that the constitutional standard, required by the First Amendment, whereby recovery of damages for certain defamatory falsehoods was prohibited unless it was proved that the falsehood was uttered with knowledge that it was false or with reckless disregard of whether it was false or not, was inapplicable since the plaintiff was not a "public official" or a "public figure," and instructed the jury in accordance with Pennsylvania libel law, which imposed liability on news media for publishing falsehoods if reasonable care was not used in ascertaining the truth of reports. The jury returned a verdict for the plaintiff, awarding general and punitive damages, and the District Court reduced the punitive damages on remittitur (289 F Supp 737). The Court of Appeals for the Third Circuit reversed, holding that the constitutional standard applied, and that the evidence was insufficient to support a verdict for the plaintiff under such standard (415 F2d 892).

On certiorari, the United States Supreme Court affirmed. Although not agreeing on an opinion, five members of the court agreed that under the restrictions upon state libel laws imposed by the constitutional guaranties of freedom of speech and of the press, the plaintiff could not recover in the case at bar.

Brennan, J., announced the judgment of the court, and in an opinion in which **Burger, Ch. J.,** and **Blackmun, J.,** joined, expressed the views that (1) the constitutional standard of knowing or reckless falsity applied whenever the allegedly defamatory statements related to the plaintiff's involvement in a matter of public or general concern, such as in the case at bar, regardless of whether the plaintiff was a "public official," a "public figure," or a "private individual," and (2) the evidence in the case at bar was insufficient to sustain an award for the plaintiff under such constitutional standard.

Black, J., concurred in the judgment on the ground that the First Amendment did not permit the recovery of libel judgments against the news media even when statements were broadcast with knowledge that they were false.

White, J., concurring in the judgment, expressed the view that absent the requisite showing of knowing or reckless falsity under the constitutional standard, the press and the broadcast media had a privilege under the First Amendment to report and comment upon official actions of public servants in full detail, with no requirement that the reputation or the privacy of an individual involved in or affected by the official action be spared from public view, which was all that was done by the defendant in the case at bar.

Harlan, J., dissenting, stated that (1) although the constitutional protection of free speech and free press prohibited the imposition of liability without fault in defamation cases, nevertheless the state should be free to impose a duty of reasonable care in defamation cases involving a private plaintiff, (2) in such cases, the plaintiff should be compensated only for actual, measurable harm which was reasonably foreseeable as a result of the publication, (3) punitive damages could be awarded if actual malice was proved, so long as they bore a reasonable and purposeful relationship to the actual harm done, and (4) the instant case should be remanded for adjudication under such principles.

Marshall, J., joined by **Stewart, J.,** dissented, expressing the view that in libel actions brought by private individuals, damages should be restricted to actual losses, with the states being left free to articulate whatever fault standard best suited the state's need, as long as absolute or strict liability was not used.

Douglas, J., did not participate.

COUNSEL

Ramsey Clark argued the cause for petitioner.   With him on the brief was Benjamin Paul.

Bernard G. Segal argued the cause for respondent. With him on the brief were Irving R. Segal, Samuel D. Slade, and Carleton G. Eldridge, Jr.

EUGENE GRIFFIN et al., Petitioners,

v

LAVON BRECKENRIDGE et al.

403 US 88, 29 L Ed 2d 338, 91 S Ct 1790

Argued January 13 and 14, 1971. Decided
June 7, 1971.

Decision: Federal civil rights statute (42 USC § 1985
(3)) authorizing recovery of damages for conspiracy
held constitutional as applied to assault of Negroes
by private white persons.

SUMMARY

Some Negroes brought an action in the United States
District Court for the Southern District of Mississippi,
seeking to recover damages from some white persons who
allegedly had conspired to deprive the plaintiffs of their
civil rights, and in furtherance of this conspiracy, had
stopped the plaintiffs' automobile on a public highway
and had detained, assaulted, beaten, and injured them.
The action was based on 42 USC § 1985(3), which
authorizes the recovery of damages where two or more
persons conspire or go in disguise on the highway or on
the premises of another for the purpose of depriving any
person or class of persons of the equal protection of the
laws or of equal privileges and immunities under the
laws. The District Court dismissed the complaint, relying upon Collins v Hardyman (1950) 341 US 651,
95 L Ed 1253, 71 S Ct 937, as a basis for holding that
§ 1985(3) applied only to conspiracies involving state
action. The Court of Appeals for the Fifth Circuit affirmed on the same grounds (410 F2d 817).

On certiorari, the United States Supreme Court re-

versed and remanded the case.   In an opinion by **Stewart,
J.**, it was held, expressing the unanimous view of the court,
that the decision in Collins v Hardyman was confined to
its own facts, that § 1985(3) was intended to reach private action, that the allegations of the plaintiffs' complaint stated a cause of action under § 1985(3), and that
the constitutionality of § 1985(3), as applied to the
present case, could be upheld on the basis of Congress'
powers under § 2 of the Thirteenth Amendment; and
it was held, expressing the view of eight members of the
court, that the constitutionality of § 1985(3) could also
be upheld on the basis of Congress' power to protect the
right of interstate travel.

Harlan, J., concurring, agreed with the court's opinion
except for the court's reliance on the right of interstate
travel.

COUNSEL

Stephen J. Pollak argued the cause for petitioners.
With him on the brief were Gary J. Greenberg and John
A. Bleveans.

W. D. Moore, by appointment of the Court, 400 US
1006, 27 L Ed 2d 620, 91 S Ct 562, argued the cause
for respondents.   With him on the brief was Helen J.
McDade.

Lawrence G. Wallace argued the cause for the United
States as amicus curiae urging reversal.   On the brief
were Solicitor General Erwin N. Griswold and Louis F.
Claiborne.

HERBERT L. ELY, Individually and as Chairman
of the Democratic Party of Arizona, Appellant,

v

GARY PETER KLAHR et al.

403 US 108, 29 L Ed 2d 552, 91 S Ct 1803

Argued March 23, 1971. Decided June 7, 1971.

Decision: Arizona Legislature held properly allowed
until November 1, 1971, to enact valid apportionment plan.

SUMMARY

On May 19, 1970, a three-judge United States District Court for the District of Arizona ordered that the
1970 Arizona legislative elections be conducted under the
Legislature's apportionment plan which the court found
to be invalid, on the stated assumption that the Arizona
Legislature would enact a valid apportionment plan by
November 1, 1971, failing which any party to the action
might apply to the court for appropriate relief (313 F
Supp 148).

On appeal, the United States Supreme Court affirmed.
In an opinion by **White, J.**, expressing the view of six
members of the court, it was held that, considering that
the 1970 elections had been held and that 1970 census
figures would be forthcoming in the summer of 1971, the
court properly allowed the Legislature until November
1 to adopt a valid apportionment statute, although the
court should make very sure that the 1972 elections are
held under a constitutionally adequate apportionment
plan.

Harlan, J., concurred in the result on the ground that
the federal courts cannot restructure state electoral
processes.

Douglas, J., joined by **Black, J.**, concurred while warning that the judicial machinery must be put into motion soon to assure that the 1972 elections are held under a valid apportionment plan.

COUNSEL

Philip J. Shea argued the cause and filed a brief for appellant.

John M. McGowan II, Special Assistant Attorney General of Arizona, argued the cause for appellees. With him on the brief was Gary K. Nelson, Attorney General.

EDGAR D. WHITCOMB, Governor of the State
of Indiana, Appellant,

v

PATRICK CHAVIS et al.

403 US 124, 29 L Ed 2d 563, 91 S Ct 1858

Argued December 8, 1970. Decided June 7, 1971.

Decision: Countywide legislative district for at-large
election of several state legislators held constitutional
althought disproportionately small number of legislators resided in ghetto.

SUMMARY

In a suit in a 3-judge United States District Court
for the Southern District of Indiana, attacking Indiana's
state legislative apportionment insofar as it created a
single district of Marion County for the at-large election
of eight state senators and 15 state assemblymen, the
court, after withholding judgment for 2 months to allow
the state legislature to correct the malapportionment according to the principles enumerated by the court, (1)
redistricted Marion County into single-member districts
on the ground that the multimember Marion County
district illegally minimized and canceled out the voting
power of the cognizable racial minority in the Marion
County ghetto, as evidenced by fewer legislators' having
resided in the ghetto than the ghetto's proportion of the
County population; and (2) redistricted the entire state
into single-member districts on the ground that the state
was malapportioned by population-per-senator variations
of 80,496 to 106,790 and population-per-assemblyman
variations of 41,449 to 53,003 (307 F Supp 1362).

On appeal, the United States Supreme Court reversed.

White, J., announced the court's judgment, and in Parts I-VI of his opinion, expressing the view of five members of the court, held that evidence of the ghetto's having fewer resident legislators than its proportion of the county population did not prove invidious discrimination against ghetto residents. In Part VII of his opinion, White, J., joined by Burger, Ch. J., Black and Blackmun, JJ., held that the District Court properly ordered state-wide reapportionment. Douglas, J., joined by Brennan and Marshall, JJ., while dissenting from the court's judgment, were in accord with the views expressed in Part VII of the opinion of White, J.

Stewart, J., dissented from Part VII of the court's opinion on the ground that a state legislative apportionment scheme is constitutional if it is rational in the light of the state's own characteristics and needs, and not such as to permit the systematic frustration of the majority's will.

Harlan, J., filed a separate opinion declaring that he would reverse and remand with directions to dismiss the complaint on the ground that the federal courts cannot restructure state electoral processes.

Douglas, J., joined by Brennan and Marshall, JJ., dissented on the grounds that multimember legislative districts are unconstitutional where there are invidious effects, and that invidious effects had been proved in this case.

COUNSEL

William F. Thompson, Assistant Attorney General of Indiana, argued the cause for appellant. With him on the briefs were Theodore L. Sendak, Attorney General, and Richard C. Johnson, Chief Deputy Attorney General.

James Manahan argued the cause for appellees. With him on the brief were James Beatty and John Banzhaf III.

William J. Scott, Attorney General, and Francis C. Crowe and Herman Tavins, Assistant Attorneys General, filed a brief for the State of Illinois as amicus curiae urging reversal, joined by the following Attorneys General: MacDonald Gallion of Alabama, G. Kent Edwards of Alaska, Gary K. Nelson of Arizona, Duke W. Dunbar of Colorado, Richard C. Turner of Iowa, A. F. Summer of Mississippi, Robert L. Woodahl of Montana, Gordon Mydland of South Dakota, Crawford C. Martin of Texas, Vernon B. Romney of Utah, and Chauncey H. Browning of West Virginia.

Charles Morgan, Jr., Reber F. Boult, Jr., David J. Vann, and Melvin L. Wulf filed a brief for the ACLU Foundation, Inc., et al. as amici curiae urging affirmance.

SAMUEL J. ABATE, etc., et al., Petitioners,

v

PAUL F. MUNDT

403 US 182, 29 L Ed 2d 399, 91 S Ct 1904

Argued November 19, 1971.   Decided June 7, 1971

Decision: County legislative districting following town
lines held constitutional, in view of longstanding
town-county co-operation, notwithstanding 11.9-
percent deviation from voting equality.

SUMMARY

In a suit brought in the New York Supreme Court,
Rockland County, to compel the Rockland County Board
of Supervisors to reapportion in accordance with constitutional requirements, the court approved a plan creating
a county legislature with districts corresponding to the
county's five towns, one legislator being assigned to the
smallest town and the number of legislators for each other
town being the number of times its population exceeded
that of the smallest town.   Rounding off fractions to the
nearest integer caused variations of 11,577 population-
per-legislator in one town to 13,020 population-per-
legislator in another town, with consequent 4.8 percent
overrepresentation of one town and 7.1 percent under-
representation of another, for a total voting inequality of
11.9 percent.   The Appellate Division affirmed (— App
Div 2d —, 305 NYS2d 102), and the Court of Appeals
affirmed (25 NY2d 309, 253 NE2d 189).

On certiorari, the United States Supreme Court affirmed.   In an opinion by **Marshall, J.,** expressing the
view of five members of the court, it was held that the
population variations were constitutionally permissible in

light of the absence of a built-in bias tending to favor any particular area or interest and the longstanding local governmental structure in which the towns and the county worked in close co-operation to provide overlapping public services.

Harlan, J., concurred in the result on the ground that federal courts cannot restructure state electoral processes.

Stewart, J., concurred in the judgment.

Brennan, J., joined by **Douglas, J.,** dissented on the ground that town lines could not be used to establish county legislative districts where the result was an 11.9-percent deviation from voting equality.

COUNSEL

Frank P. Barone argued the cause and filed a brief for petitioner Abate. Doris Friedman Ulman argued the cause and filed a brief for petitioners Molof et al. Paul H. Rivet argued the cause and filed a brief for petitioners O'Sullivan et al.

J. Martin Cornell argued the cause for respondents. With him on the brief was Arthur J. Prindle.

Louis J. Lefkowitz, Attorney General, Ruth Kessler Toch, Solicitor General Erwin N. Griswold, and Robert W. Imrie, Assistant Attorney General, filed a brief for the State of New York as amicus curiae.

UNITED STATES et al., Petitioners,

v

ANNE GOYNE MITCHELL et al.

403 US 190, 29 L Ed 2d 406, 91 S Ct 1763

Argued April 20, 1971.   Decided June 7, 1971.

Decision: Wife held liable for federal income tax on half of community income despite her subsequent exercise of Louisiana statutory right to renounce community.

SUMMARY

The present case involved an attempt by the United States to reach certain property as a means of enforcing federal income tax liability with respect to each of two women, whose marital domicil had been in Louisiana, a community property state. During each woman's marriage, there had been certain years in which the women and their husbands had failed to file any federal income tax returns. One of the women subsequently was divorced, and she formally renounced her community property rights, pursuant to Article 2410 of the Louisiana Civil Code, which granted a wife the privilege of being able to exonerate herself from the debts contracted during the marriage by renouncing the community of gains; the other woman's husband subsequently died, and she did not accept any benefits of the community. With respect to each woman, the United States sought to impose federal income tax liability allocable to half of the community income for the years in which no tax returns had been filed. With respect to the divorced woman, the Tax Court held that under Louisiana community property law, the woman had possessed an immediate vested ownership interest in half the community property and was personally liable for the tax on her share, and that this tax liability was not affected by her Article 2410 renunciation (51 T Ct 641). Similarly, with respect to the woman whose husband had died, the United States District Court for the Eastern District of Louisiana upheld the government's right to impose tax liability on the woman for her share of the community income. As to each woman, however, the Court of Appeals for the Fifth Circuit reversed the judgment below and held that a woman, by renouncing the community or by failing to accept any benefits of the community, avoided any federal income tax liability on the community income (430 F2d 1; 430 F2d 7).

On certiorari, the United States Supreme Court reversed. In an opinion by **Blackmun, J.**, expressing the unanimous view of the court, it was held (1) that since federal income tax liability depended on ownership, and since a wife, under Louisiana law, had an immediate vested ownership interest in half of the community income, the wife was personally liable for federal income tax on half of the community income, and (2) that an Article 2410 renunciation of the community could not result in any exemption from the collection of federal income tax where the liability for such tax had already attached prior to such renunciation.

COUNSEL

William Terry Bray argued the cause for the United States et al. With him on the brief were Solicitor General Erwin N. Griswold, Assistant Attorney General Walters, Matthew J. Zinn, and Crombie J. D. Garrett.

Paul K. Kirkpatrick, Jr., argued the cause and filed a brief for respondent Mitchell. Patrick M. Schott argued the cause and filed a brief for respondent Angello.

———————

STELLA CONNELL, Appellant,

v

JAMES M. HIGGINBOTHAM et al.

403 US 207, 29 L Ed 2d 418, 91 S Ct 1772

Argued November 19, 1970. Decided June 7, 1971.

Decision: Florida loyalty oath for public employees held constitutional as to pledge to support federal and state constitutions, but unconstitutional as to disavowal of belief in forceful overthrow of government.

SUMMARY

The appellant, after being hired as a substitute classroom teacher in a Florida county school system, was later dismissed for refusing to sign a statutory loyalty oath of five clauses required of all Florida public employees. An action was commenced in the United States District Court for the Middle District of Florida challenging the constitutionality of the statute and the loyalty oath upon which the appellant's employment was conditioned. The three-judge District Court declared three of the five clauses contained in the oath to be unconstitutional, but upheld the remaining clauses which required each public employee to swear or affirm (1) "that I will support the Constitution of the United States and of the State of Florida," and (2) "that I do not believe in the overthrow of the government of the United States or of the State of Florida by force or violence."

On appeal, the United States Supreme Court affirmed in part and reversed in part. In a per curiam opinion expressing the views of five members of the court, it was held that clause (1) of the oath, requiring all applicants for public employment to pledge to support the federal and state constitutions, was constitutionally valid, but that clause (2) was unconstitutional since it resulted in the teacher's summary dismissal from public employment without hearing or inquiry required by due process.

Marshall, J., joined by **Douglas** and **Brennan, JJ.**, concurring in the result and agreeing that clause (1) of the loyalty oath was constitutional, would have based the decision as to the unconstitutionality of clause (2) on the ground that belief as such cannot be the predicate of governmental action.

Stewart, J., concurring in part and dissenting in part, agreed that clause (1) was clearly constitutional, but would have remanded the controversy involving clause (2) to the District Court to give the parties an opportunity to get from the state courts an authoritative construction of the clause's meaning, the clause being constitutionally infirm if meant to embrace the teacher's philosophical or political beliefs, but being constitutionally valid if meant to merely test whether clause (1) of the oath could be taken without mental reservation or purpose of evasion.

COUNSEL

Sanford Jay Rosen argued the cause for appellant. With him on the brief were Tobias Simon and Melvin L. Wulf.

Stephen Marc Slepin argued the cause for appellees. With him on the brief were Rivers Buford, Jr., and James W. Markel.

ROBERT JOHNSON, Petitioner,

v

STATE OF MISSISSIPPI

403 US 212, 29 L Ed 2d 423, 91 S Ct 1778

Argued April 21, 1971.   Decided June 7, 1971.

Decision: Mississippi contempt conviction of civil rights
worker reversed and case remanded for hearing before unbiased judge.

SUMMARY

The petitioner, a civil rights worker, was charged with
committing an act of criminal contempt in the Circuit
Court of Grenada County, Mississippi, and the judge
thereof ordered his removal from the court. The petitioner was ordered to appear at a later date to show
cause why he should not be held in contempt, but
before that hearing was held, the petitioner filed (1) a
motion in the state court asking the judge to recuse himself and charging the judge with personal prejudice
against the petitioner, the civil rights organization that
he represented, and the lawyers' organization defending
him, and (2) a petition in a Federal District Court for
removal of the contempt proceedings. No hearing was
ever held on the motion for recusation, and the petition
for removal was denied almost 2 years later. On remand,
the same state court judge adjudged the petitioner to have
been in contempt, denying the petitioner's request for a
hearing on the merits and for an opportunity to show that
the trial judge should recuse himself, even though 5
days prior to the date of the contempt hearing the petitioner and others had filed suit in a Federal District
Court joining the state court judge as a defendant in an

action charging the state court with systematic exclusion of Negroes and women from juries, which suit resulted in the issuance of a temporary injunction against the state court judge by the District Court just 2 days prior to the contempt adjudication. On appeal, the Supreme Court of Mississippi affirmed the judgment of contempt but reduced the petitioner's sentence from 4 months to 1 month (233 So 2d 116).

On certiorari, the United States Supreme Court reversed and remanded. In a per curiam opinion expressing the unanimous view of the court, it was held that although instant punishment for contempt might sometimes be proper, under the circumstances of the case, where a hearing at a later date on the contempt charge was set, the trial judge should have recused himself, for he was so enmeshed in matters involving the alleged contemnor as to make it appropriate for another judge to sit at the contempt hearing, trial before an unbiased judge being essential to due process.

COUNSEL

Stephen W. Porter argued the cause for petitioner. With him on the brief was Richard B. Ruge.

G. Garland Lyell, Jr., Assistant Attorney General of Mississippi, argued the cause for respondent. With him on the brief was A. F. Summer, Attorney General.

HAZEL PALMER et al., Petitioners,

v

ALLEN C. THOMPSON, Mayor,
City of Jackson, et al.

403 US 217, 29 L Ed 2d 438, 91 S Ct 1940

Argued December 14, 1970. Decided
June 14, 1971.

Decision: City's closing of public swimming pools rather
than desegregating them held not violative of Thirteenth Amendment or of equal protection clause
of Fourteenth Amendment.

SUMMARY

After federal litigation had resulted in a judgment
declaring unconstitutional a Mississippi city's operation
of public swimming pools on a racially segregated basis,
four for whites only and one for Negroes only, the city
council decided not to operate public swimming pools at
all, and the pools were closed. Some Negro residents of
the city brought suit in the United States District Court
for the Southern District of Mississippi, seeking to require
the city to reopen the pools and to operate them on a
desegregrated basis. Holding the plaintiffs not entitled
to relief, the District Court held (1) that the personal
safety of the citizens of the city and the maintenance of
law and order would be endangered by the operation of
the pools on an integrated basis, and (2) that the pools
could not be economically operated on an integrated basis.
The Court of Appeals for the Fifth Circuit, sitting en
banc, affirmed by a divided vote, and rejected the contention that since the pools had been closed either in whole
or in part to avoid desegregation, the city council's action

was a denial of the equal protection of the laws (419 F2d 1222).

On certiorari, the United States Supreme Court affirmed. In an opinion by **Black, J.**, expressing the view of five members of the court, it was held that since there was substantial evidence in the record to support the conclusion that the pools were closed because the city council felt they could not be operated safely and economically on an integrated basis, and since there was no evidence in the record to show that the city was covertly aiding the maintenance and operation of pools which were private in name only, the closing of the pools did not violate either the Thirteenth Amendment or the equal protection clause of the Fourteenth Amendment.

Burger, Ch. J., concurring, joined in the court's opinion and added that the court would do a grave disservice, both to elected officials and to the public, if it were to require that every decision of local governments to terminate a desirable service be subjected to a microscopic scrutiny for forbidden motives rendering the decision unconstitutional.

Blackmun, J., concurring, joined in the court's opinion and emphasized that the city's recreational facilities other than swimming pools had been desegregated, that the pools were not an essential community service, that the pools had operated at a deficit, and that the city should not be "locked in," despite financial loss, to operate the pools for an indefinite time in the future.

Douglas, J., dissenting, relied upon the Ninth, Thirteenth, Fourteenth, and Fifteenth Amendments, and said that a state could not discontinue any of its municipal services for the purpose of perpetuating or installing apartheid or because it found life in a multiracial community difficult or unpleasant.

[Supreme Ct Sum]

White, J., joined by **Brennan** and **Marshall, JJ.,** dissenting, stated that the closing of the pools constituted a pronouncement of Negroes' unfitness to swim with whites, that the closed pools stood as mute reminders to the community of the official view of Negro inferiority, and that the city's action interposed a major deterrent to seeking judicial or executive help in eliminating racial restrictions on the use of public facilities, and, as such, was illegal under the Fourteenth Amendment.

Marshall, J., joined by **Brennan** and **White, JJ.,** dissenting, stated that when the city denied a single Negro, simply because he was a Negro, the opportunity to go swimming, the Fourteenth Amendment was violated, and that the fact that the color of his skin was used to prevent others from swimming in public pools was irrelevant.

COUNSEL

Paul A. Rosen and William M. Kunstler argued the cause for petitioners. With them on the briefs were Ernest Goodman and Arthur Kinoy.

William F. Goodman, Jr., argued the cause for respondents. On the brief were John E. Stone, Thomas H. Watkins, and Elizabeth W. Grayson.

Briefs of amici curiae urging reversal were filed by Solicitor General Erwin N. Griswold, Assistant Attorney General Leonard, and Deputy Solicitor General Wallace for the United States, and by Armand Derfner for James Moore et al.

AMALGAMATED ASSOCIATION OF STREET,
ELECTRIC RAILWAY AND MOTOR
COACH EMPLOYEES OF
AMERICA, etc., et al.,
Petitioners,

v

WILSON P. LOCKRIDGE

403 US 274, 29 L Ed 2d 473, 91 S Ct 1909

Argued December 15, 1970. Decided
June 14, 1971.

Decision: Suspended union member's breach of contract
claim against union for procuring his discharge under
union security clause held within NLRB's exclusive
jurisdiction even though predicated on union's violation of its own constitution.

SUMMARY

A union member who failed to tender his October dues
until November 10 was declared suspended from membership and at the union's request was discharged by his employer. Under the union's constitution, dues were pay-
able on the first day of the month; a member in arrears
after the 15th day of the month was not in good standing;
one allowing his arrearage to run into the second month
was debarred from benefits for one month after payment;
and one allowing his arrearage to run over the last day
of the second month suspended himself. The collective
bargaining agreement included a maintenance of membership provision. The union member sued for rein-
statement and damages in the District Court, Fourth
Judicial District, Ada County, Idaho, and recovered damages on the ground that because he was less than two

months in arrears on November 10, he was not suspended and therefore was not subject to discharge. The Idaho Supreme Court affirmed (93 Idaho 294, 460 P2d 719).

On certiorari, the United States Supreme Court reversed. In an opinion by **Harlan, J.**, expressing the views of five members of the court, it was held that (1) under the rule of San Diego Building Trades Council v Garmon (1959) 359 US 236, 3 L Ed 2d 775, 79 S Ct 773, both federal and state court jurisdiction of the claim was preempted because the union's conduct was arguably protected or prohibited by the National Labor Relations Act; and (2) no exception from this rule arose by reason of (a) the union's conduct constituting not only an unfair labor practice but also a breach of its contract with its member, (b) the necessity of the NLRB's interpreting the union constitution to determine whether the union was guilty of an unfair labor practice, or (c) the pre-Garmon decision in Association of Machinists v Gonzales (1958) 356 US 617, 2 L Ed 2d 1018, 78 S Ct 923, that a union member may sue in state court for wrongful expulsion from the union, since the Gonzales Case focused on purely union matters and did not involve a union security clause.

Douglas, J., dissented on the grounds that the Gonzales Case rather than the Garmon Case controlled, and that a state court suit can be brought where a union breaches its contract with a member by expelling him or wrongfully treating him as a nonmember.

White, J., joined by **Burger, Ch. J.**, dissented on the grounds that the Gonzales Case controlled, that state courts should not be foreclosed from granting relief for a union's deprivation of its members' state law rights under the union constitution and bylaws, and that the Garmon decision should not apply where the activity in question is only arguably protected by federal labor law.

Blackmun, J., dissented for the "basic" reasons set forth in the dissenting opinions of Douglas and White, JJ.

COUNSEL

Isaac N. Groner argued the cause for petitioners. With him on the briefs were Earle W. Putnam and Paul T. Bailey.

John L. Kilcullen argued the cause for respondent. With him on the brief were Robert W. Green and Samuel Kaufman.

Briefs of amici curiae urging reversal were filed by Solicitor General Erwin N. Griswold, Arnold Ordman, Dominick L. Manoli, Norton J. Come, and Linda Sher for the National Labor Relations Board, and by J. Albert Woll, Laurence Gold, and Thomas E. Harris for the American Federation of Labor and Congress of Industrial Organizations.

Jonathan C. Gibson filed a brief for the National Right to Work Legal Defense and Education Foundation as amicus curiae urging affirmance.

JAMES D. HODGSON, Secretary of Labor,
Petitioner,

v

LOCAL UNION 6799, United Steelworkers
of America, AFL-CIO, et al.

403 US 333, 29 L Ed 2d 510, 91 S Ct 1841

Argued March 23, 1971. Decided June 14, 1971.

Decision: Union member's failure to protest election
rule to union before filing complaint with Secretary
of Labor held to preclude Secretary's challenge to
rule in LMRDA suit.

SUMMARY

A defeated candidate for president of a union local,
having protested without success to both the local and the
international concerning the use of union facilities to pre-
pare campaign materials for his opponent, filed a complaint with the Secretary of Labor repeating this objection
and also challenging a meeting attendance requirement
imposed as a condition of candidacy for union office.
The Secretary of Labor investigated, concluded that both
objections alleged violations of § 401 of the Labor-Management Reporting and Disclosure Act, advised the union
of his conclusions, asked it to take voluntary remedial
action, and, when the union failed to comply, brought
suit against the union in the United States District Court
for the Central District of California. The court held
that the use of union facilities for the opponent's campaign was illegal, but that the meeting attendance rule
was legal. The United States Court of Appeals for the
Ninth Circuit affirmed without reaching the question
whether the attendance rule was legal (426 F2d 969).

On certiorari, the United States Supreme Court affirmed. In an opinion by **Marshall, J.**, expressing the views of seven members of the court, it was held that the union member's failure to object to the attendance rule when protesting the election to the union, while knowing of the existence of the rule, barred the Secretary from challenging it in a suit under § 402 of the Labor-Management Reporting and Disclosure Act.

Brennan, J., dissented on the ground that the Secretary may base an action for a new election on any violation uncovered in his investigation.

White, J., dissented on the ground that since the new election was validly ordered on an exhausted claim, the Secretary could insist that the new election be held legally, requiring an adjudication of the attendance rule.

COUNSEL

Deputy Solicitor General Wallace argued the cause for petitioner. With him on the brief were Solicitor General Erwin N. Griswold, Assistant Attorney General Gray, Richard B. Stone, Peter G. Nash, George T. Avery, Beate Bloch, and Cornelius S. Donoghue, Jr.

Michael H. Gottesman argued the cause for respondents. With him on the brief were Bernard Kleiman, George H. Cohen, Carl Frankel, and Jerome Smith.

COMMISSIONER OF INTERNAL REVENUE,
Petitioner,

v

LINCOLN SAVINGS AND LOAN
ASSOCIATION

403 US 345, 29 L Ed 2d 519, 91 S Ct 1893

Argued February 23, 1971. Decided
June 14, 1971.

Decision: State-chartered savings and loan association's
payment to Federal Savings and Loan Insurance
Corporation of "additional premium" under § 404
(d) of National Housing Act held not deductible for
income tax purposes as ordinary and necessary business expense.

SUMMARY

On its 1963 federal income tax return, a state-chartered
savings and loan association deducted, as an ordinary
and necessary business expense under § 162(a) of the Internal Revenue Code of 1954, an "additional premium"
paid by the taxpayer to the Federal Savings and Loan
Insurance Corporation as required by § 404(d) of the
National Housing Act, which requires that an insured
institution, in addition to paying an annual insurance
premium to be placed in the Federal Insurance Corporation's primary reserve, must also pay, with respect to any
calendar year in which it has a net account increase, an
additional premium in the nature of a prepayment of
future regular annual premiums, which additional premium is to be credited to the insurance corporation's
secondary reserve. Under the National Housing Act, the
insured institution has a property interest in its pro rata

share of the secondary reserve, with rights, under specified limited conditions, of transferring its pro rata share, of obtaining a cash refund of such share, and of receiving annual credits from the Federal Insurance Corporation's earnings to the institution's pro rata share of the secondary reserve. The Commissioner of Internal Revenue disallowed deduction of the "additional premium" payment as an ordinary and necessary business expense, and determined the resulting tax deficiency. The Tax Court upheld the deficiency (51 Tax Court 82), but the United States Court of Appeals for the Ninth Circuit reversed (422 F2d 90).

On certiorari, the United States Supreme Court reversed. In an opinion by **Blackmun, J.**, expressing the view of eight members of the court, it was held that in view of the insured institution's pro rata interest in the Federal Insurance Corporation's secondary reserve resulting from payment of "additional premiums," including the limited rights of transferability, possible refund, and possible application of its secondary reserve share to basic premium obligations, the payment of such "additional premiums" did not constitute an "expense" within the meaning of the provisions of § 162(a) of the Internal Revenue Code authorizing deduction for ordinary and necessary business expenses, but instead was capital in nature, serving to create or enhance an asset of the institution.

Douglas, J., dissented, expressing the view that the "additional premium" was paid for the purpose of obtaining insurance necessary for the success of the insured institution's business, and therefore should be considered deductible under § 162(a) of the Internal Revenue Code —the possibility that the institution might never receive its pro rata share in the Federal Insurance Corporation's secondary reserve being remote and not rendering the payment nondeductible.

COUNSEL

Matthew J. Zinn argued the cause for petitioner. With him on the brief were Solicitor General Erwin N. Griswold, Assistant Attorney General Walters, Thomas L. Stapleton, and David English Carmack.

Adam Y. Bennion argued the cause for respondent. With him on the brief were A. Calder Mackay and Victor L. Walch.

N. O. GRAHAM, Commissioner, Department
of Public Welfare, State of Arizona,
Appellant,

v

CARMEN RICHARDSON, Etc. (No. 609)

WILLIAM P. SAILER et al., Appellants,

v

ELSIE MARY JANE LEGER
and Beryl Jervis (No. 727)

403 US 365, 29 L Ed 2d 534, 91 S Ct 1848

Argued March 22, 1971. Decided
June 14, 1971.

Decision: Arizona and Pennsylvania statutes denying
welfare benefits to resident aliens who had not resided in United States for specified number of years
held unconstitutional.

SUMMARY

These cases presented the question whether the equal
protection clause of the Fourteenth Amendment prevents
a state from conditioning welfare benefits either upon
the beneficiary's possession of United States citizenship,
or if the beneficiary is an alien, upon his having resided
in the United States for a specified number of years. In
No. 609, a lawfully admitted resident alien, who had
resided continuously in Arizona since 1956 and had become permanently and totally disabled, applied for welfare benefits under the state's federally assisted program,
and met all the eligibility requirements, except that she
had not, when she first applied for benefits in 1969, re-

sided in the United States for a total of 15 years. She was denied relief solely because of an Arizona statute which conditioned eligibility either on being a United States citizen or on residing in the United States for a total of 15 years. In her class action in the United States District Court for the District of Arizona, a three-judge District Court upheld her motion for summary judgment on the ground that the state statute violated the equal protection clause of the Fourteenth Amendment (313 F Supp 34). In No. 727, the lawfully admitted aliens had resided and worked in Pennsylvania, but had been forced by illness to give up their employment. Thereafter the resident aliens, neither of whom was eligible for relief under federal programs, applied for but were denied general assistance under a Pennsylvania statute which limited general assistance to persons who qualified under the federal programs or to "those other needy persons who are citizens of the United States." In the aliens' class action in the United States District Court for the Eastern District of Pennsylvania, a three-judge District Court ruled that the statute violated the equal protection clause of the Fourteenth Amendment and enjoined its further enforcement (321 F Supp 250).

On appeal, the United States Supreme Court affirmed both judgments. In an opinion by **Blackmun, J.**, it was held (1) expressing the view of eight members of the court, that both state statutes, which denied welfare benefits to resident aliens or to aliens who had not resided in the United States for a given number of years, were unconstitutional under the equal protection clause of the Fourteenth Amendment, which encompassed aliens as well as citizens residing in a state, (2) expressing the unanimous view of the court, that since aliens lawfully within the United States had a right to enter and abide in any state on an equality of legal privileges with all citizens, both state statutes, which would make indigent and disabled aliens unable to live where they could not obtain necessary public assistance, were also unconstitutional as interfering with overriding national policies in the areas of immigration and naturalization which had been constitutionally entrusted to the Federal Government, and (3) expressing the unanimous view of the court, that § 1402(b) of the Social Security Act of 1935, as amended, providing for the Secretary of Health, Education, and Welfare's approval of any state plan for the distribution of funds under federally assisted disability welfare programs, except those plans which imposed citizenship requirements which would exclude any citizen of the United States, did not authorize Arizona to deny general assistance, merely because of their alienage, to resident aliens who had not resided within the United States for a total of 15 years.

Harlan, J., joined in holdings (2) and (3) above, and in the judgment of the court.

COUNSEL

Michael S. Flam, Assistant Attorney General of Arizona, argued the cause for appellant in No. 609. With him on the briefs were Gary K. Nelson, Attorney General, and James B. Feeley, Andrew W. Bettwy, Roger M. Horne, and Peter Sowine, Assistant Attorneys General. Joseph P. Work, Assistant Attorney General of Pennsylvania, argued the cause for appellants in No. 727. With him on the brief were Fred Speaker, Attorney General, Barry A. Roth, Assistant Deputy Attorney General, and Edward Friedman.

Anthony B. Ching argued the cause and filed a brief for appellees in No. 609. Jonathan M. Stein argued the cause for appellees in No. 727, pro hac vice. With him on the brief were Harvey N. Schmidt and Jonthan Weiss.

Jonathan Weiss filed a brief for the Legal Services for the Elderly Poor Project of the Center on Social Welfare Policy and Law as amicus curiae urging affirmance in No. 609. Robert A. Sedler and Melvin L. Wulf filed a brief for the American Civil Liberties Union as amicus curiae urging affirmance in both cases. Briefs of amici curiae urging affirmance in No. 727 were filed by Edith Lowenstein for Migration and Refugee Services, U. S. Catholic Conference, Inc., et al., and by Jack Wasserman and Esther M. Kaufman for the Association of Immigration and Nationality Lawyers.

MACIO BERNARD SIMPSON, Petitioner,

v

STATE OF FLORIDA

403 US 384, 29 L Ed 2d 549, 91 S Ct 1801

June 14, 1971

Decision: State appellate court held to have erred in rejecting accused's claim of collateral estoppel and double jeopardy without examining record of prior trial at which accused had been acquitted.

SUMMARY

Two armed men entered a store and robbed the manager and a customer. In connection with this robbery, the accused received three jury trials in the Florida state courts, each trial resulting in a general verdict. At the first trial, involving the charge of armed robbery of the manager, the accused was convicted, but the conviction was reversed on appeal because of the trial judge's failure to instruct the jury on a lesser included offense. At the second trial, also involving the charge of armed robbery of the manager, the accused was acquitted. At the third trial, involving the charge of armed robbery of the customer, the accused was convicted. On appeal to the Florida District Court of Appeal, First Circuit, the accused contended that on the basis of collateral estoppel and double jeopardy, his acquittal at the second trial of armed robbery of the manager precluded his conviction at the third trial for armed robbery of the customer, since his identity as one of the robbers was the sole disputed issue at each of the trials, but the court, affirming his conviction, rejected this contention, declined to examine the record of the second trial, and held that even if the acquittal at the second trial was entitled to collateral estoppel effect, the conviction at the first trial was equally entitled to collateral estoppel effect (237 So 2d 341). The Florida Supreme Court, by a divided vote, declined review.

Granting certiorari, the United States Supreme Court vacated the judgment below and remanded the case for further proceedings. In a per curiam opinion expressing the views of six members of the court, it was held that the prosecution could not rely upon the reversed conviction in the first trial as a basis for collateral estoppel; that unless the jury's verdict of acquittal in the second trial could have been grounded upon an issue other than that which the accused sought to foreclose from consideration, the constitutional guaranty against double jeopardy vitiated the accused's conviction; and that the court below had erred in rejecting the accused's claim of collateral estoppel and double jeopardy without examining the record of the second trial.

Brennan, J., joined by **Douglas, J.**, concurred, adding that even if collateral estoppel had been inapplicable, the double jeopardy clause precluded the accused's prosecution for the robbery of the customer.

Burger, Ch. J., joined by **Blackmun, J.**, dissented on the ground that the treatment which the court accorded to the collateral estoppel doctrine was not justified under the double jeopardy clause.

Marshall, J., did not participate.

———

LINDA JENNESS et al., Appellants,

v

BEN W. FORTSON, Secretary of State of Georgia

403 US 431, 29 L Ed 2d 554, 91 S Ct 1970

Argued March 1, 1971. Decided June 21, 1971.

Decision: Georgia election law requiring candidates who do not enter and win political party's primary but who wish to have names printed on ballots to obtain signatures of at least 5 percent of registered voters on nominating petitions held constitutional.

SUMMARY

A Georgia election law provides that a candidate for elective public office who does not enter and win a political party's primary election may have his name printed on the ballot at the general election only if he files a nominating petition signed by at least 5 percent of the number of resistered voters at the last general election for the office in question and pays a filing fee. The law, which recognizes independent candidates and provides a period of 180 days for circulating nominating petitions, does not (1) prohibit write-in votes, (2) require a candidate to be the nominee of a political party, (3) require new political parties to establish primary election machinery, (4) require petition signers to state that they intend to vote for that candidate at the election, and (5) prohibit a voter from signing as many different petitions as he wishes. Several prospective candidates and registered voters filed a class action in the United States District Court for the Northern District of Georgia, attacking the law and seeking declaratory and injunctive

[Supreme Ct Sum]

relief. The three-judge District Court entered an injunction with respect with the filing fee requirement, holding that it was unconstitutional, from which ruling no appeal was taken; but the District Court held the nominating petition requirement to be constitutionally valid (315 F Supp 1035).

On direct appeal, the United States Supreme Court affirmed. In an opinion by **Stewart, J.**, expressing the views of seven members of the court, it was held that the Georgia election law (1) did not abridge the rights of free speech and association guaranteed by the First and Fourteenth Amendments, since it did not freeze the status quo, but implicitly recognized the potential fluidity of political life, (2) did not violate the equal protection clause of the Fourteenth Amendment, since neither of the alternative methods for placing a candidate's name on the ballot could be assumed to be inherently more burdensome than the other, and (3) did not constitute invidious discrimination against a "political body" by requiring nominating petitions for its candidates whereas the name of the winner of a "political party's" primary election was printed on the ballot.

Black and **Harlan, JJ.**, concurred in the result.

COUNSEL

Peter E. Rindskopf argued the cause for appellants. With him on the brief was Howard Moore, Jr.

Robert J. Castellani, Assistant Attorney General of Georgia, argued the cause for appellee. With him on the brief were Arthur K. Bolton, Attorney General, and Harold N. Hill, Jr., Executive Assistant Attorney General.

EDWARD H. COOLIDGE, Jr., Petitioner,

v

NEW HAMPSHIRE

403 US 443, 29 L Ed 2d 564, 91 S Ct 2022

Argued January 12, 1971.   Decided June 21, 1971.

Decision: Search and seizure of automobile held unconstitutional in absence of valid warrant or exigent circumstances.

SUMMARY

Two police officers went to the accused's house to question his wife concerning a murder. After informing the officers that her husband had not been at home on the night of the murder, and after being asked whether her husband owned any guns, the wife took her husband's four guns out of a closet and gave them to the officers. After she was asked what clothes her husband had worn on the night of the murder, she produced some of his clothing and gave it to the police. She believed that she had nothing to hide, and her motive in producing the guns and clothing was to clear her husband. Several days later, police officers, having concluded that they had probable cause, obtained warrants authorizing them to arrest the accused for the murder and to search his automobile. The warrants were issued by the state attorney general, acting as a justice of the peace. Prior to issuing the warrants, the attorney general had personally taken charge of all police activities relating to the murder, and he later served as chief prosecutor at the accused's trial. The accused was arrested in his house, and officers seized his automobile, which was parked in the driveway. The automobile was subsequently towed to the police station, where it was searched and vacuumed 2 days later. At the accused's murder trial in a New Hampshire state court, vacuum sweepings obtained from the automobile were admitted in evidence against the accused, and clothing and one of the guns which his wife had given to the police were also admitted in evidence against him. He was convicted of murder, and the New Hampshire Supreme Court affirmed (109 NH 403, 260 A2d 547).

On certiorari, the United States Supreme Court reversed and remanded the case. In an opinion by **Stewart, J.**, it was held (1) in Part I, expressing the views of five members of the court, that the warrant authorizing the search of the automobile was invalid on the ground of its not having been issued by a neutral and detached magistrate, and the seizure and subsequent search of the automobile could therefore not constitutionally rest upon such a warrant, (2) in Part IID, expressing the views of five members of the court, that since the police knew of the presence of the automobile and planned all along to seize it, there were no exigent circumstances justifying their failure to obtain a valid warrant, and the fruits of the unconstitutional seizure of the automobile were inadmissible, and (3) in Part III, expressing the views of six members of the court, that the accused's wife, in bringing out the guns and clothing and handing them over to the police, was not acting as an instrument of the police and complying with a demand made by them, and that her course of conduct did not amount to a search and seizure. Also, **Stewart, J.**, joined by **Douglas, Brennan,** and **Marshall, JJ.**, expressed the views (1) in Part IIA, that the seizure and subsequent search of the automobile were not sustainable as incident to a valid arrest, (2) in Part IIB, that even if there was probable cause for the seizure or search of the automobile, a search of the automobile without a valid warrant was unconstitutional unless there were exigent circumstances making it impracticable to obtain a warrant, and that such circumstances did not exist in the present case, and (3) in Part IIC, that the doctrine of "plain view" could not justify the police seizure of the accused's automobile under the circumstances of the present case.

Harlan, J., concurred in the judgment and in Parts I, IID, and III of the court's opinion, but referred to the present state of uncertainty of—and the need for overhauling—the law of search and seizure, and expressed the view that Supreme Court decisions making the federal exclusionary rule applicable to the states should be overruled.

Burger, Ch. J., Black, J.—who was substantially joined by **Burger, Ch. J.,** and **Blackmun, J.**—and **White, J.,** each in a separate opinion, dissented from the court's judgment of reversal, and dissented, for varying reasons, from various of the court's holdings to the effect that the seizure and subsequent search of the automobile were unconstitutional. However, **Burger, Ch. J.,** joined in Part III of the court's opinion, and both **Black, J.,** joined by **Blackmun, J.,** and **White, J.,** expressed agreement with the result reached in Part III of the court's opinion.

COUNSEL

Archibald Cox, by appointment of the Court, 400 US 814, 27 L Ed 2d 42, 91 S Ct 52, argued the cause for petitioner. With him on the briefs were Matthias J. Reynolds, John A. Graf, and Robert L. Chiesa.

Alexander J. Kalinski argued the cause for respondent. With him on the brief was Warren B. Rudman, Attorney General of New Hampshire.

WEBSTER BIVENS, Petitioner,

v

SIX UNKNOWN NAMED AGENTS OF FEDERAL BUREAU OF NARCOTICS

403 US 388, 29 L Ed 2d 619, 91 S Ct 1999

Argued January 12, 1971.   Decided June 21, 1971.

Decision: Complaint alleging injuries resulting from federal narcotics agents' violation of Fourth Amendment held to state federal cause of action for damages.

SUMMARY

An action for damages was instituted in the United States District Court for the Eastern District of New York against federal narcotics agents, the plaintiff seeking recovery for humiliation and mental suffering resulting from the agents' conduct, under claim of federal authority, in connection with an arrest and search relating to alleged narcotics violations by the plaintiff.   The plaintiff alleged that the agents, acting without a warrant and without probable cause, had entered the plaintiff's apartment, had used unreasonable force in effecting the arrest, had searched the apartment, and had later interrogated the plaintiff and subjected him to a visual strip search.   The District Court dismissed the complaint on the ground, inter alia, that it failed to state a cause of action (276 F Supp 12), and the Court of Appeals for the Second Circuit affirmed on that basis (409 F2d 718).

On certiorari, the United States Supreme Court reversed and remanded.   In an opinion by **Brennan, J.**, expressing the view of five members of the court, it was held that a violation of the Fourth Amendment's command against unreasonable searches and seizures, by a federal agent acting under color of federal authority, gave rise to a federal cause of action for damages consequent upon the agent's unconstitutional conduct.

Harlan, J., concurred in the judgment, stating that federal courts had the power to award damages for violation of constitutionally protected interests, and that the traditional judicial remedy of damages was appropriate to vindicate the personal interests protected by the Fourth Amendment.

Burger, Ch. J., dissented, expressing the views that the doctrine of separation of powers would be better preserved by recommending a solution to the problem of damages caused by a federal agent's failure to obey the strictures of the Fourth Amendment to the Congress as the branch of government in which the Constitution has vested the legislative power; that with regard to deterring law enforcement officials from attempting to obtain evidence through illegal searches and seizures, the suppression doctrine, calling for the exclusion of illegally obtained evidence which would otherwise be admissible, was unsatisfactory; and that the problem could be solved by Congress' enacting legislation which would (1) waive sovereign immunity as to illegal acts of law enforcement officials committed in the performance of assigned duties, (2) create a cause of action for damages resulting from such illegal acts, (3) create a quasi-judicial tribunal to adjudicate the claims for such damages, (4) provide that this statutory remedy would be in lieu of the exclusion of evidence secured for use in criminal cases in violation of the Fourth Amendment, and (5) provide that no evidence otherwise admissible would be excluded from any criminal proceeding because of violation of the Fourth Amendment.

Black, J., dissented on the ground that while Congress

could create a federal cause of action for damages for an unreasonable search by federal officers in violation of the Fourth Amendment, it had not done so, and the creation of such a cause of action by the court was an exercise of power not given to it by the Constitution.

Blackmun, J., dissenting, stated that the judicial legislation creating the cause of action opened the door for another avalanche of new federal cases, tending to stultify proper law enforcement, and that if a truly aggrieved person had no adequate remedy, then it was for Congress and not the court to act.

COUNSEL

Stephen A. Grant argued the cause and filed a brief for petitioner.

Jerome Feit argued the cause for respondents. On the brief were Solicitor General Erwin N. Griswold, Assistant Attorney General Ruckelshaus, and Robert V. Zener.

Melvin L. Wulf filed a brief for the American Civil Liberties Union as amicus curiae urging reversal.

JOSEPH McKEIVER and Edward Terry,
Appellants,

v

STATE OF PENNSYLVANIA (No. 322)

IN RE BARBARA BURRUS et al.,
Petitioners (No. 128)

403 US 528, 29 L Ed 2d 647, 91 S Ct 1976

Argued December 9 and 10, 1970. Decided
June 21, 1971.

Decision: Jury trial in state juvenile delinquency proceedings held not required under due process clause
of Fourteenth Amendment.

SUMMARY

    These cases raised the issue whether the due process
clause of the Fourteenth Amendment affords the right
to trial by jury in state juvenile delinquency proceedings.
No. 322 involved separate proceedings against two boys,
15 and 16 years old, respectively, in the Juvenile Branch of
the Court of Common Pleas of Philadelphia County,
Pennsylvania, charging as acts of juvenile delinquency
conduct by the juvenile in one case which constituted
felonies under Pennsylvania law, and conduct amounting
to misdemeanors in the second case. The trial judge in
each case denied a request for jury trial, and adjudged the
juvenile as delinquent on the respective charges, one of
the juveniles being put on probation and the other being
committed to an institution. The Superior Court of
Pennsylvania affirmed both orders without opinion (215
Pa Super 760, 255 A2d 921; 215 Pa Super 762, 255 A2d

922). Consolidating the appeals in both cases, the Supreme Court of Pennsylvania affirmed, holding that there was no constitutional right to a jury trial in the juvenile court (438 Pa 339, 265 A2d 350). In No. 128, a group of children, ranging in age from 11 to 15 years, were charged by juvenile petitions in the District Court, Hyde County, North Carolina, with various acts amounting to misdemeanors under state law, which acts arose out of a series of demonstrations protesting school assignments and a school consolidation plan. Consolidating the several cases into groups for hearing, the trial judge excluded the general public over counsel's objection in all but two of the cases; denied a request for jury trial in each case; and entered a custody commitment order in each case, declaring the juvenile a delinquent and placing each juvenile on probation after suspending the commitments. The cases were consolidated into two groups for appeal, and the Court of Appeals of North Carolina affirmed in each instance (4 NC App 523, 167 SE2d 454; 5 NC App 487, 168 SE2d 695). Consolidating the cases into a single appeal, the Supreme Court of North Carolina deleted that portion of each order relating to the commitment, but otherwise affirmed, holding that a juvenile was not constitutionally entitled to a jury in delinquency proceedings (275 NC 517, 169 SE2d 879).

On appeal in the Pennsylvania case, and on certiorari in the North Carolina proceedings, the United States Supreme Court affirmed in each instance. A majority of the court, although not agreeing upon an opinion, agreed that the due process clause of the Fourteenth Amendment did not assure the right to jury trial in the adjudicative phase of a state juvenile court delinquency proceeding.

Blackmun, J., announced the judgment of the court, and in an opinion joined by **Burger,** Ch. J., **Stewart,** J., and **White,** J., expressed the views that (1) the fact that the due process clause of the Fourteenth Amendment imposed the Sixth Amendment right to jury trial upon the states in certain "criminal prosecutions" did not automatically require jury trial in state juvenile delinquency proceedings, the claimed right to jury trial instead depending upon ascertaining the precise impact of the due process requirement on delinquency proceedings, (2) the applicable due process standard was fundamental fairness, and (3) notwithstanding the disappointments and failures with regard to state juvenile court procedure and its idealistic hopes relating to rehabilitation, nevertheless trial by jury in the juvenile court's adjudicative stage was not a constitutional requirement, particularly since requiring jury trial might remake the juvenile proceeding into a fully adversary process, with the attendant delay, formality, and clamor of such process, and would effectively end the juvenile system's idealistic prospect of an intimate, informal protective proceeding.

White, J., concurring, stated that in view of the differences of substance between criminal and juvenile courts, due process did not require the states to afford jury trials in juvenile courts, although they were free to do so if they so chose.

Brennan, J., concurred in No. 322 and dissented in No. 128, on the grounds that (1) the due process clause did not require the states to provide jury trials on demand in juvenile delinquency proceedings so long as some other aspect of the process, such as the availability of public trial, adequately protected the interest that the Sixth Amendment jury trial provision was intended to serve, (2) since public trial was available under Pennsylvania law, the judgment in No. 322 must be affirmed, but (3) the judgment in No. 128 should be reversed, since North Carolina law either permitted or required exclusion of the general public from juvenile trials, the trial judge in the instant cases had denied public hearing, and there was no indication of any feature of North Carolina's juvenile procedure that could substitute for public or jury trial in protecting the juvenile against misuse of the judicial process.

Harlan, J., concurred in the judgments on the ground that criminal jury trials were not constitutionally required of the states, either as a matter of Sixth Amendment law or due process.

Douglas, J., joined by **Black** and **Marshall, JJ.,** dissented, expressing the view that by reason of the Sixth and Fourteenth Amendments, a juvenile was entitled to a jury trial as a matter of right where the delinquency charge was an offense that, if the person were an adult, would be a crime triable by jury, which was true in the cases at bar wherein the juveniles were subject to imprisonment or confinement for periods of from 5 to 10 years.

COUNSEL

Daniel E. Farmer argued the cause for appellants in No. 322. With him on the brief were John S. Roberts, Jr., Peter W. Brown, Harvey N. Schmidt, and James O. Freedman.

Michael Meltsner argued the cause for petitioners in No. 128. With him on the briefs were Jack Greenberg, Julius L. Chambers, James E. Ferguson II, and Anthony Amsterdam.

Arlan Specter argued the cause for appellee in No. 322. With him on the brief was James D. Crawford.

Robert Morgan, Attorney General, argued the cause for respondent, the State of North Carolina, in No. 128. With him on the brief were Ralph Moody, Deputy At-

torney General, and Andrew A. Vanore, Jr., Assistant
Attorney General.

Alfred L. Scanlan argued the cause for the National
Council of Juvenile Court Judges as amicus curiae urging
affirmance in No. 128.   With him on the brief was Martin
J. Flynn.

Briefs of amici curiae in No. 128 were filed by John
J. Droney for the Commonwealth of Massachusetts; by
Thomas C. Lynch, Attorney General, Albert W. Harris,
Jr., Assistant Attorney General, and Derald E. Granberg
and Gloria F. DeHart, Deputy Attorneys General, for
the State of California; and by Norman Lefstein for the
Public Defender Service for the District of Columbia et al.

UNITED STATES, Petitioner,

v

ROOSEVELT HUDSON HARRIS

403 US 573, 29 L Ed 2d 723, 91 S Ct 2075

Argued March 23, 1971. Decided
June 28, 1971.

Decision: Federal tax investigator's affidavit, based partially on information from informer, held sufficient to establish probable cause for search for nontaxpaid liquor.

SUMMARY

A warrant authorizing a search of the accused's premises was issued on the basis of a federal tax investigator's affidavit which recited (1) that the accused had a reputation with the investigator for over 4 years as being a trafficker of nontaxpaid distilled spirits; (2) that over this period, the investigator had received numerous items of information from all types of persons as to the accused's activities; (3) that the local constable had located a sizable stash of illicit whisky in an abandoned house under the accused's control during this period; (4) that on the date of the affidavit, the investigator had received information from an informant who feared for his life and property if his name were revealed; (5) that the investigator had interviewed this informant and had found him to be a prudent person; and (6) that the investigator had obtained from the informant a sworn verbal statement to the effect that (a) the informant had personal information of and had purchased illicit whisky from within the accused's residence for a period of more than 2 years, and most recently within the past 2 weeks, (b) the informant had knowledge of a person who had purchased illicit whisky within the past 2 days from the house, (c) the informant had personal knowledge that illicit whisky had been consumed by purchasers in a certain outbuilding, and (d) the informant had seen the accused go to another outbuilding on numerous occasions to obtain whisky for other persons. In the United States District Court for the Eastern District of Kentucky, the accused was tried for possession of nontaxpaid liquor, evidence found through the search of his premises was admitted against him, and he was convicted. The Court of Appeals for the Sixth Circuit reversed the conviction, holding that under Aguilar v Texas, 378 US 108, 12 L Ed 2d 723, 84 S Ct 1509, and Spinelli v United States, 393 US 410, 21 L Ed 2d 637, 89 S Ct 584, the investigator's affidavit was insufficient to establish probable cause for the search, and that the evidence found through the search should therefore have been suppressed (412 F2d 796).

On certiorari, the United States Supreme Court reversed the judgment of the Court of Appeals and reinstated the judgment of conviction. In an opinion by **Burger, Ch. J.**, announcing the judgment of the court, it was held, expressing the view of five members of the court, that the investigator's affidavit was sufficient to establish probable cause for the search.

In Part I of his opinion, **Burger, Ch. J.**, joined by **Black, Stewart,** and **Blackmun, JJ.**, expressed the view that the investigator's affidavit contained an ample factual basis for believing the informant which, when coupled with the investigator's own knowledge of the accused's background, afforded a basis upon which a magistrate could reasonably issue a warrant; in Part II, **Burger, Ch. J.**, joined by **Black** and **Blackmun, JJ.**, expressed the view that in assessing the reliability of the informant's information, the magistrate could properly rely on the investigator's knowledge of the accused's reputation; both in Part I and Part II, the Aguilar and Spinelli cases were distinguished; in Part III, **Burger,** Ch. J., joined by **Black, White,** and **Blackmun,** JJ., expressed the view that the fact that the informant's statements included declarations against his own penal interest, since he admitted having purchased illicit liquor, furnished reason for crediting his information and supported the magistrate's finding of probable cause for the search, it not being especially significant that neither the name nor the person of the informant was produced before the magistrate.

Stewart, J., joined in Part I of the opinion by **Burger,** Ch. J., and in the court's judgment.

White, J., joined in Part III of the opinion by **Burger,** Ch. J., and in the court's judgment.

Black, J., concurring, joined in the opinion by **Burger,** Ch. J., but would overrule the Aguilar and Spinelli Cases rather than merely distinguishing them.

Blackmun, J., concurring, joined in the opinion by **Burger,** Ch. J., but would overrule the Spinelli Case rather than merely distinguishing it.

Harlan, J., joined by **Douglas, Brennan,** and **Marshall,** JJ., dissented on the ground that the investigator's affidavit did not provide a sufficient basis for the magistrate's determination that probable cause for the search existed.

COUNSEL

Beatrice Rosenberg argued the cause for the United States. With her on the brief were Solicitor General Erwin N. Griswold, Assistant Attorney General Wilson, Richard B. Stone, and Mervyn Hamburg.

Steven M. Umin, by appointment of the Court, 400 US 955, 27 L Ed 2d 263, 91 S Ct 351, argued the cause and filed a brief for respondent.

Frank G. Carrington, Jr., and **Alan S. Ganz** filed a brief for Americans for Effective Law Enforcement, Inc., as amicus curiae urging reversal.

ALTON J. LEMON et al., Appellants,

v

DAVID H. KURTZMAN, as Superintendent
of Public Instruction of the Commonwealth
of Pennsylvania (No. 89)

JOHN R. EARLEY et al., Appellants,

v

JOAN DiCENSO et al. (No. 569)

WILLIAM P. ROBINSON, Jr., Commissioner
of Education of the State of Rhode Island,
et al., Appellants,

v

JOAN DiCENSO et al. (No. 570)

403 US 602, 29 L Ed 2d 745, 91 S Ct 2105

Argued March 3, 1971. Decided
June 28, 1971.

Decision: Pennsylvania and Rhode Island statutes under
which state aid as to secular instruction was furnished
to church-related elementary and secondary schools,
and to teachers therein, held violative of First
Amendment.

SUMMARY

These cases presented the issue whether the religion
clauses of the First Amendment were violated by state
statutes providing state aid to church-related elementary
and secondary schools, and to teachers therein, with
regard to instruction in secular matters. In Nos. 569 and
570, citizens and taxpayers of Rhode Island brought suit

against state officials in the United States District Court for the District of Rhode Island to enjoin, as repugnant to the religion clauses of the First Amendment and the due process clause of the Fourteenth Amendment, the operation of a Rhode Island statute providing for payment of up to 15-percent annual salary supplements to teachers of secular subjects in nonpublic elementary schools. Under the statute, the teacher was required to be employed in a nonpublic school at which the average per-pupil expenditure on secular education was less than the public school average; the school's financial records were subject to audit by the state; the teacher was required to teach only those subjects offered in the public schools, using teaching materials used in the public schools; and upon applying for a salary supplement, the teacher was required to first agree in writing not to teach a course in religion while receiving salary supplements. After hearing evidence which concerned the nature of secular instruction offered in Roman Catholic schools— only teachers at such schools having applied for benefits under the statute—the three-judge District Court found that the parochial school system was an integral part of the religious mission of the church, and held that the statute violated the establishment clause of the First Amendment (316 F Supp 112). In No. 89, a similar action against state officials was instituted in the United States District Court for the Eastern District of Pennsylvania by Pennsylvania residents and taxpayers, and associations thereof, challenging the constitutionality of a Pennsylvania statute providing for state reimbursement of nonpublic elementary and secondary schools for cost of teachers' salaries, textbooks, and instructional materials in specified secular subjects, but prohibiting reimbursement for any course that contained any subject matter expressing religious teaching or the morals or forms of worship of any sect. Under the Pennsylvania statute, the participating schools were required to maintain prescribed accounting procedures to identify the cost of secular educational service; such accounts were subject to state audit; reimbursement was limited to courses presented in the public schools' curricula; and textbooks and instructional materials were subject to approval by the state. The complaint alleged that church-related schools, which were the principal beneficiaries under the statute, were controlled by religious organizations, had the purpose of propagating a particular religious faith, and conducted their operations to fulfil such purpose. The three-judge District Court dismissed the complaint for failure to state a claim for relief, holding that the statute did not violate the First Amendment (310 F Supp 35).

On appeals, the United States Supreme Court affirmed in Nos. 569 and 570, and reversed in No. 89, remanding that case. In an opinion by **Burger,** Ch. J., expressing the view of seven members of the court as to Nos. 569 and 570, and of six members of the court as to No. 89, it was held that the statutes of both states were unconstitutional under the religion clauses of the First Amendment, as fostering, by their cumulative impact, excessive entanglement between government and religion, particularly in view of (1) the religious purpose and operation of church-related elementary and secondary schools, (2) the enhancement of the process of religious indoctrination resulting from the impressionable age of the pupils, particularly in elementary schools, (3) the necessity of state surveillance to insure that the teachers, who were subject to control by religious organizations, observed the restrictions as to purely secular instruction, (4) the states' examination of the parochial schools' financial records to determine which expenditures were religious and which were secular, (5) the probable intensification of political divisiveness along religious lines resulting from the annual appropriations required under the statutes, benefiting relatively few religious groups, and (6) the self-perpetuating and self-expanding propensities of the innovative statutory programs.

Douglas, J., joined by **Black, J.**, concurring, joined the court's opinion and expressed the views that (1) secular instruction in a parochial school was an integral part of religious instruction, (2) what the taxpayers gave for secular purposes under the state statutes would enable the parochial schools to use all of their own funds for religious training, and (3) the state surveillance and supervision of parochial schools required under the statutes violated the establishment clause of the First Amendment, whereas the requirement that taxpayers of many faiths contribute money for propagation of one faith violated the free exercise clause.

Marshall, J., although taking no part in the consideration or decision of No. 89, concurred in Mr. Justice Douglas' opinion covering Nos. 569 and 570.

Brennan, J., agreeing that the judgment in Nos. 569 and 570 should be affirmed, but noting that the judgment in No. 89 should be reversed outright, expressed the views that (1) secular education in parochial schools was inextricably intertwined with the schools' religious mission, (2) the statutes involved required too close proximity of government to the subsidized sectarian institutions, creating real dangers of secularization of a creed through the states' regulation and policing of the instruction and teachers of the sectarian schools, and thus offending the establishment clause of the First Amendment, (3) even if the objectionable features of the statutes as to state surveillance were eliminated, nevertheless the statutory subsidies would still be unconstitutional general subsidies of religious activities, notwithstanding that the subsidies were paid solely for secular education provided by the parochial schools, and (4) the statutes violated the principle that government may not employ religious means to serve legitimate secular interests, at least without the clearest demonstration that nonreligious means will not suffice.

White, J., concurring in part and dissenting in part, stated that (1) the state statutes did not violate the First Amendment since indirect benefit to religion from government aid to sectarian schools in performance of separable secular functions did not convert such aid into an impermissible establishment of religion, (2) considerations under the free exercise clause of the First Amendment at least counseled against refusing support for students attending parochial schools simply because in that setting they were also being instructed in the tenets of the faith they were constitutionally free to practice, (3) the Rhode Island statute involved in Nos. 569 and 570 should be sustained since the record did not establish that secular instruction could not be separated from religious instruction or that entanglement difficulties would accompany the salary supplement program, and (4) although the facial challenge to the Pennsylvania statute should be similarly rejected, nevertheless the judgment of reversal and remand in No. 89 was proper since the complaint, which was dismissed by the District Court, alleged that the schools were operated to fulfil religious purposes and that the statute financed and participated in the blending of sectarian and secular instruction, and since such allegations, if proved, would establish the unconstitutionality of the statute as applied.

COUNSEL

Henry W. Sawyer III argued the cause and filed briefs for appellants in No. 89. Edward Bennett Williams argued the cause for appellants in No. 569. With him on the brief were Jeremiah C. Collins and Richard P. McMahon. Charles F. Cottam argued the cause for appellants in No. 570. With him on the brief were Herbert F. DeSimone, Attorney General of Rhode Island, and W. Slater Allen, Jr., Assistant Attorney General.

J. Shane Creamer argued the cause for appellees Kurtzman et al. in No. 89. On the brief were Fred Speaker, Attorney General of Pennsylvania, David W. Rutstein, Deputy Attorney General, and Edward Friedman. William B. Ball argued the cause for appellee schools in No. 89. With him on the brief were Joseph G. Skelly, James E. Gallagher, Jr., C. Clark Hodgon, Jr., Samuel Rappaport, Donald A. Semisch, and William D. Valente. Henry T. Reath filed a brief for appellee Pennsylvania Association of Independent Schools in No. 89. Leo Pfeffer and Milton Stanzler argued the cause for appellees in Nos. 569 and 570. With them on the brief were Harold E. Adams, Jr., and Allan M. Shine.

Briefs of amici curiae urging reversal in No. 89 were filed by Mr. Pfeffer for the American Association of School Administrators et al.; by Henry C. Clausen for United Americans for Public Schools; by Samuel Rabinove, Arnold Forster, George Soll, Joseph B. Robison, Paul Hartman, and Sol Rabkin for the American Jewish Committee et al.; by Franklin C. Salisbury for Protestants and Other Americans United for Separation of Church and State; by J. Harold Flannery for the Center for Law and Education, Harvard University, et al.; and by Peter L. Costas and Paul W. Orth for the Connecticut State Conference of Branches of the NAACP et al.

Briefs of amici curiae urging affirmance in No. 89 were filed by Acting Solicitor General Friedman, Assistant Attorney General Ruckelshaus, Robert V. Zener, and Donald L. Horowitz for the United States; by Paul W. Brown, Attorney General of Ohio, pro se, and Charles S. Lopeman, First Assistant Attorney General, for the Attorney

General of Ohio et al.; by Levy Anderson for the City of Philadelphia; by Robert M. Landis for the School District of Philadelphia; by the City of Pittsburgh; by Bruce W. Kauffman, John M. Elliott, and Edward F. Mannino for the City of Erie; by James A. Kelly for the School District of the City of Scranton; by Charles M. Whelan, William R. Consedine, Alfred L. Scanlan, Arthur E. Sutherland, and Harmon Burns, Jr., for the National Catholic Educational Association et al.; by Ethan A. Hitchcock and I. N. P. Stokes for the National Association of Independent Schools, Inc.; by Jerome H. Gerber for the Pennsylvania State AFL–CIO; by Thomas J. Ford, Edward J. Walsh, Jr., and Theodore D. Hoffmann for the Long Island Conference of Religious Elementary and Secondary School Administrators; by Nathan Lewin for the National Jewish Commission on Law and Public Affairs; by Stuart Hubbell for Citizens for Educational Freedom; and by Edward M. Koza, Walter L. Hill, Jr., Thomas R. Balaban, and William J. Pinkowksi for the Polish American Congress, Inc., et al.

The National Association of Laymen filed a brief as amicus curiae in No. 89.

Briefs of amici curiae urging reversal in Nos. 569 and 570 were filed by Acting Solicitor General Friedman, Assistant Attorney General Gray, and Messrs. Zener and Horowitz for the United States, and by Jesse H. Choper and Messrs. Consedine, Whelan, and Burns for the National Catholic Educational Association et al.

Briefs of amici curiae urging affirmance in Nos. 569 and 570 were filed by Messrs. Rabinove, Robison, Forster, and Rabkin for the American Jewish Committee et al.; by Mr. Salisbury for Protestants and Other Americans United for Separation of Church and State; by Mr. Flannery for the Center for Law and Education, Harvard University, et al.; and by Messrs. Costas and Orth for the Con-

necticut State Conference of Branches of the NAACP
et al.

ELEANOR TAFT TILTON et al.,
Appellants,

v

ELLIOT L. RICHARDSON, Secretary of the
United States Department of Health,
Education, and Welfare, et al.

403 US 672, 29 L Ed 2d 790, 91 S Ct 2091

Argued March 2 and 3, 1971. Decided
June 28, 1971.

Decision: Higher Education Facilities Act of 1963 held
not violative of First Amendment insofar as it authorizes federal construction grants for secular facilities of church-related colleges and universities; Act's
limitation of federal interest in facilities to 20-year
period held violative of First Amendment.

SUMMARY

Taxpayers and residents of Connecticut instituted an
action in the United States District Court for the District
of Connecticut against federal officials and certain church-
related colleges and universities located in Connecticut,
challenging the constitutionality, under the religion
clauses of the First Amendment, of the Higher Education
Facilities Act of 1963, under which federal aid was granted to the defendant institutions by way of construction
grants for buildings and facilities to be used for secular
educational purposes. The Act authorizes federal grants
to institutions of higher education for construction of
academic facilities, except facilities to be used for sectarian instruction or worship, or in connection with
the program of a divinity school or department, and the
statutory restrictions as to secular use of the facilities
are enforced primarily by the government's on-site in-

spections. Under the Act, the government retains only a 20-year interest in the financed facilities, and if a facility should be used other than as a secular academic facility during such period, the United States is entitled to recover back a proportionate part of the federal grant. After hearing evidence as to the religious nature of the defendant institutions and as to their compliance with the statutory conditions, the three-judge District Court ruled that the Act authorized grants to church-related institutions, and that the Constitution was not thereby violated (312 F Supp 1191).

On appeal, the United States Supreme Court vacated and remanded for entry of an appropriate judgment. Although not agreeing on an opinion, five members of the court agreed that the religion clauses of the First Amendment were not violated by the Higher Education Facilities Act insofar as it authorizes grants to church-related colleges and universities for construction of buildings and facilities to be used exclusively for secular educational purposes, and eight members of the court agreed that the First Amendment was violated by the Act's provisions limiting the government's interest in covered facilities to a 20-year period and thereby allowing use of the facilities for sectarian purposes after such period, since such provisions operated to effect a contribution of some value to a religious body.

Burger, Ch. J., announced the judgment of the court, and in an opinion joined by **Harlan, Stewart,** and **Blackmun,** JJ., expressed the views that (1) the Act, which included church-related institutions and which reflected the legitimate secular objective of assisting in providing necessary facilities for higher education, did not have the primary effect of aiding religious purposes of the church-related institutions, even though some benefits accrued to such institutions, (2) there was no showing that religion so permeated the secular education provided by the defendant institutions as to make their secular and religious educational functions inseparable, and the Act would not be declared unconstitutional on the basis of a "composite profile" of the "typical sectarian institution," as asserted by the plaintiffs, (3) the unconstitutionality of the Act's provisions limiting the government's interest in covered facilities to a 20-year period did not require invalidation of the entire Act, (4) the administration of the Act with regard to aid to church-related institutions did not foster excessive government entanglement with religion in violation of the First Amendment, particularly since religious indoctrination was not a substantial purpose of such institutions, and since the aid, which was provided on a one-time, single-purpose basis, was directed at facilities that were religiously neutral, and (5) there was no violation of the plaintiffs' rights under the free exercise clause of the First Amendment through their compelled payment of taxes which in part financed grants under the Act, since they were unable to identify any coercion directed at the practice or exercise of their religious beliefs.

White, J., concurred in the result on the ground that legislation having a secular purpose and extending governmental assistance to sectarian schools in the performance of their secular functions did not violate the First Amendment merely because the legislative program incidentally benefited a church in fulfilling its religious mission.

Douglas, J., joined by **Black** and **Marshall, JJ.**, dissented, expressing the views that the court's proper invalidation of the statutory limitation of federal interest in subsidized facilities to a 20-year period did not save the statute as a whole; and that aid to religious schools under the Act violated the religion clauses of the First Amendment and academic freedom, since the government surveillance necessary to insure that the facilities were not used for sectarian purposes created prohibitive entanglement between government and religion, and since even if the statutory restriction as to secular use of the facilities was observed, nevertheless a religious institution, which operated on a single budget for both religious and secular teaching, was unconstitutionally aided because money saved from one item of its budget was free to be used elsewhere.

Brennan, J., dissented, stating that (1) the Act was unconstitutional insofar as it authorized grants of federal tax moneys to sectarian institutions, particularly in view of the necessarily deep involvement of government in the religious activities of such institutions through the policing of restrictions, and the fact that subsidies of tax moneys directly to a sectarian institution necessarily aided the proselytizing function of the institution, (2) the establishment clause of the First Amendment precluded the government from providing funds to sectarian universities in which the propagation and advancement of a particular religion was a function or purpose of the institution, and (3) the case should be remanded for the District Court's determination of the question whether the defendant institutions were "sectarian" institutions.

COUNSEL

Leo Pfeffer argued the cause for appellants. With him on the briefs were Peter L. Costas, Paul W. Orth, and Jerry Wagner.

Daniel M. Friedman argued the cause for appellees Richardson et al. On the brief were Solicitor General Erwin N. Griswold, Assistant Attorney General Ruckelshaus, Robert V. Zener, and Donald L. Horowitz, F. Michael Ahern, Assistant Attorney General of Connecticut, argued the cause for appellee Peterson. With him on the brief was Robert K. Killian, Attorney General. Edward Bennett Williams argued the cause for appellee colleges and universities. With him on the brief were Jeremiah C. Collins, Howard T. Owens, Lawrence W. Iannotti, and Bruce Lewellyn.

Briefs of amici curiae urging reversal were filed by Franklin C. Salisbury for Protestants and Other Americans United For Separation of Church and State, and by Peter L. Costas and Paul W. Orth for the Connecticut State Conference of Branches of the NAACP et al.

Briefs of amici curiae urging affirmance were filed by Wilber G. Katz and John Holt Myers for the American Council on Education et al., and by Nathan Lewin for the National Jewish Commission on Law and Public Affairs.

CASSIUS MARSELLUS CLAY, Jr., also known
as Muhammad Ali, Petitioner,

v

UNITED STATES

403 US 698, 29 L Ed 2d 810, 91 S Ct 2068

Argued April 19, 1971. Decided
June 28, 1971.

Decision: Draft registrant's conviction for refusing induction overturned because denial of his conscientious objector claim might have been based on Justice
Department's erroneous advice.

SUMMARY

Local Board No. 47, Louisville, Kentucky, denied a
draft registrant's application for classification as a conscientious objector. He took an administrative appeal to
the Kentucky Appeal Board, which referred his file to the
Justice Department for an advisory recommendation.
The FBI conducted the statutorily required "inquiry,"
and a hearing was held before a Justice Department-ap-
pointed hearing officer, who found that the registrant was
sincere in his objection on religious grounds to participation in war in any form, and recommended that the conscientious objector claim be sustained. Nevertheless, the
Justice Department advised the Kentucky Appeal Board
that the claim should be denied for failure to satisfy each
of the three basic tests for qualification as a conscientious
objector. The Kentucky Appeal Board denied the registrant's claim without a statement of reasons. The registrant refused to submit to induction and was convicted,
in the United States District Court for the Southern District of Texas, of wilful refusal to submit to induction.
The United States Court of Appeals for the Fifth Circuit

affirmed (397 F2d 901), and when the judgment of affirmance was set aside for a determination of his claim of illegal electronic surveillance (394 US 310, 22 L Ed 2d 297, 89 S Ct 1164), it again affirmed the conviction (430 F2d 165).

On certiorari, the United States Supreme Court reversed. In a per curiam opinion expressing the views of six members of the court, it was held that (1) since the registrant's beliefs were founded on the tenets of the Muslim religion as he understood them, they were religiously based and therefore satisfied this test for qualification as a conscientious objector; (2) since the hearing officer found that the registrant was sincere in his objections, and thus met another test for qualification as a conscientious objector, the Justice Department erred in advising the Kentucky Appeal Board to disregard this finding simply because he did not assert his claim until military service became imminent; and (3) whether or not the registrant met the third test of conscientious objection to war in any form, it was not clear that the Kentucky Appeal Board relied on some legitimate ground in denying the claim, and therefore the conviction could not stand.

Douglas, J., concurred on the ground that the First Amendment freedom of religion precluded the registrant's induction, since in accordance with the Koran he believed only in religious wars against nonbelievers.

Harlan, J., concurred on the ground that the Kentucky Appeal Board might have acted on the Justice Department's erroneous advice that the registrant's proof of sincerity was insufficient as a matter of law because his claim had not been timely asserted.

Marshall, J., did not participate.

COUNSEL

Chauncey Eskridge argued the cause for petitioner. With him on the briefs were Jack Greenberg, James M. Nabrit III, Jonathan Shapiro, and Elizabeth B. DuBois.

Solicitor General Erwin N. Griswold argued the cause for the United States. With him on the brief were Assistant Attorney General Wilson and Beatrice Rosenberg.

CHARLES HUNTER and Franklin Wright,
Petitioners,

v

TENNESSEE (No. 5085)

———

ULOUS HARRIS, Petitioner,

v

TENNESSEE (No. 5098)

———

GARFIELD HOUSTON and Earl Foster,
Petitioners,

v

TENNESSEE (No. 5101)

———

CHARLES HUNTER and Franklin Wright,
Petitioners,

v

TENNESSEE (No. 5103)

403 US 711, 29 L Ed 2d 820, 91 S Ct 2285
June 28, 1971

Decision: Death sentences vacated to allow applications
to state court for leave to supplement bills of exceptions to raise Witherspoon issues.

SUMMARY

Pending appeals in the Tennessee Supreme Court from
rape convictions and consequent death sentences, the
United States Supreme Court announced its decision in
Witherspoon v Illinois (1968) 391 US 510, 20 L Ed 2d

776, 88 S Ct 1770.   The appellants sought to raise issues under Witherspoon by supplementing their bills of exceptions, but were precluded from doing so by a Tennessee statute prohibiting the filing of bills of exceptions more than 90 days after judgment.   The Tennessee Supreme Court affirmed the convictions and sentences without considering the possible effect of Witherspoon (222 Tenn 672, 440 SW2d 1).   Pending certiorari to the United States Supreme Court, the Tennessee Legislature amended the statute to authorize the filing of bills of exceptions in criminal cases at any time, for good cause shown.

The United States Supreme Court granted certiorari, vacated the judgments, and remanded the cases to the Tennessee Supreme Court to allow the petitioners to apply under the new Tennessee statute for leave to supplement their bills of exceptions.

Black, J., dissented without opinion.

NEW YORK TIMES COMPANY,
Petitioner,

v

UNITED STATES (No. 1873)

UNITED STATES, Petitioner,

v

THE WASHINGTON POST COMPANY
et al. (No. 1885)

403 US 713, 29 L Ed 2d 822, 91 S Ct 2140

Argued June 26, 1971. Decided June 30, 1971.

Decision: Government held not entitled to injunction
against newspapers' publication of classified study
relating to Viet Nam policy.

SUMMARY

In an action in the United States District Court for the
Southern District of New York, the United States government sought an injunction against the publication by
the New York Times of the contents of a classified study
entitled "History of U. S. Decision-Making Process on
Viet Nam Policy," and in an action in the United States
District Court for the District of Columbia, the government sought a similar injunction against the Washington
Post. Each District Court denied injunctive relief. The
Court of Appeals for the District of Columbia affirmed
the judgment of the District Court for the District of
Columbia, but the Court of Appeals for the Second Circuit remanded the case to the District Court for the South-
ern District of New York for further hearings.

On certiorari, the United States Supreme Court affirmed the judgment of the Court of Appeals for the District of Columbia, but reversed the judgment of the Court of Appeals for the Second Circuit and remanded the case with directions to enter a judgment affirming the judgment of the District Court for the Southern District of New York. In a per curiam opinion expressing the view of six members of the court, it was held that the government did not meet its burden of showing justification for the imposition of a prior restraint of expression.

Black, J., joined by **Douglas, J.**, concurring, stated that under the First Amendment, the press must be left free to publish news, whatever the source, without censorship, injunctions, or prior restraints, and that the guarding of military and diplomatic secrets at the expense of informed representative government was not justified.

Douglas, J., joined by **Black, J.**, concurring, stated that the First Amendment left no room for governmental restraint on the press, and that the dominant purpose of the First Amendment was to prohibit governmental suppression of embarrassing information.

Brennan, J., concurring, stated that the First Amendment stood as an absolute bar to the imposition of judicial restraints in circumstances of the kind presented by the present cases.

Stewart, J., joined by **White, J.**, concurring, stated that the court was asked to perform a function which the Constitution gave to the Executive, not to the Judiciary, and that it could not be said that disclosure of the documents involved in the present cases would surely result in direct, immediate, and irreparable damage to the nation or its people.

White, J., joined by **Stewart, J.**, concurring, stated that although the government mistakenly chose to proceed by injunction, the court's decision did not mean that the law invited newspapers or others to publish sensitive documents or that they would be immune from criminal action if they did so.

Marshall, J., concurring, stated that under the concept of separation of power, the court did not have authority to grant the requested relief, and that the court should not take on itself the burden of enacting law, especially law which Congress had refused to pass.

Burger, Ch. J., dissenting, stated that the First Amendment right was not an absolute, and that the present cases had been decided in unseemly haste and without an adequate record.

Harlan, J., joined by **Burger, Ch. J.**, and **Blackmun, J.**, dissenting, stated that the court had been almost irresponsibly feverish in dealing with the present cases, that the scope of the judicial function in passing upon the activities of the Executive in the field of foreign affairs was very narrowly restricted, and that the doctrine prohibiting prior restraints did not prevent courts from maintaining the status quo long enough to act responsibly.

Blackmun, J., dissenting, stated that the present litigation had maintained a frenetic pace and character, that he could not subscribe to a doctrine of unlimited absolutism for the First Amendment at the cost of downgrading other provisions of the Constitution, and that there was a danger that publication of the critical documents involved in the present cases would result in the death of soldiers, the destruction of alliances, the greatly increased difficulty of negotiation with our enemies, the inability of our diplomats to negotiate, the prolongation of the war, and further delay in the freeing of United States prisoners.

COUNSEL

Alexander M. Bickel argued the cause for petitioner in No. 1873. With him on the brief were William E. Hegarty and Lawrence J. McKay.

Solicitor General Erwin N. Griswold argued the cause for the United States in both cases. With him on the brief were Assistant Attorney General Mardian and Daniel M. Friedman.

William R. Glendon argued the cause for respondents in No. 1885. With him on the brief were Roger A. Clark, Anthony F. Essaye, Leo P. Larkin, Jr., and Stanley Godofsky.

Briefs of amici curiae were filed by Bob Eckhardt and Thomas I. Emerson for Twenty-Seven Members of Congress; by Norman Dorsen, Melvin L. Wulf, Burt Neuborne, Bruce J. Ennis, Osmond K. Fraenkel, and Marvin M. Karpatkin for the American Civil Liberties Union; and by Victor Rabinowitz for the National Emergency Civil Liberties Committee.

GLOSSARY OF COMMON LEGAL TERMS

Abatement

The extinguishment of a lawsuit.

Action

A lawsuit.

Administrative determination

A decision by a government board, agency or official, rather than by a court.

Administrator

One appointed by a court to settle the estate of a deceased person. The feminine form is "administratrix."

Admiralty

The body of law governing maritime cases.

Affidavit

A sworn written statement.

Agency shop

A union-management arrangement whereby nonunion workers are employable provided that they pay to the union sums equivalent to union initiation fees and dues.

Amicus curiae

One who, not being a party to a lawsuit, assists the court in deciding the case.

Antitrust laws

Laws prohibiting restrictions on competition.

Appealable

That which may be taken to a higher court for review.

Appellant

One who appeals to a superior court from the order of an inferior court.

Appellee

A party against whom a case is appealed from an inferior court to a superior court.

Arbitration

The submission of a dispute to a selected person—not a court—for decision.

Arraign

To call a person before a judge or commissioner to answer criminal charges made against him.

Array

The whole body of persons, summoned to attend court, from whom a jury will be selected.

Assignee

One to whom property or a right is transferred.

Assignor

The transferor of property or a right.

Bareboat charter

The charter of a ship whereby the party hiring the ship must furnish the crew.

Barratry

The habitual stirring up of lawsuits.

Brief

A written legal argument submitted to the court deciding the case.

Calendar

A list of cases awaiting decision in a court.

Capital crime

An offense punishable by death.

Cause of action
A right to legal redress.

Cease-and-desist order
An order to stop doing specified acts.

Certiorari
A superior court's order to a lower court to send up the record of a case for review by the superior court.

Charter
An agreement for the hire of a ship.

Choice of remedies
An election of which form of legal redress to seek.

Civil
Not criminal, as a civil lawsuit.

Class action
A lawsuit on behalf of persons too numerous to participate actively therein.

Collapsible corporation
A corporation used to give the appearance of a long-term investment to what is actually a mere venture in the manufacture, production or construction of property, with the intention of having the profits of the venture taxed as a capital gain rather than as income.

Commerce clause
The provision of the United States Constitution giving Congress power to regulate commerce with foreign nations, among the states.

Common law
The body of the law apart from constitutions, treaties, statutes, ordinances, and regulations.

Condemnee
One whose property is condemned.

Condemnor
One who condemns property.

Continuance
A postponement of proceedings.

Copyright
The exclusive privilege of publishing literary or artistic productions.

Coram nobis
A means of challenging a court's judgment, especially in criminal cases.

Court of Appeals
See United States Court of Appeals.

Cross appeal
An appeal filed by the person against whom an appeal is taken.

Cross-licensing agreement
An agreement between patent owners licensing each to use the other's patent.

De novo
Anew or over again, such as a trial de novo.

Devise
A will provision making a gift of land.

Disputes clause
A provision in a government contract for the settlement of disputes between the contractor and the government by decision of a government board or official.

District court
A federal trial court.

Diversity case

A case decided by a federal court because the parties are citizens of different states.

Double jeopardy

Placing a person twice in jeopardy of conviction for the same offense.

En banc

With all the judges of the court sitting.

Entrapment

Inducing one to commit a crime not contemplated by him for the purpose of prosecuting him.

Equal protection

The guaranty of the United States Constitution that no person or class of persons shall be denied the same protection of the laws that is enjoyed by other persons or classes of persons in like circumstances.

Establishment clause

The provision of the United States Constitution that Congress shall make no law respecting an establishment of religion.

Federal district court

See District court.

Federal question jurisdiction

The jurisdiction of federal courts over cases presenting questions of federal law.

Felony

A crime punishable by death or by imprisonment in a state prison.

Felony murder

A homicide by a person engaged in the commission of a felony.

Forma pauperis
Without the payment of legal fees in advance.

Full faith and credit clause
The provision of the United States Constitution that full faith and credit shall be given in each state to the public acts, records, and judicial proceedings of every other state.

Habeas corpus
A judicial inquiry into the legality of the restraint of a person.

Habeas corpus ad testificandum
A procedure for moving a prisoner so that he may testify in court.

Indictment
A grand jury's accusation of crime.

Interlocutory
That which settles an intervening matter but does not decide a case.

Intestate
One who dies without leaving a valid will.

Jurisdiction of subject matter
The power to decide a certain type of case.

Laches
Delay barring the right to special forms of relief.

Legatee
One to whom personal property is given by will.

Lessee
A tenant.

Lessor
A landlord.

Libel

Written defamation; in maritime cases, a suit in court.

Lien

A charge upon property for the payment of a debt.

Local action

A lawsuit, especially one involving rights to land, which can be brought only in the place where the wrong was committed.

Maintenance

Officious intermeddling in a lawsuit by assisting one party, especially by the payment of money, to prosecute or defend, particularly where the profits of the lawsuit are to be divided.

Maintenance and cure

The legal duty of a seaman's employer to care for him during his illness.

Mandamus

A judicial command to perform an official duty.

Misdemeanor

Any crime not punishable by death or by imprisonment in a state prison.

Per curiam

By the court as a whole.

Per se

By itself.

Plaintiff

A person who brings a lawsuit.

Plenary

Full or complete.

Police power

The power inherent in the states as sovereigns and not derived under any written constitution.

Privileges and immunities clause

The provision of the United States Constitution that no state shall make or enforce any law which abridges the privileges or immunities of citizens of the United States.

Pro hac vice

For this occasion.

Pro se

For himself; in his own behalf.

Proximate cause

The immediate cause of injury.

Public defender

A lawyer employed by the public to defend persons accused of crime.

Quantum meruit

The reasonable value of services.

Recidivist

One charged with a crime similar to that for which he was previously convicted.

Recognizance

A bail bond.

Remand

To order to be sent back.

Res judicata

The doctrine that a final judgment is binding on the parties to the lawsuit and the matter cannot be relitigated.

Respondent

The defendant in an action; with regard to appeals, the party against whom the appeal is taken.

Sanction

The penalty to be incurred by a wrongdoer.

Saving clause

A statutory provision preserving rights which would otherwise be annihilated by the statute.

Seaworthy

The reasonable fitness of a vessel to perform the service which she has undertaken to perform.

Statute of frauds

A statute rendering certain types of contracts unenforceable unless in writing.

Statute of limitations

A statute fixing a period of time within which certain types of lawsuits or criminal prosecutions must be begun.

Subpoena

Legal process to require the attendance of a witness.

Subrogate

To substitute one person for another with respect to certain rights.

Subrogee

One who is substituted for another so as to gain the benefit of the latter's rights.

Substantial federal question

A question of federal law of sufficient merit to warrant decision of the case by a federal court.

Substantive offense

An offense which is complete in itself and does not depend on the establishment of another offense.

Summary judgment

A judgment without a trial.

Supremacy clause

The provision of the United States Constitution that the Constitution, federal laws enacted pursuant thereto, and federal treaties shall be the supreme law of the land, binding the judges in every state, notwithstanding any state law to the contrary.

Surety

One who binds himself with another, called the principal, for the performance of an obligation with respect to which the principal is already bound and primarily liable.

Surrogate

The judge of a court dealing largely with wills and decedents' estates.

Transitory action

An action which may be brought wherever the defendant may be served with process.

Trespass

An injury intentionally inflicted on the person or property of another.

Trier of fact

One who decides questions of fact.

United States Code

The official compilation of statutes enacted by Congress.

United States Court of Appeals

The intermediate level of federal courts above the United States District Courts but below the Supreme Court of the United States.

[Supreme Ct Sum]

United States District Court
See District court.

Unseaworthy
See Seaworthy.

USC
See United States Code.

Venue
The place where a case may be tried.

Writ of certiorari
See Certiorari.

Writ of error coram nobis
See Coram nobis.

*

TABLE OF CASES

*

INDEX

ADMINISTRATIVE LAW—Continued

Social security disability claimant, report of doctor not appearing at administrative hearing as evidence against, 251

Transportation of dangerous articles, regulation pertaining to, 277

Uninsured motorist failing to post security for claims, suspension of license and registration of, 269

Welfare funds, provision for approval of state plan for distribution of, 332

ADMIRALTY

Seaman's action for wages due, 39

ADMISSIONS AND DECLARATIONS

Informer, search based on tip including declarations against interest of, 351

Joint trial, inculpatory out-of-court statement of codefendant as admissible at, 285

AFDC PROGRAM

Refusal to permit caseworker to visit home as resulting in termination of benefits, 37

AFFIDAVIT

Oath or Affidavit (this index)

AGE

Voting age requirements, 27

AGENTS

National bank authority to operate collective investment fund, 179

AIDING AND ABETTING

Gambling, Travel Act as violated by interstate travel for purpose of, 199

ALIENS

Military service, denial of citizenship based on prior claim of exemption, 262

Physical presence as required to maintain citizenship of foreign-born child having one alien parent, 201

Refugee status as affected by firm resettlement in third country after flight, 220

Welfare benefits, residence requirement for payment of, 332

ANARCHY
Constitutionality of New York criminal anarchy statutes, 87

ANTENNA
Patent infringement case, collateral estoppel in, 243

ANTITRUST LAWS
Restraints of Trade and Monopolies (this index)

APARTHEID
Public swimming pools, city closing rather than desegregating, 321

APPEAL AND ERROR
Certiorari (this index)

Conscientious objector claim, failure to take administrative appeal from denial of, 260

Criminal Appeals Act (this index)

Death sentence vacated to allow application to supplement bill of exceptions under changed state law, 371

Direct Appeal (this index)

Discharge of jury on declaration of mistrial in criminal case, government appeal from, 58

Federal Maritime Commission, time for review of orders of, 20

Injunction with marked impact on First Amendment rights, reviewability of, 254

Interlocutory order as to production of corporate records, appealability of, 267

Mootness, dismissal of appeal on ground of, 98

Puerto Rican statute as "state statute" for appellate purposes, 13

Reapportionment plan, stay pending appeal from three-judge District Court decree as to, 294

APPORTIONMENT
County legislature electoral districts, validity of apportionment plan following town lines for, 312

Countywide multimember legislative district, validity of, 309

Stay of decree creating multimember district with instructions to devise single-member district, 294

Time for legislative enactment of apportionment plan, allowance of, 307

ASSOCIATION
Freedom of Association (this index)

ATTENDANCE AT MEETING
Union election rules, challenge to, 327

ATTENDANCE ZONES
School desegregation by assignment of students to new attendance zones, 206, 211, 214

ATTORNEY GENERAL
Warrants issued by state attorney general for arrest of accused and search of automobile, validity of, 340

ATTORNEYS
Arizona State Bar, denial of admission to, 76
New York statutory procedures for screening bar applicants, 101
Ohio State Bar procedures for screening applicants, 80
Representation by Counsel (this index)

AUTOMOBILES
Motor Vehicles (this index)

BANKRUPTCY
Accrued but unpaid vacation pay as not constituting "property" passing to trustee, 8
State suspension of driver's license for failure to satisfy accident judgment as conflicting with Bankruptcy Act, 288
Withheld taxes, priority of claim for, 161

BANKS AND BANKING
Collective investment fund, authorization of national bank to operate, 179
Savings and loan association payment of additional premium as deductible business expense, 329
Travel services for customers, standing to challenge ruling allowing national bank to provide, 15

BELIEFS
Loyalty oath embracing political or philosophical beliefs of public employees, validity of, 317
Religion and Religious Matters (this index)

BUGGING
Surveillance by transmitter concealed on informant as illegal search and seizure, 193

BUILDINGS
Higher Education Facilities Act, grants to church-related institutions under, 363

BURDEN OF PROOF
Presumptions and Burden of Proof (this index)

BURGLARY TOOLS
Search and seizure incident to arrest without probable cause, 171

BUSINESS EXPENSES
Savings and loan association, deductible business expense of, 329

BUSING OF STUDENTS
Antibusing statute, injunction against enforcement of, 216, 218
Desegregation of dual public school system, 206, 211, 214

CAPITAL PUNISHMENT
Guilty plea, death penalty as motivation for, 10
Jury, effect of single-verdict procedure or absence of standards to guide, 240
Vacation of sentence to allow application to supplement bill of exceptions under changed state law, 371

CARRIERS
Dangerous articles, regulation pertaining to transportation of, 277
Discontinuance or change in train service, duties with respect to notice of, 3
State regulation, 1

CATHOLIC SCHOOLS
State aid as to secular instruction in church-related schools, 355

CENSORSHIP
Obscenity (this index)

CENSUS
Apportionment plan, population figures as basis for, 294, 307, 309, 312

CLASS SUITS

Aliens, residence requirement for payment of welfare benefits to, 332

State denial of unemployment benefits violating Social Security Act, 230

CLAYTON ACT

Restraints of Trade and Monopolies (this index)

CODEFENDANT

Joint trial, inculpatory out-of-court statement of codefendant as admissible at, 285

COLLATERAL ESTOPPEL

Examination of record of prior trial in ruling on claim of collateral estoppel, 336

Indian lands, effect of consent judgment on claim for compensation for former, 238

Patent infringement case, prior determination of invalidity of patent as basis for pleading collateral estoppel in, 243

COLLECTIVE BARGAINING

Arbitration effect of seaman's failure to take advantage of Labor Management Relations Act provisions for, 39

Injunction against strike for union failure to make reasonable effort to reach agreement, 279

Jurisdiction of claim by member against union for procuring discharge under union security clause, 324

Political subdivision exempt from Labor-Management Relations Act, natural gas utility district as, 281

COLLECTIVE INVESTMENT FUND

National bank authority to operate collective investment fund, 179

COLLEGES AND UNIVERSITIES

Armed Forces member, jurisdiction over habeas corpus petition directed at ROTC commander by, 156

Church-related institutions, federal construction grants to, 363

COLORADO INDIAN LANDS

Res judicata effect of consent judgment on claim for compensation for former Indian lands, 238

COLORADO WATER RIGHT DETERMINATION AND ADMINISTRATION ACT OF 1969
Consent of United States to be sued in water adjudication suit, 166

COMIC STRIPS
Clayton Act as violated by corporate acquisition of comic supplement printing company, 274

COMMERCE
Interstate Commerce (this index)

COMMON CARRIERS
Carriers (this index)

COMMUNISM
Bar admission, refusal to answer questions concerning Communist Party membership as basis for denial of, 76, 80
Resettlement in third country after flight as affecting refugee status of a lien, 218

COMMUNITY PROPERTY
Income tax liability of wife as affected by renunciation of rights, 314

COMPETITION
Restraints of Trade and Monopolies (this index)

COMPTROLLER OF CURRENCY
Collective investment fund, national bank authority to operate, 179
Travel agents as having standing to challenge ruling, 15

CONFESSIONS
Diary seized during search incident to arrest, 196
Habeas corpus proceeding, raising question of voluntariness of confession in, 52
Joint trial, inculpatory out-of-court statement of codefendant as admissible at, 285

CONFRONTATION OF WITNESSES
Conspirator's statements against other conspirators, admission of, 23
Joint trial, inculpatory out-of-court statement of codefendant as admissible at, 285

CONSTITUTIONAL LAW—Continued

Firearms, violation of statute requiring registration of, 177

"Fuck the Draft," validity of conviction for disturbing peace by wearing jacket bearing words, 299

Informer, search based partly on tip from, 351

Joint trial, inculpatory out-of-court statement of codefendant as admissible at, 285

Jury and Jury Trial (this index)

Labor union furnishing legal assistance to members or controlling legal fees, injunction against, 174

Libel and slander action, "public figure" within rule requiring showing of actual malice in, 120

Loyalty oath for public employees, 317

Police Power (this index)

Religion and Religious Matters (this index)

Retroactive Application (this index)

Search and Seizure (this index)

Self-incrimination (this index)

Sidewalk assemblies "annoying" to passers-by, validity of ordinance punishing, 283

Standing to challenge constitutionality of state statute, 90

Supremacy Clause (this index)

Suspicious person ordinance as applied to parked motorist talking on two-way radio at night, 271

Uninsured motorist failing to post security for claims, suspension of license and registration of, 269

Vagueness of Statute (this index)

CONSTRUCTION OF BUILDINGS

Higher Education Facilities Act, grants to church-related institutions under, 363

CONSTRUCTION OR INTERPRETATION

Abortion statute, vagueness of, 223

Bankruptcy Act, construction of provisions of, 8

Conscientious objector claim made after receipt of induction notice, determination of, 227

Consent decree forbidding meatpackers from engaging in retail business, effect of, 291

Higher Education Facilities Act, effect of partial invalidation of, 363

Immigration and Nationality Act (this index)

CORROBORATION
Informer, necessity of corroboration of tip of, 171, 351

CORROSIVE LIQUIDS
Transportation of dangerous articles, regulation pertaining to, 277

COSTS
State statute requiring indigents to pay costs in divorce action, 137

COUNTIES
Apportionment (this index)

COURTHOUSE
"Fuck the Draft," validity of conviction for disturbing peace by wearing jacket bearing words, 299

COURT-MARTIAL
Kidnapping and rape committed on military base as within jurisdiction of, 134

COURT OF APPEALS
Improper appeal from judgment of, 13
Time for direct review of orders of United States Maritime Commission, 20

CREDITORS
Debtors and Creditors (this index)

CRIMINAL APPEALS ACT
Abortion statute, appeal from dismissal of complaint on ground of unconstitutional vagueness of, 223
Selective Service regulation, appeal from construction of, 117

CRIMINAL CONTEMPT
Contempt (this index)

CRIMINAL LAW
As to particular crimes, see more specific topics throughout this index
Double Jeopardy (this index)
Guilty Plea (this index)
Jury and Jury Trial (this index)
Mistrial, government's appeal from discharge on declaration of, 58

DRIVERS' LICENSES—Continued

Security for claims, suspension of license of uninsured motorist failing to post, 269

DRUGS

Arrest and search, damage action for injuries from invalid, 343

DUAL SCHOOL SYSTEM

Antibusing statute, injunction against enforcement of, 216

Desegregation plans, validity of, 206, 211, 214

DUE PROCESS

Abortion statute, unconstitutional vagueness of, 223

Church-related schools, state aid as to secular instruction in, 355

Conscientious objector claim made after receipt of induction notice, procedure for determination of, 227

Contempt charge against civil rights worker, bias of judge at hearing on, 319

Death penalty, single-verdict procedure or absence of standards to guide jury as affecting imposition of, 240

Illegitimate child as barred from sharing in intestate father's estate, 168

Jury trial in juvenile delinquency proceeding, right to, 346

Liquor sale to named person, posting of notice forbidding, 50

Loyalty oath for public employees, validity of, 317

Sidewalk assemblies "annoying" to passersby, validity of ordinance punishing, 283

Social security disability claimant, report of doctor not appearing at administrative hearing as evidence against, 251

Tax exemption, arbitrariness of cutoff date for, 1

Unemployment benefits, requirement of immediate payment by former employer pending appeal from award, 230

Uninsured motorist failing to post security for claims, suspension of license and registration of, 269

EAGLE RIVER

Consent of United States to be sued in supplemental water adjudication suit, 163

EAVESDROPPING

Electronic surveillance by transmitter concealed on informant as illegal search and seizure, 193

[Supreme Ct Sum]—27

EXEMPTIONS
Income Taxes (this index)
Military Service Armed Forces (this index)

EXHAUSTION OF REMEDIES
Conscientious objector claim, failure to take administrative appeal from denial of, 260
Union election rules, challenge to, 327

EXIGENT CIRCUMSTANCES
Search of automobile as affected by absence of exigent circumstances, 340

EXONERATION FROM DEBT
Income tax liability of wife as affected by renunciation of, 314

EXPENSES
Savings and loan association, deductible business expense of, 329

EXTORTION
Consumer Credit Protection Act prohibition of extortionate credit transactions, 236

FACULTY
Teachers (this index)

FAILING COMPANY
Applicability exception to Clayton Act, 274

FALSITY
Truth or Falsity (this index)

FEDERAL POWER COMMISSION
Interconnection of electric power companies, order for, 264

FEDERAL SAVINGS AND LOAN INSURANCE CORPORATION
Savings and loan association payment of additional premium as deductible business expense, 329

FELONIES
As to particular crimes, see more specific topics throughout this index
Jury trial in juvenile delinquency proceeding, right to, 346

GLASS-STEAGALL BANKING ACT OF 1933

National bank authority to operate collective investment fund, 179

GRANDFATHER CLAUSE

Exemption from income tax of certain corporations organized prior to specified date, 1

GRAND JURY

Subpoena duces tecum, appealability of order directing attempt to obtain foreign corporate records and refusing to quash, 267

GREAT SALT LAKE

Ownership of shorelands, 297

GUILTY PLEA

Indigent accused, retroactivity of decision requiring counsel for, 204

Standard for determining validity of, 10

GUNS

Firearms (this index)

HABEAS CORPUS

Armed Forces member, jurisdiction over habeas corpus petition directed at ROTC commander by, 156

Indigent accused, retroactivity of decision requiring appointed counsel for, 204

Joint trial, inculpatory out-of-court statement of codefendant as admissible at, 285

Search and seizure incident to arrest without probable cause, 171

Voluntariness of confession raising question of, 52

HAND GRENADES

Registration requirement of National Firearms Act, 177

HEALTH

Abortion statute, dismissal of indictment on ground of vagueness of, 223

HEARSAY

Administrative hearing, admissibility of report of doctor not appearing at, 251

Conspirator's statements against other conspirators as violative of right of confrontation of witnesses, 23

HEARSAY—Continued

Joint trial, inculpatory out-of-court statement of codefendant as admissible as, 285

HIGHER EDUCATION FACILITIES ACT

Church-related institutions, grants to, 363

HIGH SCHOOLS

Schools and School Districts (this index)

HIGHWAYS AND STREETS

Civil rights, recovery from private persons conspiring to deny, 305

Judicial review of routing of interstate highway through a public park, 141

Suspicious person ordinance as applied to parked motorists talking on two-way radio at night, 271

HOUSING

Referendum, requirement for approval of low-income housing project by majority vote in local, 233

HUMILIATION

Arrest and search, damage action for injuries resulting from invalid, 343

HUSBAND AND WIFE

Income tax liability of wife as affected by renunciation of community property rights, 314

Search and seizure, handing over of guns and clothing to police by wife of accused as constituting, 340

IDENTITY OR IDENTIFICATION

Double jeopardy, examination of record of prior trial in ruling on claim of, 336

Informer, search based partly on information from unnamed, 351

Search and seizure incident to arrest, legality of, 171, 196

Self-incrimination, state hit-and-run statute as violating privilege against, 256

IGNORANCE OF LAW

Transportation of dangerous articles, violating regulation pertaining to, 277

INDEX

ILLEGITIMACY
Intestate succession, statute barring illegitimate child from, 168

IMMIGRATION AND NATIONALITY ACT
Aliens (this index)

IMPORTS
Obscene matter, seizure by and forfeiture proceedings regarding, 248

IMPRISONMENT
Indigent's imprisonment for nonpayment of fines for traffic offenses, 139

INCOME TAX
Bankruptcy, priority of claim for withheld taxes in, 161
Community property, income tax liability of wife as affected by renunciation of, 314
Cutoff date for exemption purposes, arbitrariness of, 1
Savings and loan association, deductible business expense of, 329
Self-incrimination, federal wagering tax statutes as violation of privilege, 187, 190

INDEPENDENT CANDIDATES
Party primary, nominating petition requirement for candidate who does not enter and win, 338

INDIANS
Debt of Indian incurred on reservation, jurisdiction in case involving, 48
Res judicata effect of consent judgment on claim for compensation for Indian lands, 238

INDICTMENTS AND INFORMATIONS
Abortion statute, dismissal of indictment on ground of vagueness of, 223
Certiorari to review affirmance of conviction where petitioner was not charged with alleged offense, 273
Transportation of dangerous articles, prosecution for knowingly violating regulation pertaining to, 277

INDIGENTS
Poor and Poor Laws (this index)

JUVENILE DELINQUENCY

Jury trial in juvenile delinquency proceeding, right to, 346

KENYA

Subpoena duces tecum, appealability of order directing attempt to obtain foreign corporate records and refusing to quash, 267

KIDNAPPING

Court-martial, kidnapping committed on military post as within jurisdiction of, 134

KNOWLEDGE

Notice or Knowledge (this index)

KORAN

Conscientious objector claim based on tenets of Koran, 368

LABOR AND LABOR UNIONS

Antitrust suit against labor union, preponderance of evidence rule as applicable in, 128

Arbitration provisions of NLRA, effect of seaman's failure to take advantage of, 39

Bill of Rights provisions of Landrum-Griffin Act, jurisdiction of suit for violation of, 114

Collective Bargaining (this index)

Election rules of union, challenge to, 327

Legal assistance to members, injunction against furnishing of or controlling legal fees for, 174

Norris-La Guardia Act (this index)

Pickets, ordinance punishing sidewalk assemblies "annoying" to passersby as applied to, 283

Political subdivision exempt from Labor-Management Relations Act, natural gas utility district as, 281

Railroads (this index)

Regional director of NLRB, review of determination and order of, 95

Secondary boycott provision of NLRA, violation of, 33

Union security clause, jurisdiction of claim by member against union for procuring discharge under, 324

LAKES

Ownership of lands around Great Salt Lake, 297

Pollution of Lake Erie, suit by state for prevention of, 158

LANDLORD AND TENANT
Voluntary vacation of premises by tenants contesting summary eviction procedure, effect of, 98

LEAFLETS
Enjoining peaceful distribution of leaflets, 254

LEGISLATIVE DISTRICTS
Apportionment (this index)

LEGITIMATION
Illegitimate child as barred from sharing in intestate father's estate, 168

LESSER INCLUDED OFFENSES
State practice of acceptance of, 10

LIBEL AND SLANDER
Arrest, libel action for news report of, 301
Police brutality, action by police officer based on magazine article discussing report on, 123
Political candidate, charge of criminal conduct on part of, 120, 126

LICENSES
Drivers' Licenses (this index)

LIMITATION OF ACTIONS
Waiver of defense of in antitrust suit, 130

LIQUOR
Intoxicating Liquor (this index)

LITERACY TEST
Voting rights statutes provision suspending use of literacy test, 27

LOAN SHARKS
Consumer Credit Protection Act prohibition of extortionate credit transactions, 236

LOITERING
Sidewalk assemblies "annoying" to passersby, ordinance punishing, 283
Suspicious person ordinance, applicability of, 271

LONGSHOREMEN
Recovery from shipowner for injuries received from negligent act of fellow longshoreman, 62

LOTTERIES
Gambling (this index)

LOW-INCOME HOUSING
Referendum, requirement for approval of low-income housing project by majority vote in local, 233

LOYALTY OATH
Public employees, validity of loyalty oath for, 317

MAGAZINES
Press (this index)

MAGISTRATE
Attorney general, validity of warrants issued by, 340
Informer, necessity of producing before magistrate issuing search warrant name or person of, 351

MAILS
Obscene matter, distribution of, 45, 246

MALICE
Libel action, necessity of showing malice in, 120, 123, 126, 301

MASTERS
Great Salt Lake, reference to Special Master for determination of ownership of shorelands around, 297

MEATPACKING INDUSTRY
Consent decree forbidding meatpackers from engaging in retail business, effect of, 291

MENTAL SUFFERING
Arrest and search, action for injuries resulting from invalid, 343

MERCURY POISONING
Suit by state for prevention of pollution, 158

MERCY RECOMMENDATION
Death penalty, single-verdict procedure or absence of standards to guide jury as affecting imposition of, 240

MILITARY SERVICE
Armed Forces (this index)

MINORS
Children (this index)

MISDEMEANORS
Change of venue in case involving misdemeanor, 65
Jury trial in juvenile delinquency proceeding, right to, 346

MONEYLENDERS
Consumer Credit Protection Act prohibition of extortionate credit transactions as constitutional under commerce clause, 236

MONOPOLIES
Restraints of Trade and Monopolies (this index)

MOOTNESS
Dismissal of appeal, ground for, 98
Voluntary vacation of premises by tenants contesting summary eviction procedure, effect of, 98

MOTOR VEHICLES
Civil rights, recovery from private persons stopping automobile in furtherance of conspiracy to deny, 305
Imprisonment of indigent for nonpayment of fines for traffic offenses, 139
Search and seizure, legality of, 171, 340
Self-incrimination, state hit-and-run statute as violating privilege against, 256
Suspicious person ordinance as applied to parked motorists talking on two-way radio at night, 271
Uninsured Motorist (this index)

MULTIMEMBER ELECTION DISTRICT
Apportionment (this index)

MUNICIPALITY
Public swimming pools, city closing rather than desegregating, 321
Referenda on local actions, required vote of approval in, 233, 295

MURDER
Certiorari to review affirmance of conviction as improvidently granted, 273

MURDER—Continued

Fear of death penalty as motivation for plea of guilty to second degree murder, 10

Single-verdict procedure or absence of standards to guide jury as affecting imposition of death penalty, 240

MUSLIM RELIGION

Conscientious objector claim based on tenets of Muslim religion, 368

MUTUAL FUNDS

National bank's authority to operate collective investment fund, 179

MUTUALITY OF ESTOPPEL

Patent infringement case, effect of prior determination of invalidity of patent in, 243

NAMES

Informer, search based partly on tip from unnamed, 351

NARCOTICS

Damage action for injuries from invalid arrest and search, 343

Electronic surveillance by transmitter concealed on informant, 193

Search incident to arrest, retroactivity of prior decision narrowing scope of, 183

NATIONAL BANKS

Banks and Banking (this index)

NATIONAL FIREARMS ACT

Registration requirements, 177

NATIONAL HOUSING ACT

Savings and loan association payment of additional premium as deductible business expense, 329

NATURALIZATION

Aliens (this index)

NAVIGABLE WATERS

Great Salt Lake, ownership of shorelands around, 297

NEWSPAPERS

Press (this index)

OBSCENITY—Continued

"Fuck the Draft," disturbing peace by wearing jacket bearing words, 299

Libel action for new report of arrest for possessing obscene literature, 301

Mails, ban on use of, 45, 246

Search and seizure—

customs collectors, provisions as to seizure of obscene materials by, 248

pending state prosecution, suppression of obscene materials seized in connection with, 92

OHIO STATE BAR

Applicant's refusal to answer questions concerning membership in Communist Party, 80

OIL LEASES

Cancellation for failure to satisfy requirements of General Mining Act, 17

ORIGINAL JURISDICTION

Pollution, suit by state for prevention of, 158

OVERRULING DECISION

Retroactive Application (this index)

OVERTHROW OF GOVERNMENT

Loyalty oath for public employees, validity of, 317

PANIC PEDDLING

Enjoining peaceful distribution of leaflets accusing real estate broker of "panic peddling," 254

PARENT AND CHILD

Citizenship of foreign-born child with one alien parent, maintenance of, 201

Illegitimate child as barred from sharing in intestate father's estate, 168

PARKS

Interstate highway route through park, review of approval of, 141

PAROCHIAL SCHOOLS

State aid as to secular instruction in church-related schools, 355

RECUSATION
Contempt charge against civil rights worker, bias of judge at hearing on, 319

REFERENCE TO MASTER
Great Salt Lake, determination of ownership of shorelands around, 297

REFERENDUM
Bond issue or tax rate increase, validity of requiring approval by 60 percent vote in referendum on, 295

Low-income housing project, requirement for approval by majority vote in local referendum on, 233

REFUGEES
Resettlement in third country after flight as affecting status of alien, 220

REGISTRATION
Firearms, violation of statute requiring registration of, 177

Self-incrimination, federal wagering tax statutes as violating privilege of, 187, 190

Uninsured motorist, suspension of vehicle registration of, 269, 288

RELEASE OR DISCHARGE
Bankruptcy Act, state suspension of drivers' licenses as conflicting with provisions for discharge under, 288

Co-conspirator, effect of release of, 130

RELIGION AND RELIGIOUS MATTERS
Conscientious objector claims, religious freedom clause as affecting, 148, 368

Higher Education Facilities Act, grants to church-related institutions under, 363

Ministerial student exemption from military service, 260

State aid as to secular instruction in church-related schools, 355

REMOVAL OF CAUSE
Contempt charge against civil rights worker, bias of judge at hearing on, 319

REPORTS AND REPORTING
Self-incrimination, state hit-and-run statute as violating privilege against, 256

VAGUENESS OF STATUTE

Abortion statute, sufficiency of notice of governing standards under, 223

"Offensive conduct" as sufficient to inform ordinary person of permissible conduct, 299

Sidewalk assemblies "annoying" to passersby, ordinance punishing, 283

Suspicious person ordinance as applied to parked motorists talking on two-way radio at night, 271

VENUE

Misdemeanor case, change of venue in, 65

VERDICTS

Death penalty, single-verdict procedure as affecting imposition of, 240

VESTED RIGHTS OR INTERESTS

Income tax liability of wife as affected by renunciation of community property rights, 314

VIET NAM

Conscientious objections to particular war, 148

Publication of classified government study, injunction against, 373

VISA

Refugee status of alien seeking immigrant visa, 220

VOTING

Elections (this index)

WAGERING TAX

Self-incrimination, retroactivity of decision invalidating federal wagering tax statutes as violation of privilege against, 187, 190

WAGES AND SALARY

Bankruptcy Act, vacation pay as "property" passing to trustee under, 8

Teachers in church-related schools, state aid as to secular instruction by, 355

WAIVER

Estoppel and Waiver (this index)

[Supreme Ct Sum]—29

WARRANTS
Search and Seizure (this index)

WATERS
Consent of United States to be sued in water adjudication suit,
    163
Lakes (this index)

WEAPONS
Firearms (this index)

WELFARE
Poor and Poor Laws (this index)
Social Security and Unemployment Compensation (this index)

WHARF DEMURRAGE CHARGES
Finality of order of Federal Maritime Commission, 20

WHISKEY
Intoxicating Liquor (this index)

WHITE RIVER NATIONAL FOREST
Joinder of United States in supplemental water adjudication suit,
    163

WIFE
Husband and Wife (this index)

WITHERSPOON ISSUES
Vacation of death sentence to allow application to supplement bill
    of exceptions under changed state law, 371

WITHHOLDING TAXES
Bankruptcy, priority of claim for withheld taxes, 161

WITNESSES
Accused, use of prior inconsistent statements to impeach, 112
Corporation of Witnesses (this index)
Cross-Examination (this index)
Informant, unavailability of informant as affecting evidence from
    electronic surveillance by transmitter concealed on person of,
    193
Joint trial, inculpatory out-of-court statement of codefendant as
    admissible at, 285

WITNESSES—Continued

Report of doctor not appearing at administrative hearing as evidence against disability claimant, 251

Self-Incrimination (this index)

ZONING

School attendance zones, desegregation by reassignment of, 206, 211, 214